This book
BELONGS TO:

Copyright © 2021 by The Foundry Kids
The Foundry Publishing®
PO Box 419527
Kansas City, MO 64141
thefoundrypublishing.com

978-0-8341-3981-7

Printed in China

Cover Design and Interior Design: Brandon Hill
Authors: James Abbott, Tami Brumbaugh, Michaele LaVigne, Kyle Tyler
Copy Editor: Kimberly A. Crenshaw
Editor: Kyle Tyler
Senior Editor: Jeremy Bond
Publisher: Mark D. Brown

Library of Congress Cataloging-in-Publication Data
A complete catalog record for this book is available from the Library of Congress.

10 9 8 7 6 5 4 3 2 1

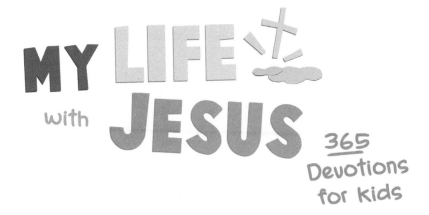

MY LIFE with JESUS

365 Devotions for kids

James Abbott
Tami Brumbaugh
Michaele LaVigne
Kyle Tyler

THE FOUNDRY
KIDS

Kansas City, Missouri

Table of Contents

How to Use this Book....

What's the goal of *My Life with Jesus* devotions?
To help kids create regular time with Jesus. The devotions will help you explore the way, truth, and life of Jesus from His birth to the coming of the Holy Spirit. What's it like having Jesus show up each day to walk by your side, build you up, and cheer you on? Let's find out. Are you ready?

Who is this for?
These devotions are for kids like you. Explore by yourself, with your family, or with a friend.

How does it work?
The book is divided into 52 weeks. Each week explores a different story or passage from the Bible. Each week has the same routine:

- On the first day of each week, you'll just read and reflect on the passage. You can use the *5 What's* to help you know what to look for as you read. (Get help from the tools on page v.)

- For Days 2-7 of each week, you'll read a short devotional inspired by the Bible passage you read on Day 1.

- Go back and read the Day 1 Scripture as often as you'd like.

Holy Qs! and Blessing
Holy Qs! are one or two questions to help you think about your life with Jesus each day. Blessings are special words spoken to people, reminding them of their connection to God and their purpose. Each day you'll find a blessing that does the same for you.

Should I just start on Week 1?
Yep. The book follows the life of Jesus from His birth, to His resurrection, to the coming of the Holy Spirit. So, starting with Week 1 is the easiest way to go no matter what time of year you pick up the book.

Options for Advent and Lent:
If you want to read these devotions to be in sync with Advent and Lent, then you have a couple of options:

- If you are starting at the beginning of Advent, which is also the start of the Church year, start with Week 1.

- If you'd like to start reading during Lent (the weeks leading up to Easter), then think about starting with Week 42. This is when the book starts to explore the events leading up to the resurrection of Jesus.

Advent and Lent are special times throughout the year when we focus on a particular part of Jesus's story. Advent is a time of preparing and leading us into the Christmas season. Lent is a time of connecting to Jesus's story during the time around His death and resurrection, leading us into the Easter season.

HOLY Qs!

In 1729 (Whoa! That was a long time ago.), John and Charles Wesley, two Christian brothers, started a club with a few friends at their college. This wasn't a chess club or a football club or a music club. This was a club for the friends to help each other live a life with Jesus. They would meet several nights a week and read Scripture, receive communion, pray, and talk about life together.

The club started meeting more and more. Some people even made fun of how much they met together and nicknamed them the "Holy Club." As they met, they asked each other a set of very specific questions—22 questions, to be exact—that helped everyone think about their life with Jesus.

Even after all these years, these questions can be really helpful. Of course, answering 22 "Holy Club Questions" every day is a lot. And this was like 300 years ago, so the way we talk is a little different. So, we changed them up just a little. We're calling them Holy Qs! and there are one or two each day for you to answer. Sometimes they go right along with the devotion, and sometimes they're just there to get you thinking about your life with Jesus in fresh new ways. All 22 Holy Qs! are listed below. And you'll find them throughout the book.

1. Have my words matched my actions? Does who I say I am and how I act line up?
2. How can I be honest and trustworthy this week?
3. How will I be a good friend and listener?

HOLY Qs!

4. How have I been trustworthy recently?

5. How can I keep from letting things like popularity or friends determine how I act?

6. How can God's love give me confidence today?

7. How does what I learned from Scripture inspire my thoughts and actions?

8. What habits help me spend time getting to know God through Scripture?

9. What have I been enjoying about prayer recently?

10. Who in my life needs to hear about Jesus? How can they hear it from me?

11. How can the way I spend my money reflect my relationship with Jesus?

12. God cares about our whole life, not just the spiritual parts. What healthy habits do I need to work on?

13. How can I be obedient to God this week?

14. What can I do to make wise choices this week?

15. Is anything in my life really hard right now? Am I talking to God about it? Who else can I talk to?

16. Have I been jealous, grumpy, or really hard on anyone? What can I do about it?

17. What's a healthy or helpful way I can use my spare time?

18. When good things happen, how do I give God the credit?

19. How can I learn from others this week?

20. Is there anyone I'm struggling to get along with? What am I going to do about it?

21. What am I thankful for? How can I show how thankful I am this week?

22. How does my relationship with Jesus impact my daily life in real ways?

The 5 What's

The 5 What's is a simple set of questions to guide your reading of any passage of Scripture, including the ones in this book. They help us explore, understand, and embrace a passage of Scripture.

What's That Word?

We all run into words we don't understand. If you see a word that doesn't make sense, then dig around to find out what it means. Ask a friend or adult. Look in the back of your Bible. Or, with permission, look it up online.

What's Happening in the Passage?

Who are the people? Who's talking? Where are they? What are they up to? Is this a story, a poem, a parable, or something else? Look for fun details and try to understand the people in the passage. Imagine yourself as someone in the story.

What's Happening in the Bible?

How can other stories in the Bible help you understand this passage better? This might be the hardest question to answer yourself. We'll help you out with this question in lots of the devotions each week. You can also just think about any other Bible stories that come to mind when you read this one. The whole Bible works together for one purpose.

What's This Say about God?

God reveals himself through the Bible. Reading the Bible is one of the best ways we have to get to know God better. Look for what He's doing or saying in each Scripture. What's the passage say about His character or love?

What's This Say about Us?

As we learn about God, we learn about ourselves and we react to His love for us. How does the passage change you? What do you do now? How do you live in God's love from here? How does this Scripture inspire your life with Jesus?

Lectio Divina

That's a nifty phrase! It's Latin. It's pronounced LEX-ee-oh di-VEEN-a and means "spiritual reading." It's like using the Bible to help you pray. Prayer is more than just talking to God. It's also the act of spending focused time with God. Lectio Divina helps us focus our time with God using five simple actions.

Read

Read the passage. Then, read it again slowly. Read it knowing God has something to say to you through these Scriptures.

Think

What words or moments stand out to you? Give yourself time to really think about what you're reading, what's happening, and why it could be important for you.

Speak

What do you want to say to God because of what you read? Do you have questions? Something to confess or request? Something that gets you excited? Talk to Jesus about it.

Listen

Sit quietly. You've read, you've thought, you've talked. Now, just be there, in God's presence. Listen. This might be hard at first, but that's okay. Resting in God's presence can bring so much joy.

Go

Keep the Scripture in mind as you go. Maybe you learned some things you can do in your life right now. Maybe it's a new way of thinking. Let it encourage you today. As you go, may God's Word go with you.

Savior, King, and Friend

What's it mean to have a life with Jesus? What's it mean to be a follower of Jesus, have a relationship with Jesus, or be saved? These are all ways we describe what it means to be Christian. Here's another way to think about it: Being a Christian means Jesus is your Savior, King, and Friend.

Savior

God's love for you is enormous. His Son is proof. Jesus brings God's love straight to you. His love is even stronger than sin. Ask and He forgives. He gives you new life and eternal life. God loves you as Savior.

King

You are God's creation. His power surrounds you. His beautiful design, perfect rule, and loving attention are all over His kingdom. His power provides, inspires, and restores. He is worthy of our worship. God loves you as King.

Friend

God knows you. He listens. He speaks. He comforts. He stays with you through good times and bad times. His love and presence are right here, right now. He is the best and truest Friend. God loves you as Friend.

God's Love. Our Love.

Jesus loves you as your Savior, He loves you as your King, and He loves you as your Friend. We respond to God's love with our own love. We love Jesus as our Savior, the only one who gives us new life. We love Jesus as our King, giving Him our worship and following His authority. We love Jesus as our Friend, talking, listening, and loving what He loves.

Loving God as our Savior, King, and Friend helps us understand what it means to be a Christian. Next time you're asked what it means to be Christian, you'll know what to say. "It means Jesus is my Savior, King, and Friend!"

Weekly Scriptures

WEEK 1 Day 1
THE MESSIAH IS PROPHESIED

This week's passage is from the Old Testament. Can you discover what it has to do with the life of Jesus? Enjoy God's love for you!

JEREMIAH 33:14-16

14 "The day will come, says the LORD, when I will do for Israel and Judah all the good things I have promised them.
15 "In those days and at that time
I will raise up a righteous descendant from King David's line.
He will do what is just and right throughout the land.
16 In that day Judah will be saved,
and Jerusalem will live in safety.
And this will be its name:
'The LORD Is Our Righteousness.'"

Day 2
HERE WE GO

JEREMIAH 33:14-16

What's something you had to spend a lot of time preparing for? Let's learn a phrase together. "Prevenient grace" (Pre-VEEN-ee-ent grace). This is a phrase we use when we talk about God preparing a way for us. God was preparing the world for Jesus years and years before Jesus was born. God spoke through the prophet Jeremiah hundreds of years before Mary and Joseph were even around, and the prophet told everyone that a King was coming.

God prepares a way for you, too. God prepared you for a relationship with Him, and He is going before you every day. You'll never go anywhere God hasn't gone, or speak with anyone that God hasn't spoken to. That doesn't mean things will always be easy, but God will always be there. He is preparing the way for you to spread the love and good news of Jesus to the world. How is it comforting to know that God not only goes with you, but goes before you?

HOLY Qs!

- When good things happen, how do I give God the credit?
- What am I thankful for? How can I show how thankful I am this week?

BLESSING

Go following the way of the Savior, walking in the truth of the King, and living the life of the Friend. May your thoughts, words, and actions reflect the love of Jesus.

WHAT'S MY PLAN?

JEREMIAH 33:14-16

If you knew what was going to happen in the future, what would you do differently? In the Bible, God chose certain people to be His messengers. Many times those messengers, called prophets, would have something to tell about the future. Jeremiah was one of those prophets, with one of those messages. God had promised a leader for Israel. We often read this passage during Advent—the season of preparing that leads us to Christmas—because Jesus was the one being promised. Hundreds of years before Jesus was born, He was promised. You may be starting to read this book in the weeks before Christmas or you may be starting in another time of year. Whenever it is, look for God's promises to us every day.

Jesus was promised to us out of love. God loved His people enough to know they would need a Savior. We recognize God's love for us by seeing how His amazing plans unfolded. God still loves His people. And God still has plans for us—plans for us to live in a relationship with Jesus. Now, instead of telling us the future through prophets, He is with us every day as we live in that relationship. God's loving plan for you is to know Jesus! How's the plan coming?

HOLY Qs!

- *How can God's love give me confidence today?*
- *Have I been jealous, grumpy, or really hard on anyone? What can I do about it?*

BLESSING

Go following the way of the Savior, walking in the truth of the King, and living the life of the Friend. May your thoughts, words, and actions reflect the love of Jesus.

Day 4

MY PLACE IN HIS KINGDOM

JEREMIAH 33:14-16

Who are Israel and Judah? God's people—the descendants of Abraham—were split into 12 tribes. All the tribes together were called Israel (named after Abraham's grandson)—and one of those tribes was called Judah. Judah is where Bethlehem is, where Jesus was born. When the Bible talks about Israel, it's talking about the people of God. Now, the people of God are called Christians. Abraham may not be your great-great-great-great-great grandfather, but you're still part of God's people!

Being a Christian isn't about where you were born, or who your grandfather is. It's about having a relationship with Jesus. (Turn to page vii to learn more about that.) Some of us get to be raised in homes with other Christians, and we get to learn from our earliest days what a relationship with Jesus is. Others don't learn until later in life. Some just haven't learned it yet. But there's a place for all of us in God's kingdom. How's that feel?

HOLY Qs!

- *Who in my life needs to hear about Jesus? How can they hear it from me?*

BLESSING

Go following the way of the Savior, walking in the truth of the King, and living the life of the Friend. May your thoughts, words, and actions reflect the love of Jesus.

WHAT KIND OF HERO?

JEREMIAH 33:14-16

What do you remember about King David's story in the Old Testament? It's pretty awesome. We can't recap the whole thing here, but let's just say he was a conquering hero king in the history of God's people, and his name was about as famous as anyone's could be. To be associated with King David was pretty high praise. So here's this prophecy saying that the one who would save God's people would be from King David's line (line means family). Yes! Finally! A new hero!

Being part of King David's family made Jesus seem pretty legit. People would be more likely to believe in Jesus because of His connections to David. What about you? What made you interested in Jesus in the first place? Is there a certain story you really like? Is there another Christian who got you excited about Him? What is it about Jesus that makes you want to pay attention to and follow Him?

HOLY Qs!

- *Is anything in my life really hard right now? Am I talking to God about it? Who else can I talk to?*

BLESSING

Go following the way of the Savior, walking in the truth of the King, and living the life of the Friend. May your thoughts, words, and actions reflect the love of Jesus.

Day 6
EXPECT THE UNEXPECTED

JEREMIAH 33:14-16

Take a quick look at yesterday's devotion. Remember the hero talk? Hold on, though. From what you know about Jesus, did He show up to be a conquering hero king? Actually, it was a little bit different from what everyone expected. Jesus was going to have a tough time convincing the world He was the Promised One from King David's line, because He wasn't going to be the warrior David was. Jesus would use love and peace, rather than swords and armies. He was definitely a hero, just not the kind of King people were expecting.

All throughout Jesus's ministry, He did things in ways people didn't expect. The more you read this book, and the Scriptures in it, the more familiar you'll get with those stories. If we live our life with Jesus, then we'll be the same way. When people expect us to get mad, we can respond with peace. When people expect us to take revenge, we can be kind instead. What are other ways following Jesus makes us different than people might expect?

HOLY Qs!

- *How does what I learned from Scripture inspire my thoughts and actions?*
- *How have I been trustworthy recently?*

BLESSING

Go following the way of the Savior, walking in the truth of the King, and living the life of the Friend. May your thoughts, words, and actions reflect the love of Jesus.

Day 7
HE'S COMING AGAIN

JEREMIAH 33:14-16

What's your favorite part of preparing for Christmas? We can think about Christmas at any time of year. As we learned in Day 3, the season when we prepare to celebrate Jesus's birth is called Advent. There's actually one other time we use this word. Did you know there's a second advent? It's the time when we're waiting and preparing for Jesus to come again. We're living in that time right now! That doesn't mean we can just sit around and wait for Him to show up, though. Nope. We have a job to do.

So how can you prepare for Jesus to come again? You can start right now. Love Jesus with your whole self. Love the people around you with all your words and actions. Tell people about Jesus's love and your relationship with Him. Show Jesus's love always, even when it's hard. You're helping prepare the world for Jesus to come again.

HOLY Qs!

- *How does my relationship with Jesus impact my daily life in real ways?*
- *God cares about our whole life, not just the spiritual parts. What healthy habits do I need to work on?*

BLESSING

Go following the way of the Savior, walking in the truth of the King, and living the life of the Friend. May your thoughts, words, and actions reflect the love of Jesus.

7

WEEK 2 Day 1
JOHN THE BAPTIST PREPARES THE WAY

It's a new week in your life with Jesus! Use the *5 What's or Lectio Divina* to guide your reading today. Enjoy God's love for you!

MARK 1:1-8 (NIV)

¹ The beginning of the good news about Jesus the Messiah, the Son of God, ² as it is written in Isaiah the prophet:

"I will send my messenger ahead of you, who will prepare your way"— ³ "a voice of one calling in the wilderness,
'Prepare the way for the Lord, make straight paths for him.'"

⁴ And so John the Baptist appeared in the wilderness, preaching a baptism of repentance for the forgiveness of sins. ⁵ The whole Judean countryside and all the people of Jerusalem went out to him. Confessing their sins, they were baptized by him in the Jordan River. ⁶ John wore clothing made of camel's hair, with a leather belt around his waist, and he ate locusts and wild honey. ⁷ And this was his message: "After me comes the one more powerful than I, the straps of whose sandals I am not worthy to stoop down and untie. ⁸ I baptize you with water, but he will baptize you with the Holy Spirit."

PUZZLE PARTNER

MARK 1:1-8

What's the biggest puzzle you've ever done? God would be a really good puzzle partner. It would be fun to dump out 5,000 pieces and go to work alongside Him. He certainly has experience seeing the big picture and creating a way for people and events to come together. When we look at the prophecy at the beginning of this Scripture, we can see how God knew Jesus was needed to save us. So He got to work preparing for His Son's arrival. And talk about patience! He had Isaiah in place to prophesy about John the Baptist 700 years before John even arrived! John then prepared the way for Jesus.

Trusting God to guide you as you put the pieces of your life together is challenging. It is hard to be patient. It's impossible to know what's coming next. But doing the puzzle of your life together with God is how it was intended. He knows what He's doing. As you make decisions, and choose what's next, always follow your puzzle partner.

HOLY Qs!

- *How can God's love give me confidence today?*
- *God cares about our whole life, not just the spiritual parts. What healthy habits do I need to work on?*

BLESSING

Go following the way of the Savior, walking in the truth of the King, and living the life of the Friend. May your thoughts, words, and actions reflect the love of Jesus.

Day 3
WE NEED DIRECTIONS

MARK 1:1-8

Think of a place that's confusing to get around. A mirror maze? An airport? A new school? Some schools seem like a maze. People can get mixed up and go the wrong way. It's helpful when there is someone in the hallway who can point you in the right direction so you can get to class. John the Baptist was like the person in the hallway (except . . . he wore clothing made of camel hair). He saw people going the wrong direction. He told them to repent and then pointed them in the right direction toward Jesus. Repent means to change your mind or turn away from doing wrong.

There are times you may make wrong choices. That does not mean you are stuck going the wrong way. You can change your mind. Turn around. Learn from your mistakes and go the other way. Jesus helps you with this, as your Savior. Read more about that on page vii. Who are the trustworthy people in your life who would be like John the Baptist and direct you back to Jesus?

HOLY Qs!

- *What can I do to make wise choices this week?*
- *How can I learn from others this week?*

BLESSING

Go following the way of the Savior, walking in the truth of the King, and living the life of the Friend. May your thoughts, words, and actions reflect the love of Jesus.

CAMEL HAIR IS JUST FINE

MARK 1:1-8

Who is this John the Baptist character? Our Scripture gives us a great picture of him. He wore clothes made out of camel hair with a leather belt around his waist. No t-shirt and jeans for this guy! And forget about pizza or hamburgers. John ate locusts and wild honey. Locusts are like grasshoppers, and can swarm together in huge numbers and destroy crops. But they don't sound very tasty. John lived in the wilderness, so he probably did not have many food and clothing options. People from town would not have been impressed by the way he looked or by his wealth. But John was ready to listen, and God used him to prepare the way for Jesus. People from all over Judea and Jerusalem listened to his message.

It doesn't matter what you wear or eat. It doesn't matter where you live or how much money you have. If you are willing and ready to listen, God can speak through you. You can help show people who Jesus is.

HOLY Qs!

- *Have my words matched my actions? Does who I say I am and how I act line up?*
- *Who in my life needs to hear about Jesus? How can they hear it from me?*

BLESSING

Go following the way of the Savior, walking in the truth of the King, and living the life of the Friend. May your thoughts, words, and actions reflect the love of Jesus.

Day 5
BAPTIZED AND LOVING IT

MARK 1:1-8

Who do you know named John? It's a very common name, even in the Bible. The John in our Scripture is set apart because he was known as John the Baptist. He clearly felt that baptism was important. Anyone who is a Christian—someone who loves Jesus as Savior, King, and Friend—can be baptized. Or, a baby can be baptized by parents who are committing to raise that baby to love Jesus. Baptism is a way to declare our love for Jesus to the world, and a way to receive His grace.

Have you been baptized? Were you just a cute little baby, or do you remember it? If you've not been baptized and you're interested, who could you talk to about it? When we read about baptism in the Bible, we can remember our own baptism, or we can talk to someone else about theirs. Ask a parent or sibling if they remember their baptism. Thank God for His good grace that is given to us through baptism.

HOLY Qs!

- *How does what I learned from Scripture inspire my thoughts and actions?*

BLESSING

Go following the way of the Savior, walking in the truth of the King, and living the life of the Friend. May your thoughts, words, and actions reflect the love of Jesus.

PREPARE TO PREPARE

MARK 1:1-8

If you have a nativity scene in your home at Christmas, where do you put it? Each nativity is a little different, but they mostly have the same characters: Mary, Joseph, and baby Jesus go in a stable. You might also have shepherds, wise men, an angel, and possibly even sheep or donkeys. If there was an extended nativity set, another figurine could be John the Baptist. He prepared the way for Jesus and announced that Jesus was coming. He explained how great Jesus was. John baptized with water, but Jesus would baptize people with the Holy Spirit.

Think about how your family prepares for Christmas. There are so many fun activities during that time of year. What are some of your favorites? None of us are figures in a nativity scene, not Joseph or Mary or baby Jesus or the shepherds, but we can still play a role in Jesus's story. John prepared the way for people to know Jesus then. How can you prepare the way for people to know Jesus now?

HOLY Qs!

- *What habits help me spend time getting to know God through Scripture?*
- *What's a healthy or helpful way I can use my spare time?*

BLESSING

Go following the way of the Savior, walking in the truth of the King, and living the life of the Friend. May your thoughts, words, and actions reflect the love of Jesus.

Day 7
KIND OF A BIG DEAL

MARK 1:1-8

What's your favorite pair of shoes? Now, consider what they've stepped on. Dusty roads, mud, puddles, gum, bird droppings, worms, squashed bugs—your shoes go through it all. Ew. It is no wonder we don't go barefoot outside very often. Read verse 7. During the time Jesus and John were alive, untying someone else's sandals was considered such a low job that only servants were required to do it. Huge crowds gathered to hear John speak, but he wanted them to redirect their focus back to Jesus. He explained that he was not even worthy to untie the straps of Jesus's sandals. That was a big statement. John didn't want the praise. Jesus was the one to worship. Jesus was the big deal.

A life with Jesus is amazing and awesome *because* of Jesus. His love transforms us. You're a big deal because He's a big deal. Let those around you see your life with Jesus. Let the love of Jesus fill you up, and people around you will see how big of a deal Jesus really is.

HOLY Qs!

- *How can I keep from letting things like popularity or friends determine how I act?*
- *How does my relationship with Jesus impact my daily life in real ways?*

BLESSING

Go following the way of the Savior, walking in the truth of the King, and living the life of the Friend. May your thoughts, words, and actions reflect the love of Jesus.

WEEK 3 Day 1
THE WORD

It's a new week in your life with Jesus! Use the *5 What's or Lectio Divina* to guide your reading today. Enjoy God's love for you!

JOHN 1:1-5

¹ In the beginning the Word already existed.
  The Word was with God,
  and the Word was God.
² He existed in the beginning with God.
³ God created everything through him,
  and nothing was created except through him.
⁴ The Word gave life to everything that was created,
  and his life brought light to everyone.
⁵ The light shines in the darkness,
  and the darkness can never extinguish it.

Day 2
BIO BOOKS

JOHN 1:1-5

Have you ever read a biography? That's a book about someone's life, written by an author who knew or studied a lot about that person. There are four books in the Bible that are a little like biographies, because they tell the story of Jesus's life.

We call these books the Gospels, and they were written by four different men: Matthew, Mark, Luke, and John. Gospel is a word that means "good news." Sometimes we call them by different names. We might say the Gospel of John, or simply John. Each of these four books tell the good news about Jesus, each in a slightly different way.

These four men all knew the same Jesus, and many of the stories they tell are the same. But each got to know Jesus a little differently, and they let us see what they saw in Jesus's life. Why is learning about the life of Jesus important? Each day as you read you will get to know Him more from the stories His friends tell.

HOLY Qs!

- *How can I learn from others this week?*

BLESSING

Go following the way of the Savior, walking in the truth of the King, and living the life of the Friend. May your thoughts, words, and actions reflect the love of Jesus.

PRETTY BIG DEAL

JOHN 1:1-5

Usually stories start at the beginning. But there is one very famous story that starts with the words "In the beginning." What comes to your mind when you hear those words?

The very first sentence of the Bible begins this way: "In the beginning God created the heavens and the earth" (Genesis 1:1). Look at John 1:1. How did John begin his story? The very same way! John was writing in the Greek language, and he used the word *Logos* (LOG-oss) to describe Jesus. "In the beginning the *Logos* already existed. The *Logos* was with God, and the *Logos* was God." Logos means "word," and words are very important. Words help us understand things, create things, put things in order, and talk with one another.

How does Jesus help us understand who God is? How does knowing Jesus change the way we talk to other people? How does He help us decide what's important? See, Jesus being the Word, the *Logos*, is actually a pretty big deal!

HOLY Qs!

- *What have I been enjoying about prayer recently?*
- *What can I do to make wise choices this week?*

BLESSING

Go following the way of the Savior, walking in the truth of the King, and living the life of the Friend. May your thoughts, words, and actions reflect the love of Jesus.

Day 4
A LIGHT IN THE DARKNESS

JOHN 1:1-5

What's the darkest place you've ever been? We almost always have some kind of light around us, even in the dark—a candle, a lamp, a flashlight, or even the moon. It only takes a small amount of light to help us see in the dark. No matter how dark it is, or how long the darkness lasts, darkness can't make light darker.

It's just the opposite! Light always makes darkness lighter.

John describes Jesus as the Light that comes into the darkness and makes it brighter. It's a way to help us understand Jesus. Light leads us through dark, and Jesus leads us through life. Things can feel dark—confusion, fear, selfishness, and pain. But Jesus gives us what we need to get through them, even defeat them, and live in the goodness of a relationship with Him. We'll call that "the light!" Where have you seen His light in a dark place in your life before?

HOLY Qs!

- *Is anything in my life really hard right now? Am I talking to God about it? Who else can I talk to?*

BLESSING

Go following the way of the Savior, walking in the truth of the King, and living the life of the Friend. May your thoughts, words, and actions reflect the love of Jesus.

GOD WITH US. FOR REAL.

JOHN 1:1-5

"So the Word became human and made his home among us. He was full of unfailing love and faithfulness. And we have seen his glory, the glory of the Father's one and only Son." —John 1:14

Like Jeremiah, Isaiah was one of the prophets who shared God's promises about Jesus. Hundreds of years before Jesus was born, Isaiah said a baby would be born and be called Immanuel (Isaiah 7:14). In Hebrew, Immanuel means "God with us."

Once again, John is reaching back into old Scripture to help us understand who Jesus is. Jesus is the Word who helped to begin and create our whole world. He is the Light of the World that can never go dark. And He is God with Us, Immanuel, who made His home among us.

Is it hard for you to imagine God being *with us*, in this room right now? If it is, you're not alone. In fact, Jesus became human to show us just how with us our God is. Why is God being *with us* so important?

HOLY Qs!

- *Who in my life needs to hear about Jesus? How can they hear it from me?*

BLESSING

Go following the way of the Savior, walking in the truth of the King, and living the life of the Friend. May your thoughts, words, and actions reflect the love of Jesus.

Day 6
BECOMING HUMAN

JOHN 1:1-5

"So the Word became human and made his home among us. He was full of unfailing love and faithfulness. And we have seen his glory, the glory of the Father's one and only Son."—John 1:14

Have you ever heard the word "incarnation" (in-car-NAY-shun)? It means "made into flesh." For thousands of years Christians have been puzzling over the mystery we call the incarnation—how God was made into flesh, made human.

Do you know any newborn babies? Jesus was carried in His mother's belly, He was born as a tiny baby, and He grew up, just like you. At one time, Jesus was the same age you are now, and probably did a lot of the same things you do. Jesus is God, but He definitely knows what it's like to be human. How does knowing Jesus was once a kid just like you change the way you think about Him?

HOLY Qs!

- *How can God's love give me confidence today?*

- *How does what I learned from Scripture inspire my thoughts and actions?*

BLESSING

Go following the way of the Savior, walking in the truth of the King, and living the life of the Friend. May your thoughts, words, and actions reflect the love of Jesus.

INTO THE NEIGHBORHOOD

JOHN 1:1-5

"The Word became flesh and blood, and moved into the neighborhood. We saw the glory with our own eyes, the one-of-a-kind glory, like Father, like Son, Generous inside and out, true from start to finish."—John 1:14, The Message

Who are the people you know best? How have you gotten to know them so well? They're probably family members who live with you, or friends that you spend time with often. It's a lot harder to get to know someone well from far away.

When Jesus became human, He moved in close to be near us. He moved into our world, our neighborhood with our dirt and trees, food and water, hunger and laughter, friendship and family. What do you have in common with Jesus? While His body was human, He was like no other human anyone had ever known or will ever know. His love and generosity help us know who God really is. How do we still see that love and generosity?

HOLY Qs!

- *What habits help me spend time getting to know God through Scripture?*
- *How does my relationship with Jesus impact my daily life in real ways?*

BLESSING

Go following the way of the Savior, walking in the truth of the King, and living the life of the Friend. May your thoughts, words, and actions reflect the love of Jesus.

WEEK 4 Day 1
JESUS'S BIRTH

It's a new week in your life with Jesus! Use the *5 What's or Lectio Divina* to guide your reading today. Enjoy God's love for you!

LUKE 2:1-20

[1] At that time the Roman emperor, Augustus, decreed that a census should be taken throughout the Roman Empire. [2] (This was the first census taken when Quirinius was governor of Syria.) [3] All returned to their own ancestral towns to register for this census. [4] And because Joseph was a descendant of King David, he had to go to Bethlehem in Judea, David's ancient home. He traveled there from the village of Nazareth in Galilee. [5] He took with him Mary, to whom he was engaged, who was now expecting a child.

[6] And while they were there, the time came for her baby to be born. [7] She gave birth to her firstborn son. She wrapped him snugly in strips of cloth and laid him in a manger, because there was no lodging available for them.

[8] That night there were shepherds staying in the fields nearby, guarding their flocks of sheep. [9] Suddenly, an angel of the Lord appeared among them, and the radiance of the Lord's glory surrounded them. They were terrified, [10] but the angel reassured them. "Don't be afraid!" he said. "I bring you good news that will bring great joy to all people. [11] The Savior—yes, the Messiah, the Lord—has been born today in Bethlehem, the city of David! [12] And you will recognize him by this sign: You will find a baby wrapped snugly in strips of cloth, lying in a manger."

[13] Suddenly, the angel was joined by a vast host of others—the armies of heaven—praising God and saying, [14] "Glory to God in highest heaven, and peace on earth to those with whom God is pleased." [15] When the angels had returned to heaven, the shepherds said to each other, "Let's go to Bethlehem! Let's see this thing that has happened, which the Lord has told us about." [16] They hurried to the village and found Mary and Joseph. And there was the baby, lying in the manger. [17] After seeing him, the shepherds told everyone what had happened and what the angel had said to them about this child. [18] All who heard the shepherds' story were astonished, [19] but Mary kept all these things in her heart and thought about them often. [20] The shepherds went back to their flocks, glorifying and praising God for all they had heard and seen. It was just as the angel had told them.

Day 2
DON'T MISS IT

LUKE 2:1-20

Here's something super cool about Scripture: the parts that we might just skip through are actually powerful for us to read. It's almost like a treasure hunt! Check out verses 1-4. Typically, we might skip past this to get to the awesome story of the shepherds, but what can you find in these opening verses that might be important?

This chapter starts with the names of people and places because these are real people and real places. The readers of Luke could quickly see that Jesus and His family were very real, and very relatable. There's also an important connection to who Jesus's family was. (Look back at Week 1, Day 5 to remember; then look at verses 3 and 4. What hero king was Jesus related to?)

As you read Scripture, take the time to really read all of it. Even the parts that might seem boring have some amazing things for you to uncover. Scripture is a gift, revealing something about who God is in every part. Everything you read can shape who you are.

HOLY Qs!

- *Have my words matched my actions? Does who I say I am and how I act line up?*
- *How does what I learned from Scripture inspire my thoughts and actions?*

BLESSING

Go following the way of the Savior, walking in the truth of the King, and living the life of the Friend. May your thoughts, words, and actions reflect the love of Jesus.

Day 3
EYEWITNESS

Luke was an incredible guy. He was a doctor and highly educated. One theory suggests he was hired by Theophilus (thee-AH-fil-us— say that name 3 times fast!) to go and investigate the stories about Jesus to see if they were true. He was very careful to interview as many people as possible to get the full story. Can you imagine getting to talk to these shepherds and hear them tell the story? That's part of why Luke's gospel is so powerful. The shepherds are first-hand eyewitnesses of the events that happened!

We are eyewitnesses for Jesus. We get to tell His story. People who want to know what Jesus is all about will hear about it from us and see it in our actions. The way we love people. The way we care for others' needs. The way we honor our parents. They will know because of the loving relationship we have with Jesus. How will you show who Jesus is this week?

HOLY Qs!

- *Who in my life needs to hear about Jesus? How can they hear it from me?*
- *Have I been jealous, grumpy, or really hard on anyone? What can I do about it?*

BLESSING

Go following the way of the Savior, walking in the truth of the King, and living the life of the Friend. May your thoughts, words, and actions reflect the love of Jesus.

Day 4
EXTRAORDINARY ORDINARY

LUKE 2:1-20

The shepherds were out at night. In the dark! Umm, scary! Would you be scared to be out in a field in the dark? Well, they were probably used to it. They did this all the time. This was a pretty ordinary night for them. But that's just when things changed.

What does your ordinary day look like? Sometimes, when we are doing ordinary things, God breaks into our lives and does extraordinary things. The shepherds certainly were not expecting an angel. Or a whole host (group) of angels. God wants us to live ready. We never know when He is going to come into our ordinary life and do something extraordinary. As you pray today, ask God to prepare you for the extraordinary work He wants to do in your life. You could have a really big impact on someone else, or on the world, when you think you're just having a normal day. Can you think of a time this has happened to you?

HOLY Qs!

- *When good things happen, how do I give God the credit?*
- *What am I thankful for? How can I show how thankful I am this week?*

BLESSING
Go following the way of the Savior, walking in the truth of the King, and living the life of the Friend. May your thoughts, words, and actions reflect the love of Jesus.

BEST FRIEND MATERIAL

LUKE 2:1-20

What's your best friend's name? What do you love to do together? Did you know God's love for you can be like a best friend? Yes, He loves you as His child, but He also loves you as a best friend would. He loves to be with you. He loves to know everything about you. Best friend stuff.

It's not surprising that the shepherds were freaked out by the angel God sent. Who expected that to happen on a quiet night in the country? The bright lights of the angel against the dark night sky probably looked pretty crazy. That's why the words God gave the angel to speak first were words of comfort. "Don't be afraid!" Comforting words from a friend. God wanted them to know He was for them and with them. God is the best friend you could have. Just like He was with the shepherds, He is for you and with you. Even right now as you read this, He is for you and with you. How do you like that?

HOLY Qs!

- *God cares about our whole life, not just the spiritual parts. What healthy habits do I need to work on?*

- *How will I be a good friend and listener?*

BLESSING

Go following the way of the Savior, walking in the truth of the King, and living the life of the Friend. May your thoughts, words, and actions reflect the love of Jesus.

Day 6
THAT'S CRAZY GOOD NEWS

LUKE 2:1-20

Have you ever had good news? Like you got a test back and did better than expected? Maybe you got good news about having a new baby brother or sister. Maybe you have had good news about a fun vacation you get to go on. What good news have you had? How did it make you feel? Pick three words that really describe how you felt when you heard your good news.

Now pick three words that describe how you think the shepherds felt when they got their good news. God announced to them the good news that the Savior of the world was here. Ok, for real, this is the crazy best news the world has ever received. Ever. Can you imagine what that felt like? Now here's good news about that good news: It's for you, too! Jesus came because He loves us. He loves you, friend. The Savior of the entire world loves you. That's good news! How will living in Jesus's love inspire you today?

HOLY Qs!

- *How can God's love give me confidence today?*
- *What habits help me spend time getting to know God through Scripture?*

BLESSING

Go following the way of the Savior, walking in the truth of the King, and living the life of the Friend. May your thoughts, words, and actions reflect the love of Jesus.

TRUTH TELLER

LUKE 2:1-20

Check out verses 11-12 and 16. The angels tell the shepherds exactly what they will find. They will find Jesus wrapped up cozy in a manger. The shepherds headed into town and found exactly what they were told. God's message proved trustworthy.

God is a truth teller and promise keeper. Only a true God, a true King of the world, could have told them exactly where to go and exactly who they'd find. Like the shepherds did that night, you can trust God. You can follow God. When He speaks to you, when He leads you, trust and follow. With a love like His, you can be confident He'll lead you the right way. His love for you is huge. So, trust Him and follow Him. He's a King who knows. He's a Friend who leads. He is good!

HOLY Qs!

- *How can I be obedient to God this week?*
- *What can I do to make wise choices this week?*

BLESSING

Go following the way of the Savior, walking in the truth of the King, and living the life of the Friend. May your thoughts, words, and actions reflect the love of Jesus.

WEEK 5 Day 1
PROPHECY OF SIMEON

It's a new week in your life with Jesus! Use the *5 What's or Lectio Divina* to guide your reading today. Enjoy God's love for you!

LUKE 2:25-35

[25] At that time there was a man in Jerusalem named Simeon. He was righteous and devout and was eagerly waiting for the Messiah to come and rescue Israel. The Holy Spirit was upon him [26] and had revealed to him that he would not die until he had seen the Lord's Messiah. [27] That day the Spirit led him to the Temple. So when Mary and Joseph came to present the baby Jesus to the Lord as the law required, [28] Simeon was there. He took the child in his arms and praised God, saying,

[29] "Sovereign Lord, now let your servant die in peace,
as you have promised.
[30] I have seen your salvation,
[31] which you have prepared for all people.
[32] He is a light to reveal God to the nations,
and he is the glory of your people Israel!"

[33] Jesus' parents were amazed at what was being said about him. [34] Then Simeon blessed them, and he said to Mary, the baby's mother, "This child is destined to cause many in Israel to fall, and many others to rise. He has been sent as a sign from God, but many will oppose him. [35] As a result, the deepest thoughts of many hearts will be revealed. And a sword will pierce your very soul."

ALWAYS. ALWAYS. ALWAYS.

LUKE 2:25-35

Can you remember the feeling you have when you wake up Christmas morning? It's finally here! You might feel a little bit like Simeon. He had been waiting a long time for the Messiah to finally arrive. He was getting old. But the Holy Spirit had told Simeon he would get to meet Jesus, and he was led to the temple by the Spirit the day Jesus's parents brought Him in. It finally happened. Simeon had lived to see the long-awaited promise arrive.

It's hard to be patient when we're waiting on something big, especially when it's been promised. And sometimes it doesn't always come right when we're expecting. Here's the thing, even if it's not exactly how you expected, God always keeps His promises. God has a history—throughout the Bible and beyond—of making promises to His people and always, always, always coming through. What does this mean? He can be trusted. Today, you can have peace knowing your God can always be trusted.

HOLY Qs!

- *How can I be honest and trustworthy this week?*
- *What's a healthy or helpful way I can use my spare time?*

BLESSING

Go following the way of the Savior, walking in the truth of the King, and living the life of the Friend. May your thoughts, words, and actions reflect the love of Jesus.

Day 3
LIVING THE PRAYER LIFE

LUKE 2:25-35

What does someone do if they are completely committed to God? Simeon was righteous and devout. In other words, he was a godly man that was totally committed. The Holy Spirit spoke, and Simeon was ready to listen and obey. His prayer life must have been pretty amazing. Not only did he talk with God, he heard from God and was so locked in on that relationship that he was able to tell what the Holy Spirit was leading him to do.

How's your prayer life? We get to know God through Scripture, and through other Christians, but we also grow closer to God by really spending time with God. That includes speaking in our prayers, and listening in our prayers. Imagine having a prayer life so active that we were totally in tune with what God was saying to us, and what God wanted us to do. Simeon is a great role model of prayer. Be reminded that Jesus is real. You ready to talk to Him?

HOLY Qs!

- *What have I been enjoying about prayer recently?*

- *What habits help me spend time getting to know God through Scripture?*

BLESSING

Go following the way of the Savior, walking in the truth of the King, and living the life of the Friend. May your thoughts, words, and actions reflect the love of Jesus.

REALLY GREAT

LUKE 2:25-35

Yesterday we talked about hearing God through prayer. It's one thing to hear from God, but how we react to hearing from God is another thing. Simeon was led by the Holy Spirit. He had been waiting all that time to meet the Messiah. Imagine if he had woken up that day and said, "You know what? I'm sick of all this waiting. I'm not going to the temple today! I'm taking a day off." What would he have missed?

Name a time you had to obey when it wasn't your favorite thing to do. Being obedient is not always easy. God often doesn't lead us to do things the way we would choose to do them. But, since God really is our good King, obeying Him is a joyful thing! We listen, pray, talk, get close to God, and obey when He leads us because we know He leads out of love. Simeon obeyed, and his lifelong pursuit of meeting the Messiah happened. God has something pretty great in store for you. But you've got a part to play. Trust, and obey.

HOLY Qs!

- *How can I be obedient to God this week?*
- *How can I learn from others this week?*

BLESSING

Go following the way of the Savior, walking in the truth of the King, and living the life of the Friend. May your thoughts, words, and actions reflect the love of Jesus.

Day 5
REVEALING GOD

LUKE 2:25-35

What do you want to know about God? Check out verse 32. The Messiah was the Savior the Jewish people were waiting for. Simeon, who had dedicated his life to the coming of the Messiah, said, "He is a light to reveal God to the nations." We don't celebrate Jesus because He came to do a few miracles or tell some great stories. This verse is important in helping people understand Jesus's purpose on earth. Jesus came to reveal God to us and to save us from our sins. When we see Jesus, His character, and the way He lived His life, we see God. That is something to celebrate!

Now, in your life with Jesus, you get to do the same thing. It's about the way you live your life, the way you treat people, the way you love. You have an opportunity, a calling, to reveal God. People can see who God is through you. Through your relationship with Jesus. Whoa! That's a big deal. How will people see God through you today?

HOLY Qs!

- *Have my words matched my actions? Does who I say I am and how I act line up?*

- *How will I be a good friend and listener?*

BLESSING

Go following the way of the Savior, walking in the truth of the King, and living the life of the Friend. May your thoughts, words, and actions reflect the love of Jesus.

EVERYBODY EVERYWHERE

LUKE 2:25-35

Who is a person you know who lives the farthest away from you? Let's point out something in verses 31-32: "All people" and "to the nations." God is God of the whole world. All the nations. We know that. But to the people in the temple hearing what Simeon was saying, it would have been pretty wild. Most everyone believed the Messiah was coming to save the Jewish people. That's not the whole world. Luke made sure that his whole audience, not just the Israelites, knew that Jesus was for them, too.

Is there anyone in your life that seems like they're a really long way from God? Someone who doesn't know Jesus? Maybe someone that doesn't really care to? Maybe it's someone in your family or at school. Maybe you can't even see a way in your head that they would ever know Jesus. Guess what? Jesus is for them, too.

HOLY Qs!

- *Is there anyone I'm struggling to get along with? What am I going to do about it?*

- *Who in my life needs to hear about Jesus? How can they hear it from me?*

BLESSING

Go following the way of the Savior, walking in the truth of the King, and living the life of the Friend. May your thoughts, words, and actions reflect the love of Jesus.

Day 7
IT'S TOUGH SOMETIMES

LUKE 2:25-35

What's something in your life that has been hard to get through? In verse 35 Simeon tells Mary, "a sword will pierce your very soul." Ouch! He wasn't talking about a real sword piercing Mary. Rather, Simeon was speaking as a prophet (a messenger from God) about how difficult Jesus's life was going to be. People wouldn't believe Him. He would be rejected. Eventually, He would be killed. Mary was going to have to watch all of this happen. For a mother, this would be devastating.

Jesus's life was not going to be easy, and He never promises an easy life for His followers. Sometimes, following Jesus is very hard. Sometimes, we feel like we don't fit in because we follow Jesus. Sometimes, we have to make choices that don't feel like the fun choice because we follow Jesus. But every time it's hard, remember that Jesus has been there. He understands. He goes with you into those hard things. He's with you before and after. His love for you never changes, no matter how hard things get.

HOLY Qs!

- *How can I keep from letting things like popularity or friends determine how I act?*
- *What can I do to make wise choices this week?*

BLESSING

Go following the way of the Savior, walking in the truth of the King, and living the life of the Friend. May your thoughts, words, and actions reflect the love of Jesus.

WEEK 6 Day 1
PROPHECY OF ANNA

It's a new week in your life with Jesus! Use the *5 What's or Lectio Divina* to guide your reading today. Enjoy God's love for you!

LUKE 2:36-40

[36] Anna, a prophet, was also there in the Temple. She was the daughter of Phanuel from the tribe of Asher, and she was very old. Her husband died when they had been married only seven years. [37] Then she lived as a widow to the age of eighty-four. She never left the Temple but stayed there day and night, worshiping God with fasting and prayer. [38] She came along just as Simeon was talking with Mary and Joseph, and she began praising God. She talked about the child to everyone who had been waiting expectantly for God to rescue Jerusalem.
[39] When Jesus' parents had fulfilled all the requirements of the law of the Lord, they returned home to Nazareth in Galilee. [40] There the child grew up healthy and strong. He was filled with wisdom, and God's favor was on him.

Day 2
HE SEES YOU

LUKE 2:36-40

Has someone ever read a story to you, and you could tell they skipped a part? Maybe it was getting late and they were struggling to keep their eyes open. They thought they could skip to the end without you noticing. There is a scene in Jesus's story that often gets skipped as well. It's about something amazing that happened when Jesus was 40 days old. Last week, you were able to explore part of it when you studied the story of Simeon. The Scripture this week reveals there was another person, Anna, who celebrated Jesus's arrival. She played an important role in sharing news about Jesus with people who were waiting to hear about a Savior.

As a kid, you might feel like this sometimes. Overlooked. Anna's story isn't long, or full of action, but it's important. God does not create people who are unnecessary to His story. Everyone He creates is important and loved. That includes you.

HOLY Qs!

- *How can I keep from letting things like popularity or friends determine how I act?*

- *How can God's love give me confidence today?*

BLESSING

Go following the way of the Savior, walking in the truth of the King, and living the life of the Friend. May your thoughts, words, and actions reflect the love of Jesus.

WORSHIP ISN'T STINKY

LUKE 2:36-40

Have you ever had a day where everything went wrong? Some days just stink. Well, Anna had some stinky years. Her husband died after they had only been married seven years. That was really hard because she would have no one to provide for her and no one to carry on the family name. Instead of becoming bitter, Anna decided to turn to God for healing. She dedicated her life to Him.

We can learn a lot from Anna about how to handle hard times. She turned to God and worshiped through it all. God is more than able to handle your worries, fears, and pain. Talk to God about your aching heart. Praying and writing in a journal are great ways to express your feelings. God can also work through other people to give you guidance and relief. You are not alone! Give those stinky days to God. Worship can keep you going.

HOLY Qs!

- God cares about our whole life, not just the spiritual parts. What healthy habits do I need to work on?

- Is anything in my life really hard right now? Am I talking to God about it? Who else can I talk to?

BLESSING

Go following the way of the Savior, walking in the truth of the King, and living the life of the Friend. May your thoughts, words, and actions reflect the love of Jesus.

Day 4
WHO'S THAT?

LUKE 2:36-40

At the age of 84, Anna's physical hearing might have been fading. But she had no problem hearing God. This passage says Anna never left the temple. She just stayed there all day and night praying, worshiping, and learning from God. This deepened her relationship with God. They were close friends.

Think about older adults in your life who seem to spend incredible amounts of time praying, worshiping, and learning from God. Maybe they actually spend lots and lots of time at your church building fixing things up, teaching others, or helping the community. Maybe they do most of their work for Jesus outside the church building. How do you see adults around you living their lives with Jesus? How do they inspire you or teach you? How do their lives help inspire your life with Jesus?

HOLY Qs!

- *What habits help me spend time getting to know God through Scripture?*

- *What's a healthy or helpful way I can use my spare time?*

BLESSING

Go following the way of the Savior, walking in the truth of the King, and living the life of the Friend. May your thoughts, words, and actions reflect the love of Jesus.

SPREAD THE WORD

LUKE 2:36-40

Who is a woman in your life that has shown you Jesus's love? There are only a handful of women in the Bible who are called prophets Anna was the first female prophet mentioned in the New Testament. She spoke everything God told her to speak. After meeting Mary, Joseph, and Jesus, she began praising God. She knew there were many people who were waiting for a Savior. She was thrilled that God had allowed her to share the good news about Jesus's arrival.

Good news is meant to be shared. If you played a game you thought was amazing, you would want to tell others all about it so they could play. You wouldn't want your friends to miss out. Well, this is better than any game. This is Jesus! There are still people who do not know what a life with Jesus is all about. If you have the desire to tell others about Him, but are not sure how to explain what it means to be a Christian, check out page vii for some ideas.

HOLY Qs!

- *Who in my life needs to hear about Jesus? How can they hear it from me?*

BLESSING

Go following the way of the Savior, walking in the truth of the King, and living the life of the Friend. May your thoughts, words, and actions reflect the love of Jesus.

Day 6
HANGING OUT IN WORSHIP

LUKE 2:36-40

What's your favorite way to worship God? Anna spent every day worshiping. God granted her the honor of being a witness when Mary and Joseph brought Jesus to the temple. Anna and Simeon got to be witnesses that baby Jesus was the Messiah. Imagine what they would have missed if they decided they were too busy to worship in the temple that day.

We often think people are awesome if they have busy and exciting lives. By today's standards, Anna's lifestyle might seem boring. Not all of us are called to spend every moment of every day at church. But we can follow Anna's example and be fully devoted to God, worshiping each day. What are some ways you can worship Jesus every day, even if you aren't hanging out at church? How can you worship at school? How can you worship outside? How can you worship at home? He deserves our every-single-day worship!

HOLY Qs!

- *Have my words matched my actions? Does who I say I am and how I act line up?*
- *How does what I learned from Scripture inspire my thoughts and actions?*

BLESSING

Go following the way of the Savior, walking in the truth of the King, and living the life of the Friend. May your thoughts, words, and actions reflect the love of Jesus.

NOT SO FAMOUS

If you were famous, what would it be for? Do you realize Anna is only mentioned in three verses in the Bible? She was the daughter of Phanuel, who had never even been mentioned before. She was from one of the less famous tribes in Israel, Asher. She was single, a widow, and old. But God has a history of working through people who didn't seem very important. David began as a shepherd boy. The disciples were fishermen before they became famous to us. God often chooses humble people to make a difference, so there is no question about the source of their power. Anna became a witness and a prophet for our Savior. Not bad for someone who didn't seem famous.

You do not have to come from a famous family. You do not have to be the best basketball player, singer, or student. He loves you because He created you. What is important is that you follow God and let His love work through your life. He can do big things. See what happens.

HOLY Qs!

- How can I learn from others this week?
- How does my relationship with Jesus impact my daily life in real ways?

BLESSING

Go following the way of the Savior, walking in the truth of the King, and living the life of the Friend. May your thoughts, words, and actions reflect the love of Jesus.

WEEK 7 Day 1
THE MAGI

It's a new week in your life with Jesus! Use the *5 What's or Lectio Divina* to guide your reading today. Enjoy God's love for you!

MATTHEW 2:1-14 (NIV)

¹ After Jesus was born in Bethlehem in Judea, during the time of King Herod, Magi from the east came to Jerusalem ² and asked, "Where is the one who has been born king of the Jews? We saw his star when it rose and have come to worship him."
³ When King Herod heard this he was disturbed, and all Jerusalem with him. ⁴ When he had called together all the people's chief priests and teachers of the law, he asked them where the Messiah was to be born. ⁵ "In Bethlehem in Judea," they replied, "for this is what the prophet has written:
⁶ "'But you, Bethlehem, in the land of Judah, are by no means least among the rulers of Judah; for out of you will come a ruler who will shepherd my people Israel.'"

⁷ Then Herod called the Magi secretly and found out from them the exact time the star had appeared. ⁸ He sent them to Bethlehem and said, "Go and search carefully for the child. As soon as you find him, report to me, so that I too may go and worship him."

⁹ After they had heard the king, they went on their way, and the star they had seen when it rose went ahead of them until it stopped over the place where the child was. ¹⁰ When they saw the star, they were overjoyed. ¹¹ On coming to the house, they saw the child with his mother Mary, and they bowed down and worshiped him. Then they opened their treasures and presented him with gifts of gold, frankincense and myrrh. ¹² And having been warned in a dream not to go back to Herod, they returned to their country by another route.

¹³ When they had gone, an angel of the Lord appeared to Joseph in a dream. "Get up," he said, "take the child and his mother and escape to Egypt. Stay there until I tell you, for Herod is going to search for the child to kill him."

¹⁴ So he got up, took the child and his mother during the night and left for Egypt.

Day 2
WHAT'S A MAGI?

MATTHEW 2:1-14

Some Bible translations call them kings, others say wise men. The word Matthew uses is *magi*, a title used for those who studied the stars. These were educated men. Although they weren't scientists like the ones we have today, they had studied the stars their whole lives. They had memorized the patterns of the stars and constellations. They knew how the night sky changed with the different seasons. They gave stars names, and measured their distances from one another.

Then one night, these men saw something that made them sit up and take notice. A brand new star showed up! Most people probably didn't even notice a new star up in the sky with all the rest. But the Magi were paying attention. The God who created the sun, the moon, and the stars was making a big announcement. Do you think God has ever tried to get your attention?

HOLY Qs!

- *When good things happen, how do I give God the credit?*

BLESSING

Go following the way of the Savior, walking in the truth of the King, and living the life of the Friend. May your thoughts, words, and actions reflect the love of Jesus.

THE GOD OF SURPRISES

MATTHEW 2:1-14

One thing you'll quickly learn is that God is very surprising. God never seems to do what we would do if we were God. He does things we don't expect, even things we don't understand.

For hundreds of years God had been promising that a new king, the Messiah, would come. God spoke through prophets and Scripture. But no one expected God to speak through stars! And certainly no one who followed God expected God to share the best secret in the world with *magi*. These men were not Jewish; they were not part of God's chosen people. They probably had heard stories about Israel's God, but the people in their country practiced a different religion.

But this surprising God decided to talk to them in the language they understood best: the stars. Their story reminds us that God wants all people to know and see God. And God will always do surprising things to make that happen. How might God use you to reach out to someone in an unexpected way?

HOLY Qs!

- *What habits help me spend time getting to know God through Scripture?*

BLESSING

Go following the way of the Savior, walking in the truth of the King, and living the life of the Friend. May your thoughts, words, and actions reflect the love of Jesus.

Day 4
EPIPHANY!

MATTHEW 2:1-14

Have you ever heard the word "epiphany" (e-PIF-a-nee)? It's not something that happens to you every day. An epiphany is a huge, life-changing experience. It's like when the mystery is solved, or the light bulb goes on. The missing piece is found, and suddenly every-thing makes sense. An epiphany is what happens to make people say, "Ah-ha!" or "Eureka!"

For thousands of years, Christians have used the word Epiphany to tell the story of the magi. They had an "ah-ha moment" that changed their lives forever. And it has been so important to the church that they gave this day its own special holiday on January 6. It begins a season of Epiphany that lasts several weeks, until Ash Wednesday. These days remind us that God is still working in the world, showing us who God is.

Think about your own life. Have you ever had an epiphany moment? A moment when you suddenly understood some-thing about God that you didn't before? Epiphany is God's gift to everyone, not just magi!

HOLY Qs!

- God cares about our whole life, not just the spiritual parts. What healthy habits do I need to work on?
- What's a healthy or helpful way I can use my spare time?

BLESSING

Go following the way of the Savior, walking in the truth of the King, and living the life of the Friend. May your thoughts, words, and actions reflect the love of Jesus.

STEPPING OUT

MATTHEW 2:1-14

What's the longest trip you've ever taken? A life-changing discovery can make you do crazy things. After their epiphany the magi decided they had to go honor this new king. They purchased very expensive gifts and got ready for a *really* long trip. If you look on a world map, you can see how far it is from Iran to Jerusalem. Traveling by camel, this could have taken a year or more!

The magi took a huge risk and made big sacrifices to do this. They probably had some family or friends who thought they were crazy. But they were determined. They knew how important it was, even if they didn't know what to expect.

The magi were courageous, trusting, and full of faith. Don't you want those words to describe you? Following God looks like this most of the time. We don't know everything, but what we do know, we want more of! Think about times you've been courageous, trusting, and full of faith recently.

HOLY Qs!

- *How can I be obedient to God this week?*

BLESSING

Go following the way of the Savior, walking in the truth of the King, and living the life of the Friend. May your thoughts, words, and actions reflect the love of Jesus.

Day 6
WHAT KIND OF KING?

MATTHEW 2:1-14

Whew! After the longest road trip ever, the magi were in the city of Jerusalem, home of King Herod's palace. But to their surprise (and King Herod's!), the new baby King was not born into a royal family at all. Instead, they found Him in a small house in the village of Bethlehem, outside of the big city. This is our first clue that King Jesus is not like any king we've ever known.

It may not have been the king they expected, but when the magi saw Him they were filled with joy. Something surprising and wonderful was happening. Even the stars knew about this child! Filled with wonder, they gave their gifts and worshiped a toddler.

Talk about surprising! Some of the first people to worship Jesus were from a different culture, spoke a different language, and came from a country far away. This King Jesus is not like other kings—He's the King for *all* people. How can you help share the news of King Jesus with someone from somewhere else in the world?

HOLY Qs!

- *Is there anyone I'm struggling to get along with? What am I going to do about it?*
- *How can the way I spend my money reflect my relationship with Jesus?*

BLESSING

Go following the way of the Savior, walking in the truth of the King, and living the life of the Friend. May your thoughts, words, and actions reflect the love of Jesus.

JESUS THE REFUGEE

MATTHEW 2:1-14

What do you see when you think of a bad king? King Herod was a terrible king. He cared more about his own comfort and power than anything else. He told the magi he wanted to worship the baby King, but he actually wanted to kill Him.

God warned the magi and Joseph in dreams so they could escape. Jesus's parents packed up everything they could carry, and left as quickly as possible. They went to the nearby country of Egypt as refugees. A refugee is a person who leaves their home country because it is not safe. Today there are more than 70 million refugees around the world who had to leave their homes because they were in danger. Many of them are children, just like Jesus was.

What do you think Jesus's parents were thinking while sneaking out for safety? Jesus knows what fear feels like. Jesus knows what it is like to depend on the kindness of strangers. Jesus is King of refugees, too.

HOLY Qs!

- *How can I keep from letting things like popularity or friends determine how I act?*
- *How does what I learned from Scripture inspire my thoughts and actions?*

BLESSING

Go following the way of the Savior, walking in the truth of the King, and living the life of the Friend. May your thoughts, words, and actions reflect the love of Jesus.

JESUS AT THE TEMPLE AS A BOY

LUKE 2:41-52

⁴¹ Every year Jesus' parents went to Jerusalem for the Passover festival. ⁴² When Jesus was twelve years old, they attended the festival as usual. ⁴³ After the celebration was over, they started home to Nazareth, but Jesus stayed behind in Jerusalem. His parents didn't miss him at first, ⁴⁴ because they assumed he was among the other travelers. But when he didn't show up that evening, they started looking for him among their relatives and friends.

⁴⁵ When they couldn't find him, they went back to Jerusalem to search for him there. ⁴⁶ Three days later they finally discovered him in the Temple, sitting among the religious teachers, listening to them and asking questions. ⁴⁷ All who heard him were amazed at his understanding and his answers.

⁴⁸ His parents didn't know what to think. "Son," his mother said to him, "why have you done this to us? Your father and I have been frantic, searching for you everywhere."

⁴⁹ "But why did you need to search?" he asked. "Didn't you know that I must be in my Father's house?" ⁵⁰ But they didn't understand what he meant. ⁵¹ Then he returned to Nazareth with them and was obedient to them. And his mother stored all these things in her heart. ⁵² Jesus grew in wisdom and in stature and in favor with God and all the people.

Day 2
IT'S A PARTY!

LUKE 2:41-52

Have you ever had a party? Maybe a birthday party? How about a big family reunion? It's so much fun to get people from all over together. What's an awesome party you've been to? What made the celebration so great?

Jesus and His family were following the law of Moses from the book of Exodus (23:14-17 to be exact). They were getting together with other Jews from all over the region for the Passover Feast (we'll talk more about this tomorrow). That's a big party. Let's point out something huge here: God likes to party. He loves to get His people together in celebration and joy. This is a huge part of God's character that most people miss. In the kingdom of God, in the heart of God, there is a place for partying! How's that feel? What do you think God likes to celebrate most?

HOLY Qs!

- *How can God's love give me confidence today?*
- *What have I been enjoying about prayer recently?*

BLESSING

Go following the way of the Savior, walking in the truth of the King, and living the life of the Friend. May your thoughts, words, and actions reflect the love of Jesus.

Day 3

PASS ME OVER

LUKE 2:41-52

Let's learn about Passover. What do you know about Moses? Do you remember when they were in Egypt and Pharaoh wouldn't listen to God? There were 10 plagues. How many can you name? Look at Exodus chapters 7—11 for the full list. The last plague involved death, but God told the Israelites to place the blood of a lamb on their door. Then death would pass over (Passover!) their houses and no one would die that night. So God's people did just that. Now, years later, they still celebrate life in God with the Passover festival.

We celebrate life in God, too. But instead of the blood of a lamb on our door, we celebrate our Savior, Jesus, who gave His blood on the cross to save us from death. We have new life in Jesus! That's why Jesus is sometimes called the Lamb. If you want to learn more about knowing Jesus as your Savior, turn to page vii. How does Jesus give you new life?

HOLY Qs!

- *What am I thankful for? How can I show how thankful I am this week?*
- *What habits help me spend time getting to know God through Scripture?*

BLESSING

Go following the way of the Savior, walking in the truth of the King, and living the life of the Friend. May your thoughts, words, and actions reflect the love of Jesus.

Day 4
WHERE'D YOU GO?

LUKE 2:41-52

What does it mean to be trustworthy? Look at verses 43-44. In Jesus's culture it was not unusual for His parents to not know where He was for a while. At His age, 12, He would have been trusted to spend even a couple of days away from His parents, with relatives or friends. That's why they didn't miss Him at first. It wasn't bad parenting. It was trust.

Of course, after a while, they did start to miss Jesus. They tracked Him down and asked Him what He was up to. He gave them the perfect answer in verse 49. He was doing exactly what God—His Father—wanted Him to do. Even away from His parents, Jesus could be trusted to make the right choices. That's not always easy. We can learn from Jesus, even when He was a kid. Being trustworthy means that even when you could get away with doing something wrong or not so great, you make the right choice anyway. When you pray today, ask for the courage to be trustworthy, no matter the situation.

HOLY Qs!

• *How can I be honest and trustworthy this week?*

• *How have I been trustworthy recently?*

BLESSING

Go following the way of the Savior, walking in the truth of the King, and living the life of the Friend. May your thoughts, words, and actions reflect the love of Jesus.

Day 5
I DON'T GET IT

LUKE 2:41-52

What's something that's kind of hard for you to understand? Math? Spelling? Trying to understand why they can't create a cereal that doesn't get so soggy in milk? Truth is, there's a lot we don't understand. And the older we get, the more we realize how much we don't know.

If you find yourself not understanding life, or a situation you're in, or even something God is doing, you aren't alone. Look at verses 49-50. Mary and Joseph felt the same. Proverbs 3:5 says that we can trust God instead of our own understanding of things. Why? Because we don't always understand what God is up to. There's no way we could, because we aren't God! We can trust that God is good, though. God is leading us through life with never-ending wisdom and love. Yesterday we talked about being trustworthy. Today, be reminded that God is trustworthy and always good!

HOLY Qs!

- Is anything in my life really hard right now? Am I talking to God about it? Who else can I talk to?

- How does my relationship with Jesus impact my daily life in real ways?

BLESSING

Go following the way of the Savior, walking in the truth of the King, and living the life of the Friend. May your thoughts, words, and actions reflect the love of Jesus.

FROM ME TO WE

LUKE 2:41-52

Okay, so this is gonna hurt. Life is not all about you. No, really, it's not. Too harsh? One of the hardest things for us to learn is obedience, which means doing something even if it's not our first choice. Ever had an adult say, "I'm so tired of you obeying me all the time!" Never happened. We naturally want to do our own thing. My way. When I want, how, when, where, and if I want. Me, me, me. Sin makes us naturally inclined toward selfishness.

Look at verse 51. Jesus was an obedient kid. He obeyed His parents, and God. Being in a relationship with Him and getting to know Him more leads to our obedience, too. When we see that life isn't about just doing whatever we want, we can begin to live into all the great things God has for us. Life is actually better when we aren't just doing our own thing. So, whether it's following God or a trusted adult, obedience is a big deal. Jesus taught us how to value it!

HOLY Qs!

- How can I learn from others this week?

- How can I be obedient to God this week?

BLESSING

Go following the way of the Savior, walking in the truth of the King, and living the life of the Friend. May your thoughts, words, and actions reflect the love of Jesus.

Day 7
GROWING PAINS

LUKE 2:41-52

What's the best thing about being a kid and not being a grown-up yet? What's the hard part about it? Growing up can be difficult—like getting more chores. It can also be super fun—like getting more privileges. It's both. Sometimes it can even be both at the same time. Crazy, right?

Jesus grew. In verse 52 we read that He grew in wisdom. We also know that He grew in trustworthiness. Stature means that as He grew, the people around Him trusted Him. They knew He was a good person. Not just in public, but all the time. He also had hard experiences. It definitely wasn't easy growing up in those days. It was hard work just to survive. So Jesus knows what you're going through. He had growing pains, too. What can we learn from verse 52 about the way Jesus grew up? What would it take for us to say, "I grew up like Jesus"?

HOLY Qs!

- *Have I been jealous, grumpy, or really hard on anyone? What can I do about it?*
- *What can I do to make wise choices this week?*

BLESSING

Go following the way of the Savior, walking in the truth of the King, and living the life of the Friend. May your thoughts, words, and actions reflect the love of Jesus.

WEEK 9 Day 1
BAPTISM OF JESUS

It's a new week in your life with Jesus! Use the *5 What's or Lectio Divina* to guide your reading today. Enjoy God's love for you!

MARK 1:9-11

9 One day Jesus came from Nazareth in Galilee, and John baptized him in the Jordan River. 10 As Jesus came up out of the water, he saw the heavens splitting apart and the Holy Spirit descending on him like a dove. 11 And a voice from heaven said, "You are my dearly loved Son, and you bring me great joy."

Day 2
LIVING THE JESUS LIFE

MARK 1:9-11

What's something Jesus did that you try to do? Jesus didn't just teach us what to do. He *showed* us what to do. He modeled a Christian life for us. With the help of the Holy Spirit, we can live the same way Jesus lived. When He was baptized by John the Baptist, we received a great example of this modeling. Jesus could have just told everyone, "Go and be baptized." But instead He showed everyone what it meant and looked like to be baptized.

Our words matter, but our actions must match them. The best way we can teach our friends, family, and neighbors about Jesus is to live like He did. We don't just talk about Christian life. We *live* Christian life. This starts with a relationship with Jesus. Check out page vii to learn more. Then, part of that relationship is learning about the way Jesus lived, and following His example. This includes baptism, but it's also about our life every day. How do you live like Jesus?

HOLY Qs!

- What can I do to make wise choices this week?
- How can the way I spend my money reflect my relationship with Jesus?

BLESSING

Go following the way of the Savior, walking in the truth of the King, and living the life of the Friend. May your thoughts, words, and actions reflect the love of Jesus.

BAPTISM AND ANOTHER BIG WORD

MARK 1:9-11

Time to learn a new word. "Sacrament" (SACK-ruh-ment). A sacrament is an important action in the church that is a special way of receiving God's grace. Sacraments are always done with other Christians around, in a group or community (church). Sacraments usually have some important words that are said. Sacraments are things that Jesus both told us that we are to do and showed us how to do.

Baptism is one of the sacraments in the church. Do you know the other? (Hint: Check out Week 44.) God's grace is given to us through the sacraments. God's presence is with us in the sacraments. We can live our whole lives in God's presence, but there's something special about what the Spirit does in us through baptism. Have you been baptized? If so, what do you remember about it? Why did you do it? Talk with a trusted adult or pastor to help you remember. If you haven't been, are you interested in baptism?

HOLY Qs!

• *How can God's love give me confidence today?*

BLESSING

Go following the way of the Savior, walking in the truth of the King, and living the life of the Friend. May your thoughts, words, and actions reflect the love of Jesus.

Day 4
RIVER OF FREEDOM

MARK 1:9-11

What do you think of when you hear the word "freedom"? The Jordan River shows up several times in the Bible. It holds a special place in the history of the Israelites because Joshua led them across the Jordan after 40 years in the desert, on their journey to finally receive their promised land. (Check out Joshua 3 for that story.) Because of this story, the Jordan River can be associated with freedom. They crossed out of life in the desert into the freedom of a good life in their new home.

Thousands of years later, Jesus was baptized in that same river . . . the river that represents freedom. Baptism is a way of announcing our life with Jesus to the whole world. We want to tell everyone how good He is. In our relationship with Jesus, we are given freedom! Freedom from life controlled by sin. Let's celebrate! Jesus was baptized in the river of freedom, and came to set people free. What else about your relationship with Jesus gives you freedom?

HOLY Qs!

- *What's a healthy or helpful way I can use my spare time?*
- *How does what I learned from Scripture inspire my thoughts and actions?*

BLESSING

Go following the way of the Savior, walking in the truth of the King, and living the life of the Friend. May your thoughts, words, and actions reflect the love of Jesus.

WELCOME TO THE FAMILY

MARK 1:9-11

What are three things you love about your family? Being a part of a family can be a huge blessing. Healthy families offer support, love, and maybe even chocolate chip cookies. Take a look at verse 11. When Jesus was baptized, God claimed Him, out loud, as His own Son. Pretty sweet. When you were baptized, or when you get baptized someday, you might not hear God's voice booming from heaven, but the celebration will be just as real!

You don't have to be baptized to be in God's family, but baptism is a very public way of celebrating your place as a child of God. Don't just quietly be a Christian. Tell people about it. Celebrate it! We do that through baptism. We also do that through our words and actions each day. It's like bragging on someone in your family. "See that firefighter? Yeah, that's my mom. She's cool." "See those beautiful mountains? Yeah, made by my God. God is cool." How excited are you to be a part of God's family?

HOLY Qs!

- *When good things happen, how do I give God the credit?*
- *Who in my life needs to hear about Jesus? How can they hear it from me?*

BLESSING

Go following the way of the Savior, walking in the truth of the King, and living the life of the Friend. May your thoughts, words, and actions reflect the love of Jesus.

Day 6
WE'RE BEST FRIENDS

MARK 1:9-11

Why are you and your best friend best friends? What makes your friendship such a good one? Jesus is our Savior, saving us from a life controlled by sin. He's our King, wise and strong. But He's also our Friend. He knows all about being a best friend. Best friends stay with you no matter what, even when things are really hard. Best friends like to hang out. Best friends don't stop being your friend if you get angry. Best friends give you good advice.

When Jesus was baptized, the Holy Spirit joined Him in verse 10. The Holy Spirit is the way God stays with us as a Friend. The Holy Spirit goes before us and prepares a way for us. The Holy Spirit is with us every day and night. The Holy Spirit guides us to wise choices. A friend that never leaves and always has what's best for us in mind. What a gift! What do you love about having Jesus as a friend?

HOLY Qs!

- How will I be a good friend and listener?
- Have I been jealous, grumpy, or really hard on anyone? What can I do about it?

BLESSING

Go following the way of the Savior, walking in the truth of the King, and living the life of the Friend. May your thoughts, words, and actions reflect the love of Jesus.

Day 7

WHEN GOD SPEAKS

MARK 1:9-11

What do you think God's voice sounds like? Try it out loud. Wouldn't it be great if God just spoke out loud whenever we needed to hear something important? Things sure would be a lot easier if we didn't have to guess what the right choice was, or what we think God is thinking. God often speaks to us in different ways. You may go your whole life without ever hearing God speak out loud. But as you learn how to listen for His leading, you might realize God is speaking to you every single day.

God puts wise people in our life—parents, pastors, grandparents, Sunday school teachers, and others who guide us. God gives us the Bible, a book full of wisdom that teaches us who God is. In prayer, in quiet times, God can make things clear to us. God speaks to us through all of these things. Through songs, sermons, nature, other Christians, and so many other ways, God speaks. In your prayer today, ask Jesus to help you hear clearly when He speaks.

HOLY Qs!

- *What have I been enjoying about prayer recently?*
- *How can I learn from others this week?*

BLESSING

Go following the way of the Savior, walking in the truth of the King, and living the life of the Friend. May your thoughts, words, and actions reflect the love of Jesus.

65

WEEK 10 Day 1
TEMPTATION OF JESUS

MATTHEW 4:1-11

¹ Then Jesus was led by the Spirit into the wilderness to be tempted there by the devil. ² For forty days and forty nights he fasted and became very hungry. ³ During that time the devil came and said to him, "If you are the Son of God, tell these stones to become loaves of bread." ⁴ But Jesus told him, "No! The Scriptures say,
'People do not live by bread alone, but by every word that comes from the mouth of God.'"
⁵ Then the devil took him to the holy city, Jerusalem, to the highest point of the Temple, ⁶ and said, "If you are the Son of God, jump off! For the Scriptures say, 'He will order his angels to protect you. And they will hold you up with their hands so you won't even hurt your foot on a stone.'"
⁷ Jesus responded, "The Scriptures also say, 'You must not test the LORD your God.'"
⁸ Next the devil took him to the peak of a very high mountain and showed him all the kingdoms of the world and their glory. ⁹ "I will give it all to you," he said, "if you will kneel down and worship me."
¹⁰ "Get out of here, Satan," Jesus told him. "For the Scriptures say, 'You must worship the LORD your God and serve only him.'"
¹¹ Then the devil went away, and angels came and took care of Jesus.

CARTOON TEMPTATION

MATTHEW 4:1-11

What's your favorite cartoon? Some cartoons show the devil as a tiny guy in a red suit holding a pitchfork. He sits on someone's shoulder, whispering into his or her ear. A little cartoon angel sometimes sits on the other shoulder with a halo and a harp. It's like the two are equally powerful and they're trying to convince someone to do one thing or another. This is, of course, not how temptation really works. You won't find any cartoons in this passage.

God is more powerful than any evil. The enemy can be very convincing, but God gives us the power to resist temptation when we're struggling to make the right choice. What can you find in this story that can help you when you're facing temptation? Remember that God can give you the strength you need. Dive deeper into the Word and ask Jesus to help you stay strong. On your own, temptation to do wrong might seem too strong. With God working through you, the devil does not stand a chance.

HOLY Qs!

- How can I be obedient to God this week?

- Is anything in my life really hard right now? Am I talking to God about it? Who else can I talk to?

BLESSING

Go following the way of the Savior, walking in the truth of the King, and living the life of the Friend. May your thoughts, words, and actions reflect the love of Jesus.

Day 3
STRONGER AND STRONGER

MATTHEW 4:1-11

The first verse in our passage might seem a bit confusing. Do you think the Spirit really led Jesus into the wilderness to be tempted by the devil? It seems like the Spirit would lead Jesus *away* from temptation. At this point in Jesus's life, He had just been baptized. He heard God say how much He loved Him and was pleased with Him. The devil wanted to stop Jesus. God allowed the devil to tempt Jesus in order to strengthen Him and prepare Him for ministry.

It is important for us to know that God never tempts us. When we are tempted, we can rely on God to guide us through. In those times, we get stronger. The closer we walk with God, the stronger we get in resisting temptation. God can help us face temptation and use the experience for us to grow and build His kingdom. Can you think of a time God helped you through temptation? How are you stronger now?

HOLY Qs!

- *How does what I learned from Scripture inspire my thoughts and actions?*

BLESSING

Go following the way of the Savior, walking in the truth of the King, and living the life of the Friend. May your thoughts, words, and actions reflect the love of Jesus.

Day 4
STONE-COLD TEMPTATION

MATTHEW 4:1-11

Imagine how hungry you would be if you did not eat for 40 days and 40 nights! That is how long Jesus fasted in the wilderness. What kind of food would you miss the most? Jesus gave up food to focus on God. The devil knew that Jesus was very hungry, so he tempted Him with food. It seems harmless, but bread was not the issue. Jesus was sent to earth to be a man, not Superman. He had access to power, but it was to serve others, not himself. Turning stones into bread would have been a self-centered use of power. It also would have been a distraction from Jesus's time with God. Jesus quoted Scripture to fight temptation.

If you feel like you are being tempted, you can find power through the Bible. Quoting or reading Scripture can help you focus your thoughts on God. Scripture is powerful! What temptations are you facing? What Scripture could you memorize this week?

HOLY Qs!

- *What habits help me spend time getting to know God through Scripture?*
- *What can I do to make wise choices this week?*

BLESSING

Go following the way of the Savior, walking in the truth of the King, and living the life of the Friend. May your thoughts, words, and actions reflect the love of Jesus.

Day 5
THAT'S TOTAL TRUST

MATTHEW 4:1-11

Has anyone ever tricked you? After his failed attempt to get Jesus to turn stones into bread, the devil tried to convince Jesus to jump off the highest part of the temple. He copied Jesus's Scripture-quoting tactic with a verse from Psalm 91. He wanted Jesus to test God's protection. The devil also tried to attack Jesus's pride by saying, "*if you are the Son of God.*" He knew very well who Jesus really was. The devil was tempting Jesus to show people that He was God's Son. What a dramatic scene it would be to jump from the temple top and have angels save Him. Jesus again used Scripture in His refusal and was obedient to God.

If you've ever felt attacked or tricked, Jesus understands. The devil was trying to do this very thing to Him. So take a look at verse 7. Jesus had total trust in God. He didn't need God to prove it. When you are tempted, how can having total trust in God help you fight temptation and make the right choice?

HOLY Qs!

- *How can I keep from letting things like popularity or friends determine how I act?*
- *How can God's love give me confidence today?*

BLESSING

Go following the way of the Savior, walking in the truth of the King, and living the life of the Friend. May your thoughts, words, and actions reflect the love of Jesus.

Day 6
RICHES AND POWER

MATTHEW 4:1-11

Who are some of your role models? Jesus came to earth in human form so He could relate to us. He experienced great pain for our benefit. When the devil tried to tempt Jesus the third time, he clearly misread Jesus's character. He offered Jesus kingdoms and glory if He would just bow down and worship him. The devil must have been very desperate at this point. Jesus gave up His heavenly kingdom to join us on earth. Seriously. He did not care about riches and power. He had a humble heart.

Jesus came to earth so we could see how to live in God's love. We don't need to be obsessed with riches and power. Those things don't love us the way God loves us. Thanks to Jesus, we know how to move past selfishness and serve others. How can riches and power get in the way of our life with Jesus? How does God's love keep us focused on Him?

HOLY Qs!

- *Have my words matched my actions? Does who I say I am and how I act line up?*

- *How does my relationship with Jesus impact my daily life in real ways?*

BLESSING

Go following the way of the Savior, walking in the truth of the King, and living the life of the Friend. May your thoughts, words, and actions reflect the love of Jesus.

Day 7
WINNER WINNER

MATTHEW 4:1-11

What's one of your favorite movies? Does it have a happy or sad ending? After tempting Jesus three times, the devil finally catches on. Jesus knows how to defend himself with Scripture and does not give into temptation. The devil leaves, and angels come to take care of Jesus. Did you catch that? Jesus goes through a lot in this passage, but He comes out victorious. He wins! The devil loses. That doesn't mean it was easy, but it is a simple truth worth remembering. Jesus is gonna win. Sin and evil are gonna lose.

Of course we like movies with happy endings. We like to celebrate victories! When we live a life with Jesus as our Savior, King, and Friend, we get to live a life of victory. That doesn't mean we always get what we want, or everything is always easy. But if Jesus is our reason for living the way we do, we're going to have lots of victories to celebrate. What victories can you celebrate right now?

HOLY Qs!

- God cares about our whole life, not just the spiritual parts. What healthy habits do I need to work on?
- When good things happen, how do I give God the credit?

BLESSING

Go following the way of the Savior, walking in the truth of the King, and living the life of the Friend. May your thoughts, words, and actions reflect the love of Jesus.

WEEK 11 Day 1
FOLLOWING JESUS

It's a new week in your life with Jesus! Use the *5 What's or Lectio Divina* to guide your reading today. Enjoy God's love for you!

MATTHEW 4:17-24

[17] From then on Jesus began to preach, "Repent of your sins and turn to God, for the Kingdom of Heaven is near."
[18] One day as Jesus was walking along the shore of the Sea of Galilee, he saw two brothers—Simon, also called Peter, and Andrew—throwing a net into the water, for they fished for a living.
[19] Jesus called out to them, "Come, follow me, and I will show you how to fish for people!" [20] And they left their nets at once and followed him.
[21] A little farther up the shore he saw two other brothers, James and John, sitting in a boat with their father, Zebedee, repairing their nets. And he called them to come, too. [22] They immediately followed him, leaving the boat and their father behind.
[23] Jesus traveled throughout the region of Galilee, teaching in the synagogues and announcing the Good News about the Kingdom. And he healed every kind of disease and illness. [24] News about him spread as far as Syria, and people soon began bringing to him all who were sick. And whatever their sickness or disease, or if they were demon possessed or epileptic or paralyzed—he healed them all.

Day 2
JESUS'S ONE SERMON

MATTHEW 4:17-24

When have you heard something that made you change your mind? Read verse 17. Peter, Andrew, James, and John heard something that made them change their whole lives. The verse right before our reading tells us about the one sermon that Jesus kept preaching over and over. "Repent, for the kingdom of heaven is near." Do you remember what "repent" means? It might sound like a serious, spiritual word. But it really just means "to turn around," or even "to change your mind."

What does Jesus want people to change their minds about? That the kingdom of heaven is *near*. The "kingdom of heaven" is another way of saying where God is. Most thought God could only come to really good, rich, or powerful people. Or, people thought you had to do something really special for God to come. But this was Jesus's sermon: "Change your mind! Turn from sin. God is near to <u>you</u> now!" How does Jesus's sermon change your mind?

HOLY Qs!

- *How can I keep from letting things like popularity or friends determine how I act?*

- *God cares about our whole life, not just the spiritual parts. What healthy habits do I need to work on?*

BLESSING

Go following the way of the Savior, walking in the truth of the King, and living the life of the Friend. May your thoughts, words, and actions reflect the love of Jesus.

A NEW KIND OF KINGDOM

MATTHEW 4:17-24

Take a look at verse 17 again. What do you think of when you hear "the kingdom of heaven"? Some people might imagine a city of clouds up in the sky, or the place where we live with God after we die. In the Gospels we hear a lot about the kingdom of heaven, also called the kingdom of God. But these words meant something very different to Jesus and His followers.

The prophets (like Isaiah and Jeremiah) talked about the kingdom of God for hundreds of years. It was not so much a place, but a way things should be. It is anywhere God is King, where things happen the way God wants. The prophets said all things will be made right when the kingdom of God comes to earth. Sick people will be healed! Poor people will get enough to eat! Powerful people will not bully weak people! When have you seen the kingdom of God on earth? How can you be a part of the kingdom of God?

HOLY Qs!

- How can I be honest and trustworthy this week?
- Have I been jealous, grumpy, or really hard on anyone? What can I do about it?

BLESSING

Go following the way of the Savior, walking in the truth of the King, and living the life of the Friend. May your thoughts, words, and actions reflect the love of Jesus.

Day 4
WHAT'S A DISCIPLE?

MATTHEW 4:17-24

Imagine if there was one person who promised to train you to do what he or she does. Who would you want it to be? Who do you want to learn to be like? If you agreed to learn from this person, you would be his or her *disciple*. It may be a lot of work to learn everything, but it would also be a big compliment to be chosen. When a teacher chooses a disciple, the teacher is saying, "I believe you have what it takes to do what I do. You can become like me."

This is what Jesus was doing on the beach of the Sea of Galilee. Jesus saw Peter, Andrew, James, and John on the beach doing their work as fishermen. But He knew they could do more than that. If they followed Jesus, they could learn to do what Jesus was doing. They could even learn how to *live* like Jesus. What would your life look like if you were Jesus's disciple? (Hint: You can be!)

HOLY Qs!

- *How have I been trustworthy recently?*
- *What am I thankful for? How can I show how thankful I am this week?*

BLESSING

Go following the way of the Savior, walking in the truth of the King, and living the life of the Friend. May your thoughts, words, and actions reflect the love of Jesus.

SICK PEOPLE WELCOME

MATTHEW 4:17-24

Do you remember a time you've been really sick? What was it like? Being sick is not fun. But when Jesus was alive, being sick was even worse. Doctors didn't know as much as they know now. There weren't very many medicines to help people get well. Many people stayed sick for a long time, or just died. But it gets worse. Many people used to think that if you got sick, you had done something bad to deserve it. Sick people stayed at home so they wouldn't make other people sick. But they also stayed home because they didn't want healthy people pointing fingers at them and making them feel bad all the time.

Jesus welcomes everyone—healthy or sick, perfect or not perfect. Jesus isn't someone we go to after we get everything right. Jesus is the One we go to who *makes* everything right! How does it feel knowing Jesus will *always* welcome you?

HOLY Qs!

- *How can I learn from others this week?*

BLESSING

Go following the way of the Savior, walking in the truth of the King, and living the life of the Friend. May your thoughts, words, and actions reflect the love of Jesus.

Day 6
PRESENT AND POWERFUL

MATTHEW 4:17-24

Remember what the prophets said the kingdom of God, or kingdom of heaven, would be like? (Look back on Day 3 of this week if you need a reminder.) Now, do you remember what Jesus's one sermon was? (Check back on Day 2 of this week.)

Jesus preached, "Change your minds! The kingdom of heaven is near you now!" But He didn't just *talk* about God being near. He *proved it*. Wherever Jesus was, things happened the way God wanted. Sick people were welcomed and healed. Poor people got enough to eat! (We'll hear about that later.) Powerful people weren't able to bully weak people! (We'll hear more about that later, too.)

Jesus shared the presence and power of God with everyone. Anyone who was with Jesus was *with God*. All of God's power and all of God's love is present in Jesus. Can you think of a time when you knew God was present and powerful in your life?

HOLY Qs!

- *How does my relationship with Jesus impact my daily life in real ways?*
- *How can the way I spend my money reflect my relationship with Jesus?*

BLESSING

Go following the way of the Savior, walking in the truth of the King, and living the life of the Friend. May your thoughts, words, and actions reflect the love of Jesus.

Day 7
PEOPLE FISHING

MATTHEW 4:17-24

Have you ever caught a fish? Did you use a fishing pole or a net? Whatever you use to fish, there has to be bait, the thing the fish want to eat. This is what makes them come into the net or bite the hook. Peter, Andrew, John, and James caught fish using nets. But when Jesus asked them to be His disciples, He said He would teach them a new way of fishing—for people!

Do you think Jesus wanted His disciples to catch people in a net, like they did with the fish? (No!) Jesus used analogies (an-AL-o-gees) and metaphors (MET-uh-fors) a lot when He talked. These are big words that are basically ways of describing things that are similar, but not the same.

Fish see the bait and follow after it. Jesus wants people to see what they need, and follow after it too. The disciples were going to help people hear the good news about Jesus, so they could know and follow Jesus too. Can you think of anyone who has done this for you?

HOLY Qs!

- *Who in my life needs to hear about Jesus? How can they hear it from me?*

BLESSING

Go following the way of the Savior, walking in the truth of the King, and living the life of the Friend. May your thoughts, words, and actions reflect the love of Jesus.

79

THE WEDDING AT CANA

JOHN 2:1-11

¹ The next day there was a wedding celebration in the village of Cana in Galilee. Jesus' mother was there, ² and Jesus and his disciples were also invited to the celebration. ³ The wine supply ran out during the festivities, so Jesus' mother told him, "They have no more wine."

⁴ "Dear woman, that's not our problem," Jesus replied. "My time has not yet come."

⁵ But his mother told the servants, "Do whatever he tells you."

⁶ Standing nearby were six stone water jars, used for Jewish ceremonial washing. Each could hold twenty to thirty gallons. ⁷ Jesus told the servants, "Fill the jars with water." When the jars had been filled, ⁸ he said, "Now dip some out, and take it to the master of ceremonies." So the servants followed his instructions.

⁹ When the master of ceremonies tasted the water that was now wine, not knowing where it had come from (though, of course, the servants knew), he called the bridegroom over. ¹⁰ "A host always serves the best wine first," he said. "Then, when everyone has had a lot to drink, he brings out the less expensive wine. But you have kept the best until now!"

¹¹ This miraculous sign at Cana in Galilee was the first time Jesus revealed his glory. And his disciples believed in him.

WELP, I'M CONVINCED

In the days before this party, Jesus gathered His disciples for the very first time. Imagine if Jesus showed up at your house and said, "Hey, come follow me!" Would you follow right away? Would you be waiting to see something to convince you that following Jesus had been the right move? The disciples were curious enough to follow. They wanted to see what Jesus was up to.

Turns out, Jesus was up to something big. The next day Jesus blew their minds. He performed a miracle by turning water into something it's not—wine! The disciples were probably rubbing their eyes and saying, "Okay. Hold on. Did He just do that? For real?!" What would you have said? Check out verse 11. The disciples believed. Even though they had only been with Him a short time, they began to put their trust in Him. What they saw convinced them. What have you seen from Jesus that has you convinced He's the one to follow?

HOLY Qs!

- How can I keep from letting things like popularity or friends determine how I act?
- Is anything in my life really hard right now? Am I talking to God about it? Who else can I talk to?

BLESSING

Go following the way of the Savior, walking in the truth of the King, and living the life of the Friend. May your thoughts, words, and actions reflect the love of Jesus.

Day 3
EXTRA-ORDINARY

JOHN 2:1-11

What does the word "miracle" mean? Did you use the word "unexpected" in your definition? What about "extraordinary?" When something is extraordinary that means it's beyond ordinary. It's not a thing that normally happens. Take this story for example. Why don't you take a glass of water, try really hard, and turn it into grape juice? Did it work? Didn't think so. If it did, you're gonna be famous.

This miracle kicks off Jesus's journey as a miracle worker. He spent a lot of time doing the impossible. They weren't tricks. They weren't just things to make Him popular. Jesus's miracles were all about revealing God by loving others. This wedding party was His first miracle. His extraordinary power revealed His glory. Jesus was the Messiah. Jesus lived a real life, but He lived it doing the extraordinary. What is something extraordinary God has done in your life?

HOLY Qs!

- How does my relationship with Jesus impact my daily life in real ways?
- When good things happen, how do I give God the credit?

BLESSING

Go following the way of the Savior, walking in the truth of the King, and living the life of the Friend. May your thoughts, words, and actions reflect the love of Jesus.

IT'S THE LITTLE THINGS

JOHN 2:1-11

Can you remember a time you had to work really hard? Check out verses 6-8. Jesus gives the servants at the party some instructions: "Fill up those jars, dip a little out, and serve it to the master of the party." This was hard work. Those were 30-gallon jugs. That's a lot of little jars and trips to the water well to get those things full. Imagine being one of the servants. Did they have a clue what Jesus was about to do?

They didn't fully understand His plan, but they did as Jesus asked. They worked hard. Then boom! The unexpected happened. The extraordinary. Look what they would have missed had they not obeyed Him. When we follow Jesus and live in obedience, even though we may not always understand what's going on, there may be something unexpected and extraordinary just about to happen. In what ways is Jesus asking you to obediently follow Him?

HOLY Qs!

- How can I be obedient to God this week?

- God cares about our whole life, not just the spiritual parts. What healthy habits do I need to work on?

BLESSING

Go following the way of the Savior, walking in the truth of the King, and living the life of the Friend. May your thoughts, words, and actions reflect the love of Jesus.

Day 5
SHARING THE AMAZING

JOHN 2:1-11

Check out verses 9-11. There's a really cool part of this story that's easy to overlook. The host of the party tastes the wine that Jesus just created from water. He's blown away by the quality of the wine. People usually served the best stuff first, and then left the bad tasting wine for later in the party. But Jesus created something unexpectedly amazing. He always does. The party would continue and everyone would share the amazing-ness Jesus created.

The same is true for us. When we follow Jesus, He lets us be a part of the amazing-ness He is up to. Then, we can share that story with others. Everything He does is worth talking about. What amazing thing has Jesus done that is worth telling others about?

HOLY Qs!

- *How does what I learned from Scripture inspire my thoughts and actions?*
- *Who in my life needs to hear about Jesus? How can they hear it from me?*

BLESSING

Go following the way of the Savior, walking in the truth of the King, and living the life of the Friend. May your thoughts, words, and actions reflect the love of Jesus.

YOU WON'T BE NEEDING THAT

JOHN 2:1-11

The jars used to turn the water into wine were used for the ceremonial cleansing that would take place at the party. This was an Old Testament law that made people clean. Not clean on the outside like after you take a shower. The obedience of following this law brought cleanliness on the inside, forgiveness of sin. This was one of the ways people tried to get right with God before Jesus came to earth.

Now, Jesus was using the jars to say to the people, "When I'm done here, you won't be needing those anymore." In other words, being clean from sin would now come from a relationship with Jesus instead of through laws, rituals, and ceremonies. This miracle revealed that Jesus was way more important than *just* a miracle worker. He was a destroyer of sin and a cleanser of people's lives. Just like the jars, He gives life a new purpose. To learn more about a new life and purpose with Jesus, check out page vii.

HOLY Qs!

- *What habits help me spend time getting to know God through Scripture?*

- *What can I do to make wise choices this week?*

BLESSING

Go following the way of the Savior, walking in the truth of the King, and living the life of the Friend. May your thoughts, words, and actions reflect the love of Jesus.

Day 7
JESUS REVEALED

JOHN 2:1-11

What's something about you that would surprise your friends? Look at verse 11. This miracle revealed the glory of Jesus. The disciples learned a little something about who Jesus really was. His disciples were already following Him, but after they saw this miracle, they really believed.

There's a difference between believing in Jesus because that's what you've been taught, and believing in Jesus because you have experienced Him for yourself. Many of us who are raised in Christian homes start out following Jesus because that's what the trusted adults all around us are doing. At some point, though, we'll take that relationship to the next level. We'll believe for ourselves because we'll see who Jesus truly is. That's what happened for the disciples at this wedding. Maybe for you it'll be a miracle. It might just be the way Jesus comforts you in a hard time, or answers prayer, or the closeness you feel to Him during worship. What is it for you?

HOLY Qs!

- How can God's love give me confidence today?
- What have I been enjoying about prayer recently?

BLESSING

Go following the way of the Savior, walking in the truth of the King, and living the life of the Friend. May your thoughts, words, and actions reflect the love of Jesus.

WEEK 13 Day 1
JESUS HEALS MANY

LUKE 4:31-35, 38-40

[31] Then Jesus went to Capernaum, a town in Galilee, and taught there in the synagogue every Sabbath day. [32] There, too, the people were amazed at his teaching, for he spoke with authority.
[33] Once when he was in the synagogue, a man possessed by a demon—an evil spirit—cried out, shouting, [34] "Go away! Why are you interfering with us, Jesus of Nazareth? Have you come to destroy us? I know who you are—the Holy One of God!"
[35] But Jesus reprimanded him. "Be quiet! Come out of the man," he ordered. At that, the demon threw the man to the floor as the crowd watched; then it came out of him without hurting him further.

[38] After leaving the synagogue that day, Jesus went to Simon's home, where he found Simon's mother-in-law very sick with a high fever. "Please heal her," everyone begged. [39] Standing at her bedside, he rebuked the fever, and it left her. And she got up at once and prepared a meal for them.
[40] As the sun went down that evening, people throughout the village brought sick family members to Jesus. No matter what their diseases were, the touch of his hand healed every one.

Day 2
MORE POWERFUL THAN MUSCLES

LUKE 4:31-35, 38-40

What does the word "powerful" make you think of? Big muscles? An important person? A fast car? We can use "powerful" to describe any of these, and we wouldn't be wrong. But when we use the word "powerful" to describe Jesus, it gets taken to a whole new level. Look at verses 33 and 34. This impure spirit, full of evil thoughts and hurtful plans, is clearly afraid of Jesus. It's afraid Jesus has come to destroy it.

In the face of the most terrible, evil, awful things in the world, Jesus still stands as the most powerful. The things that scare us the most—like the people might have been afraid of this spirit— aren't even close to the power that Jesus has. Jesus is so powerful that even the evil spirits are afraid of Him. Jesus is God in the flesh, and commands ultimate power. How can knowing how powerful Jesus is change the way you face things you're afraid of?

HOLY Qs!

- *Is anything in my life really hard right now? Am I talking to God about it? Who else can I talk to?*

BLESSING

Go following the way of the Savior, walking in the truth of the King, and living the life of the Friend. May your thoughts, words, and actions reflect the love of Jesus.

THAT'S NEXT LEVEL

LUKE 4:31-35, 38-40

Here's a tip for you: Next time you get asked to do a job, like clean your room or something, do a crazy-good job of it. Like, dust, vacuum, organize, sweep, squeegee— do it all. It will blow people's minds that you took everything to the next level. And it will be very Jesus-like of you. We don't know how clean Jesus kept His room, but He was all about taking things to the next level. He often did more than what was expected.

When the impure spirit approached Jesus and interrupted His teaching, we know Jesus was plenty powerful enough to quiet it down. And He did. No problem. He could have stopped there and gone back to teaching, but instead He healed the man right there in front of everyone. The impure spirit was gone. The man was okay. Jesus wasn't satisfied just doing what was expected; He did so much more. What do you think the man thought of Jesus after that? How can you do more than is expected?

HOLY Qs!

- *How can I be obedient to God this week?*
- *Is there anyone I'm struggling to get along with? What am I going to do about it?*

BLESSING

Go following the way of the Savior, walking in the truth of the King, and living the life of the Friend. May your thoughts, words, and actions reflect the love of Jesus.

Day 4
GOD AND THE DOCTOR

LUKE 4:31-35, 38-40

What happened the last time you went to see a doctor or nurse? Did she or he make you worse or better? Does your doctor give out toys or candy? Doctors and nurses are all about healing. We don't always want to go see them because sometimes healing or staying healthy is uncomfortable, but they do what it takes to keep us well.

Did you know Jesus still heals? Sometimes it's immediate like in this passage of Scripture. Often, He heals through a doctor who gives you medicine, performs surgery, or helps you get better in other ways. As a Christian, you can give thanks to God. Through science, God helps us discover new ways of making people well. "Thanks for creating the doctors and nurses who care for us." "Thanks for the trusted adults who stayed with me through my healing." As Christians, we give our praise to Jesus for the blessings in our lives, like doctors and nurses. Take time today to thank God for being the ultimate healer.

HOLY Qs!

- What am I thankful for? How can I show how thankful I am this week?
- When good things happen, how do I give God the credit?

BLESSING

Go following the way of the Savior, walking in the truth of the King, and living the life of the Friend. May your thoughts, words, and actions reflect the love of Jesus.

Day 5
THE GREAT HEALER

LUKE 4:31-35, 38-40

In verse 38 Jesus continues to heal. Earlier it was an impure spirit. Now it's a high fever. What happens when *you* get a fever? Everybody's body reacts differently. But a high fever isn't good for anyone. Peter (The Scripture says "Simon." Peter was known by two different names.) was likely afraid his mother-in-law, his wife's mother, would not get better. But Jesus, the great healer, was there for them.

There are lots of different healing miracles highlighted in the book of Luke. Check this out: Luke himself was a doctor! (Colossians 4:14) Clearly he valued these miracles and wanted the world to know about them. What do you think Luke was trying to tell his readers about Jesus by telling story after story of healing? Knowing that Jesus healed so many, what does it tell you about Him? What does it tell you that Jesus valued? Why are stories of healing great for revealing both His power *and* His love?

HOLY Qs!

- *What have I been enjoying about prayer recently?*
- *How does my relationship with Jesus impact my daily life in real ways?*

BLESSING

Go following the way of the Savior, walking in the truth of the King, and living the life of the Friend. May your thoughts, words, and actions reflect the love of Jesus.

Day 6

PETER THE CONFIDENT

LUKE 4:31-35, 38-40

Do you know any other stories about Peter? Walking on water (Matthew 14)? Asking for a bath (John 13)? Cutting off an ear (John 18)? Peter was full of life and usually very willing to take a chance in the name of Jesus. He struggled with doubt at times, but was willing to listen to Jesus, to learn, and to let the Holy Spirit's power do mighty works within him. So, it's not surprising that Peter would ask Jesus to help his mother-in-law. He knew what Jesus was capable of.

How wonderful would it be to be so confident in Jesus that we could go to Him with anything? Any problem. Anything we're facing. Any joys. Any sadness. We could just know that Jesus can give us what we need to handle it. Peter and his family knew it. Knowing Peter the way we do, we can see he was pretty sure that Jesus would come through when he asked. How does Peter's story give you confidence today?

HOLY Qs!

- *God cares about our whole life, not just the spiritual parts. What healthy habits do I need to work on?*

BLESSING

Go following the way of the Savior, walking in the truth of the King, and living the life of the Friend. May your thoughts, words, and actions reflect the love of Jesus.

WOW. WORD TRAVELS FAST.

LUKE 4:31-35, 38-40

What would happen in your town if a famous person showed up in a local restaurant? Word would probably travel pretty fast. People would want to come see. By the end of this passage, Jesus has healed the man of an impure spirit, and He's healed Peter's mother-in-law. Word starts traveling. People begin finding out about the healings. They grab their sick and hurting friends and relatives and say, "We've gotta go see this guy!" Word got out quickly about Jesus's power and love.

When people get access to that kind of power and love, they want to be around it. Jesus works through us to bring love, kindness, peace, joy, confidence, power, and yes, sometimes even healing, to the world around us. When people experience these things through God's people, the word will get out. People will want more, and we can point them to Jesus. Where have you seen Jesus working through love, kindness, peace, joy, confidence, power, or healing?

HOLY Qs!

- *Who in my life needs to hear about Jesus? How can they hear it from me?*

BLESSING

Go following the way of the Savior, walking in the truth of the King, and living the life of the Friend. May your thoughts, words, and actions reflect the love of Jesus.

WEEK 14 Day 1
THE BEATITUDES

It's a new week in your life with Jesus! Use the *5 What's or Lectio Divina* to guide your reading today. Enjoy God's love for you!

MATTHEW 5:3-10

3 God blesses those who are poor and realize their need for him,
  for the Kingdom of Heaven is theirs.
4 God blesses those who mourn,
  for they will be comforted.
5 God blesses those who are humble,
  for they will inherit the whole earth.
6 God blesses those who hunger and thirst for justice,
  for they will be satisfied.
7 God blesses those who are merciful,
  for they will be shown mercy.
8 God blesses those whose hearts are pure,
  for they will see God.
9 God blesses those who work for peace,
  for they will be called the children of God.
10 God blesses those who are persecuted for doing right,
  for the Kingdom of Heaven is theirs.

Day 2
BLESSING PARTY

MATTHEW 5:3-10

This week focuses on a passage of Scripture called the Beatitudes (bee-AT-it-toods). This comes from a Latin word that means "happy" or "blessed." So, the Beatitudes are a list of blessings. Sometimes people read them like they're a list of ways to live. That would be weird. Are we all supposed to be poor and sad and hungry all the time? Nopers.

Because it's a list of blessings, we read the Beatitudes as ways that God blesses us. This is not a list of really hard things we have to do. It's a list of ways God shows up in our lives. It's how Jesus chose to open up the greatest sermon ever preached. Being a Christian isn't just a big list of rules to follow. It's a hopeful, joy-filled, freedom-loving relationship with Jesus full of blessings! The Beatitudes get the blessing party started. What blessings can you celebrate this week? Say thanks to Jesus!

HOLY Qs!

- *How can God's love give me confidence today?*

- *Is anything in my life really hard right now? Am I talking to God about it? Who else can I talk to?*

BLESSING

Go following the way of the Savior, walking in the truth of the King, and living the life of the Friend. May your thoughts, words, and actions reflect the love of Jesus.

Day 3
COMFORTERS AREN'T JUST BLANKETS

MATTHEW 5:3-10

When's the last time you were really sad? Check out verse 4. "Mourn" means being extra sad. The second beatitude tells us that God will comfort us when we mourn. There are many things that Christians might mourn. We could be sad about the effects of sin in the world. We could be sad about the way a person or group of people are being treated. We could be sad about someone we lost. It's okay to be sad.

This Scripture gives us hope in our sadness. Instead of just sitting around waiting for the sadness to go away, we can rely on Jesus. He knows all about sadness. He will comfort us. He will be with us when we mourn. We can also take this hope and offer it to others. We can be with our friends when they are sad. We can offer the hope of Jesus through our presence, our actions, and our words. Jesus is the great Comforter. Who do you know who might need Jesus's comfort in their sadness right now? How can you help? How does Jesus comfort you?

HOLY Qs!

- *How can I be obedient to God this week?*
- *Who in my life needs to hear about Jesus? How can they hear it from me?*

BLESSING

Go following the way of the Savior, walking in the truth of the King, and living the life of the Friend. May your thoughts, words, and actions reflect the love of Jesus.

Day 4
MEEK AIN'T WEAK

MATTHEW 5:3-10

What does it mean to be humble? The third beatitude is about being humble (or "meek" in other translations). To be meek is to be gentle and humble. Meekness doesn't mean weakness. Weakness is about not having power. Meekness is about giving our power over to God. The meek trust God instead of their own power. Because God's power is centered in love, He does big things through gentle and humble people. That's what makes this a blessing.

Jesus was gentle and humble. He was born a baby from a town that wasn't very popular. People talked bad about Him and were even really violent with Him. He knew that God was doing great things through Him, blessing the whole world through Him. God's powerful humility and gentle spirit changes people. It will change the earth. How do you see God using gentleness and humility to change the world?

HOLY Qs!

- Have my words matched my actions? Does who I say I am and how I act line up?

- Is there anyone I'm struggling to get along with? What am I going to do about it?

BLESSING

Go following the way of the Savior, walking in the truth of the King, and living the life of the Friend. May your thoughts, words, and actions reflect the love of Jesus.

Day 5
FILLED UP

MATTHEW 5:3-10

What is your favorite meal to have someone make for you? Some people (maybe you have a dad or grandma like this) love to cook, and they love to fill the bellies of the people at their table. Special requests? Sure! Waffles AND pancakes AND French toast AND bacon AND sausage?! Bring it on! Do you know anyone who cooks like that? Maybe that's a good picture of what God is like.

Check out verse 6. This doesn't mean you need to be hungry and thirsty all the time. It means God is ready to fill you up! To be spiritually hungry and thirsty means to want more and more of your relationship with God. You'll want to be closer to God. You'll want to worship more. You'll want more of what's right and just. You'll want to read Scripture more. Worship is like chocolate, and Scripture like popcorn, and prayer like ice cream! The more we know God, the closer we'll want to get. He loves us and will keep on meeting us and filling us with more and more of His love. How could God fill you up this week?

HOLY Qs!

- *How will I be a good friend and listener?*
- *What am I thankful for? How can I show how thankful I am this week?*

BLESSING

Go following the way of the Savior, walking in the truth of the King, and living the life of the Friend. May your thoughts, words, and actions reflect the love of Jesus.

NOT YOUR BLOOD PUMPER

MATTHEW 5:3-10

What are three things about you that someone wouldn't be able to know just by looking at you? Check out verse 8. This week is not about your actual heart, like the thing that is pumping blood to the rest of your body. When you hear Scripture or other Christians talk about your heart, what they really mean is who you are. Jesus made it clear. He can change people in very real ways, but He wasn't talking about their hairstyle.

Remember, the Beatitudes are not about what we can do, but about what Jesus can do for us and through us. Jesus changes us at the very core of who we are. A pure heart means a life that is filled with Jesus. Jesus becomes the most important thing to us. We love Him, talk to Him often, and ask Him to guide our decisions. Jesus purifies our hearts, clearing the way for us to get even closer to God. How has Jesus changed you on the inside?

HOLY Qs!

- *How does what I learned from Scripture inspire my thoughts and actions?*

- *What can I do to make wise choices this week?*

BLESSING

Go following the way of the Savior, walking in the truth of the King, and living the life of the Friend. May your thoughts, words, and actions reflect the love of Jesus.

Day 7
PEACE AND PERSECUTION

MATTHEW 5:3-10

What's a way you've found it difficult to be a Christian? This whole week has been about God's blessings, but that doesn't mean being a Christian is always easy. Sometimes, it's actually pretty tough. Sometimes, choosing to be like Jesus isn't the popular decision. Being a peacemaker might land you in persecution territory. Persecution (purs-eh-CUE-shun) is being treated poorly because of your faith.

Maybe, up to this point in your life, it hasn't ever been super difficult to follow Jesus. So let's just get this out there: It will be at some point. But when it's difficult, God is still there. Jesus understands persecution, and He and His blessings won't leave you during the difficult times. Actually, you may find yourself growing even closer to God when things get tough. The kingdom of heaven is yours. You won't be overlooked. He's with you. Talk to a trusted adult about a time it was difficult to follow Jesus. How did they grow in their faith because of that time?

HOLY Qs!

- *How can I keep from letting things like popularity or friends determine how I act?*
- *Have I been jealous, grumpy, or really hard on anyone? What can I do about it?*

BLESSING

Go following the way of the Savior, walking in the truth of the King, and living the life of the Friend. May your thoughts, words, and actions reflect the love of Jesus.

WEEK 15 Day 1
THE TEN COMMANDMENTS

This week's passage is from the Old Testament. Can you discover what it has to do with the life of Jesus? Enjoy God's love for you!

EXODUS 20:1-17

¹ Then God gave the people all these instructions:
² "I am the LORD your God, who rescued you from the land of Egypt, the place of your slavery.
³ "You must not have any other god but me.
⁴ "You must not make for yourself an idol of any kind or an image of anything in the heavens or on the earth or in the sea. ⁵ You must not bow down to them or worship them, for I, the LORD your God, am a jealous God who will not tolerate your affection for any other gods. I lay the sins of the parents upon their children; the entire family is affected—even children in the third and fourth generations of those who reject me. ⁶ But I lavish unfailing love for a thousand generations on those who love me and obey my commands.

7 "You must not misuse the name of the LORD your God. The LORD will not let you go unpunished if you misuse his name.

8 "Remember to observe the Sabbath day by keeping it holy. 9 You have six days each week for your ordinary work, 10 but the seventh day is a Sabbath day of rest dedicated to the LORD your God. On that day no one in your household may do any work. This includes you, your sons and daughters, your male and female servants, your livestock, and any foreigners living among you. 11 For in six days the LORD made the heavens, the earth, the sea, and everything in them; but on the seventh day he rested. That is why the LORD blessed the Sabbath day and set it apart as holy.

12 "Honor your father and mother. Then you will live a long, full life in the land the LORD your God is giving you.

13 "You must not murder.

14 "You must not commit adultery.

15 "You must not steal.

16 "You must not testify falsely against your neighbor.

17 "You must not covet your neighbor's house. You must not covet your neighbor's wife, male or female servant, ox or donkey, or anything else that belongs to your neighbor."

BECOMING FREE

EXODUS 20:1-17

Can you think of a rule you *like*? We have rules at school, rules for the dinner table, even rules on the playground. We might see these rules as things that stop us from doing what we want. But good rules can also give us freedom to *be* who we want.

The group of people called the Israelites, or the Jewish people, were all slaves in Egypt. God used Moses to lead all of them into freedom, and you can read the amazing story in Exodus chapters 1—15. When they were slaves, they were treated as less than human. The Egyptians used their own freedom and power to steal, cheat, lie, and even kill the Israelites.

But when God freed the Israelites, God wanted to show them what real *freedom* was like. God gave them these Ten Commandments so they could live free of fear, free of hatred, and free of fighting. God also gave them freedom to know love, to have rest, and to care for one another. Where have you seen this kind of real freedom in your life?

HOLY Qs!

- *Have my words matched my actions? Does who I say I am and how I act line up?*
- *What can I do to make wise choices this week?*

BLESSING

Go following the way of the Savior, walking in the truth of the King, and living the life of the Friend. May your thoughts, words, and actions reflect the love of Jesus.

Day 3
COVENANT PEOPLE

EXODUS 20:1-17

Have you ever heard the word "covenant" (KUH-vuh-nunt)? It's an important idea for understanding our life with Jesus. A covenant is a commitment in a relationship that will never be broken. Most things in our world work by contract. A contract says I will do this, if you do that. I will mow the lawn, *if* you pay me $10. But in a covenant someone says, "I promise to do this no matter what happens."

Some people think that the Ten Commandments work like a contract. They think if people follow God's rules, then God will love them. But God already made the choice to free the Israelite people, to love them, and to be their God. Following the Ten Commandments did not start their relationship with God. But it did show the people what it was like to be in relationship with God and do things God's way.

God made a forever commitment to the Israelites, and Jesus brings that commitment to all of us. How does knowing that Jesus will never leave you shape your life with Him?

HOLY Qs!

- *How can God's love give me confidence today?*
- *How can I be obedient to God this week?*

BLESSING

Go following the way of the Savior, walking in the truth of the King, and living the life of the Friend. May your thoughts, words, and actions reflect the love of Jesus.

WHO GOD IS

EXODUS 20:1-17

How did you learn who God is? The Israelites knew about God from the stories of their ancestors, Abraham, Isaac, and Jacob. You can read their stories in Genesis 12—50. But the Egyptians believed in many different gods. They prayed and made sacrifices to statues of these gods because they were afraid of making them angry. When God rescued the Israelites from Egypt, He wanted them to know who the real God was. God told them to call God "Yahweh" (YAH-way), which means "I am that I am" (Exodus 3:14). Yahweh is holy love, justice, mercy, and power all in one.

The people had never known a God like this before. So the first three commandments taught them how to do life with this God. This God is the only God. This God cannot be made small enough to fit into a statue. The name and reputation of Yahweh is too perfect to throw in the mud. What we know about God shows up in the way we treat God. How does what you know about God show up in your life?

HOLY Qs!

- *How have I been trustworthy recently?*

BLESSING

Go following the way of the Savior, walking in the truth of the King, and living the life of the Friend. May your thoughts, words, and actions reflect the love of Jesus.

Day 5
A GIFT AND A SIGN

EXODUS 20:1-17

Take a deep breath. How do you like to rest and relax after hard work? In Hebrew the word *shabbot*, which we call "Sabbath," literally means "to stop." Sabbath is stopping from work to receive rest. It might seem strange that God would give a rule about this. But remember, the Israelite people used to be slaves. They were never allowed to stop working! The ability to stop and rest is a gift for free people to enjoy. In Psalm 23 we are reminded that God is our good shepherd who helps us rest and cares for us. This is the gift of Sabbath.

But Sabbath is also a sign of trust. People have always worked hard to have food, safety, and money. And people have always worried that they will not have enough. So they work just a little bit more, and a little bit more, but never really stop. But when we practice Sabbath, it is a sign that we trust God can give us enough of what we need. How can you practice Sabbath?

HOLY Qs!

- *God cares about our whole life, not just the spiritual parts. What healthy habits do I need to work on?*

- *What's a healthy or helpful way I can use my spare time?*

BLESSING

Go following the way of the Savior, walking in the truth of the King, and living the life of the Friend. May your thoughts, words, and actions reflect the love of Jesus.

Day 6
HELLO, NEIGHBOR

EXODUS 20:1-17

What makes someone a good neighbor? God cares deeply about how humans treat one another. This is why God wants us to respect our parents. This is why God tells us not to steal, murder, cheat, lie, and be obsessed with stuff that isn't ours. When the Israelites were slaves, every person had to fight to survive. Families were often pulled apart. But in God's new way of life, He wanted families to stay together and care for one another. Everyone was to look out for each other, not just themselves.

In God's covenant, the people were learning to live more like God. They were learning to love one another. God was teaching people how to be good neighbors. And this is the lesson Jesus continued to teach hundreds of years later. How can you be a good neighbor this week? How have you been a good neighbor in the past?

HOLY Qs!

- *How can the way I spend my money reflect my relationship with Jesus?*

- *Have I been jealous, grumpy, or really hard on anyone? What can I do about it?*

BLESSING

Go following the way of the Savior, walking in the truth of the King, and living the life of the Friend. May your thoughts, words, and actions reflect the love of Jesus.

Day 7
JESUS AND THE BIG TEN

EXODUS 20:1-17

What is something you do better now than you did two years ago? Everyone grows and changes as they get older; this is how it's supposed to be. After hundreds of years of practicing the Ten Commandments, God knew His people needed to keep growing. It's not that the rules were bad, but they could only do so much. It's hard to create enough rules to tell you all the things you *should* do.

Jesus teaches that loving God and being a good neighbor is more about what you *do* than what you *don't* do. Actually, it's more about who you *are*. Next week we will keep reading Jesus's most famous sermon. You will notice He talks about the Ten Commandments. But Jesus doesn't just give us more rules, He invites us to keep growing in God's love. Jesus helps us *become* the kind of loving people that are good neighbors. How is Jesus helping you grow in God's way of doing things?

HOLY Qs!

- *Is there anyone I'm struggling to get along with? What am I going to do about it?*
- *When good things happen, how do I give God the credit?*

BLESSING

Go following the way of the Savior, walking in the truth of the King, and living the life of the Friend. May your thoughts, words, and actions reflect the love of Jesus.

WEEK 16 Day 1
ANGER

It's a new week in your life with Jesus! Use the *5 What's or Lectio Divina* to guide your reading today. Enjoy God's love for you!

MATTHEW 5:21-26

21 "You have heard that our ancestors were told, 'You must not murder. If you commit murder, you are subject to judgment.' 22 But I say, if you are even angry with someone, you are subject to judgment! If you call someone an idiot, you are in danger of being brought before the court. And if you curse someone, you are in danger of the fires of hell.

23 "So if you are presenting a sacrifice at the altar in the Temple and you suddenly remember that someone has something against you, 24 leave your sacrifice there at the altar. Go and be reconciled to that person. Then come and offer your sacrifice to God.

25 "When you are on the way to court with your adversary, settle your differences quickly. Otherwise, your accuser may hand you over to the judge, who will hand you over to an officer, and you will be thrown into prison. 26 And if that happens, you surely won't be free again until you have paid the last penny."

Day 2
OH! NOW I GET IT!

MATTHEW 5:21-26

What's your best subject in school? Imagine a 3rd grader studying math. He struggles for weeks on his own with multiplication and can't fully get it. One day the teacher stands up and goes through some simple rules for math that make it clear. That day he finally gets it! He even says out loud, "Oh! Now I get it!" (Which is a bad idea because he has to stand on the line at recess for speaking without his hand raised. Remember, always raise your hand in class.)

In the sermon we're digging into for a few weeks—the Sermon on the Mount—Jesus helps the people understand the law they've always followed in brand new ways. Before this, they didn't really get it. Then, the teacher (Jesus) stood up. He told them what the law really meant. The people listening were probably like the boy in math class. "Oh! Now I get it!" (Except they didn't have to miss recess.) Jesus is a great teacher. What is something you'd like Jesus to help you understand better?

HOLY Qs!

- Have I been jealous, grumpy, or really hard on anyone? What can I do about it?
- What am I thankful for? How can I show how thankful I am this week?

BLESSING

Go following the way of the Savior, walking in the truth of the King, and living the life of the Friend. May your thoughts, words, and actions reflect the love of Jesus.

Day 3
ANGER TAKES HOLD

MATTHEW 5:21-26

Ever been mad at someone? Maybe a parent, brother, sister, or friend? Why were you mad? What did you do when you got mad? Did you get them back, tell on them, maybe even try to hurt them? This week, Jesus points out that when we act in anger, bad things can happen. When we allow anger to stay inside us, we can end up doing something hurtful. Hurtful to ourselves, hurtful to others, and even hurtful to God.

Jesus isn't teaching that anger is sinful. He's showing us where hurting others begins. It begins when we allow anger to stay in us. When we don't forgive, anger takes hold and begins to control our actions, turning us into someone who doesn't make wise decisions. Jesus can help us overcome our anger, instead of letting it control us. He can help us forgive. Do you have anyone you are angry with? How can God help you with the next step?

HOLY Qs!

- *How can I learn from others this week?*

- *How does my relationship with Jesus impact my daily life in real ways?*

BLESSING

Go following the way of the Savior, walking in the truth of the King, and living the life of the Friend. May your thoughts, words, and actions reflect the love of Jesus.

Day 4
WORDS ARE IMPORTANT

MATTHEW 5:21-26

Ever had someone say something mean to you? How'd you feel? Owen and his friends were playing football one day. It was the last play. The game was tied. 21-21. Owen ran deep. Sam threw the ball to him. And he dropped it! It was an easy catch. But he dropped it. Sam got super mad, called Owen a name, and said, "How could you drop that?!" Owen felt so hurt. Sam didn't know it, but those words really hurt.

Words are important. Kind words can stay with someone for a long time. So can mean words spoken out of anger. Jesus wants us to see how important it is to allow Him to fill us with His love so we'll be more careful with our words. When we feel loved, we're filled with love. If we are filled with the love of Jesus instead of filled with anger, the words we speak will prove it! Think of a time recently you were frustrated. How could you have handled it with kind words?

HOLY Qs!

- *How will I be a good friend and listener?*

BLESSING

Go following the way of the Savior, walking in the truth of the King, and living the life of the Friend. May your thoughts, words, and actions reflect the love of Jesus.

Day 5

WARNING

MATTHEW 5:21-26

At the bottom of a mountain path leading up a steep incline is a sign that says, "Do not hike this trail without plenty of water." It's a warning. It's dangerous to head up that mountain if you can't stay hydrated. What sort of warning signs have you seen before? The words spoken by Jesus in this sermon are partly words of warning. He's making it very clear what sort of danger we're in if we allow anger to control our words and actions.

There is nothing good at the end of the story if we follow our anger. Lots of little things might make us angry, but Jesus can give us self-control. It's a gift of the Holy Spirit. Hear Jesus's words in this week's passage and pay attention to the warning signs that say, "Danger! Do not follow your anger." Let's pray today and ask for this self-control that comes only from Him, so we're ready to face the anger when it comes. Is there someone you need to apologize to for saying something out of anger?

HOLY Qs!

- Is anything in my life really hard right now? Am I talking to God about it? Who else can I talk to?

- Have my words matched my actions? Does who I say I am and how I act line up?

BLESSING

Go following the way of the Savior, walking in the truth of the King, and living the life of the Friend. May your thoughts, words, and actions reflect the love of Jesus.

Day 6
STOP

MATTHEW 5:21-26

Another warning sign. This one says, "Stop!" Check out verses 23-24. Jesus tells us here that we're not really going to be able to worship if we're blocked up with anger at someone. That broken relationship will just be there, eating at us from the inside, until we stop and seek reconciliation (RECK-un-sill-ee-A-shun). This word means making a relationship good and right.

Jesus is all about making relationships right. He came so that we could know God and be close to God and be reconciled (made right) with God. Then, because Jesus focuses on our relationships with God and with others, He wants our relationships with others to be right as well. At least, we can do our part. Other people may not always want to fix a relationship, but we can come to them with grace and love and offer reconciliation. What's it take to make a relationship right again?

HOLY Qs!

- Is there anyone I'm struggling to get along with? What am I going to do about it?

BLESSING

Go following the way of the Savior, walking in the truth of the King, and living the life of the Friend. May your thoughts, words, and actions reflect the love of Jesus.

NOT MY FAVORITE

MATTHEW 5:21-26

It's pretty easy to get over being angry at a friend. But being angry at someone you don't really get along with, that's a lot harder. Is there someone you don't really get along with right now? You may not have an "enemy," but there may be someone who isn't really your favorite person these days. Check out verse 24. Jesus tells us to be reconciled (there's that word again) with anyone who has something against you.

You don't always have to get along with everyone in the world. But if you are holding onto anger inside for any other person, this anger will keep you from getting closer to God. Anger in our life impacts our relationships. If we hold onto anger, it can shape the way we think and act, even toward the people we're not angry at. Don't let your relationship with whoever isn't your favorite person keep you from really worshiping God. Who is this person? How can you pray for that person today?

HOLY Qs!

- *How can God's love give me confidence today?*
- *What have I been enjoying about prayer recently?*

BLESSING

Go following the way of the Savior, walking in the truth of the King, and living the life of the Friend. May your thoughts, words, and actions reflect the love of Jesus.

WEEK 17 Day 1
LOVE FOR ENEMIES

It's a new week in your life with Jesus! Use the *5 What's or Lectio Divina* to guide your reading today. Enjoy God's love for you!

MATTHEW 5:38-48

38 "You have heard the law that says the punishment must match the injury: 'An eye for an eye, and a tooth for a tooth.' 39 But I say, do not resist an evil person! If someone slaps you on the right cheek, offer the other cheek also. 40 If you are sued in court and your shirt is taken from you, give your coat, too. 41 If a soldier demands that you carry his gear for a mile, carry it two miles. 42 Give to those who ask, and don't turn away from those who want to borrow.

43 "You have heard the law that says, 'Love your neighbor' and hate your enemy. 44 But I say, love your enemies! Pray for those who persecute you! 45 In that way, you will be acting as true children of your Father in heaven. For he gives his sunlight to both the evil and the good, and he sends rain on the just and the unjust alike. 46 If you love only those who love you, what reward is there for that? Even corrupt tax collectors do that much. 47 If you are kind only to your friends, how are you different from anyone else? Even pagans do that. 48 But you are to be perfect, even as your Father in heaven is perfect."

Day 2
SO THAT'S A SERMON

MATTHEW 5:38-48

What's something memorable you heard in a sermon at church? Could have been from kid's worship, family worship, or even church camp. Our passage this week is from a very important sermon Jesus preached called the Sermon on the Mount. The last couple of weeks in Matthew 5, and next week in Matthew 6, are also from this sermon. Jesus taught a lot of important lessons in this sermon.

Preaching sermons is something a pastor is called to do. It continues the ministry Jesus began. Sermons take a lot of work to prepare, education to know how to study, a lot of prayer, and the Holy Spirit to direct the pastor's words. Next time you hear a sermon, listen a little closer. You could even take notes or draw what you're hearing. Then, tell your pastor what you heard. Your pastor will really love it! Plus, talking with your pastor is a great way to grow in your life with Jesus.

HOLY Qs!

- *What am I thankful for? How can I show how thankful I am this week?*

- *How can the way I spend my money reflect my relationship with Jesus?*

BLESSING

Go following the way of the Savior, walking in the truth of the King, and living the life of the Friend. May your thoughts, words, and actions reflect the love of Jesus.

117

Day 3
FINDING LOVE IN THE LAW

MATTHEW 5:38-48

Think of a time a parent or teacher gave you instructions that you didn't really understand. How did you handle it? Back in the Old Testament, God's people were given some specific laws that helped them live a godly life. Even the very thing Jesus talks about in verse 38 is mentioned in the Law (Exodus 21:23-25). The Law was very important to God's people, but eventually many people began to misunderstand it. They started to misuse it.

People sometimes used those Exodus verses as excuses to get revenge on their enemies, but that law was given to make sure people weren't punished too harshly when they did something wrong. Jesus took these old laws and helped people understand that God is ultimately about love. Jesus brought a new way to understand the Law. In fact, the best way to understand the Law is to really know Jesus. Understanding Scripture reveals who God really is. How do you see God's love revealed in the passage? What else does it show you about Him?

HOLY Qs!

- *How does what I learned from Scripture inspire my thoughts and actions?*
- *How can I learn from others this week?*

BLESSING

Go following the way of the Savior, walking in the truth of the King, and living the life of the Friend. May your thoughts, words, and actions reflect the love of Jesus.

Day 4
YOU DID WHAT?

What makes a good leader? The Jewish people were expecting Jesus to come and be a conquering hero king. They wanted Him to fight their enemies! They didn't really understand the kind of leader Jesus had come to be. When He preached this message of loving enemies, there were a lot of people who didn't like it. How could He lead them in taking down their bad guys if He was telling everyone to love their enemies?

Being a Christian means you're going to have lots of opportunities to make decisions that aren't anything like people would expect. Imagine a kid at school is mean to you . . . and you're nice to him in return. Whoa. Friends might want you to say something hateful in return, but you react with grace and patience. People might think you're crazy! People thought that about Jesus, too. He was showing them the way to the Father, and that included love for enemies. How will you react differently this week?

HOLY Qs!

- *How does my relationship with Jesus impact my daily life in real ways?*
- *How can I keep from letting things like popularity or friends determine how I act?*

BLESSING

Go following the way of the Savior, walking in the truth of the King, and living the life of the Friend. May your thoughts, words, and actions reflect the love of Jesus.

Day 5
TWO MILES AND COUNTING

MATTHEW 5:38-48

Ever heard the phrase "go the extra mile for someone"? What does it mean? Check out verse 41. The Romans were the rulers, and people didn't like it very much. The Roman soldiers were allowed to make someone carry their things for them. That's one thing on a list of, like, a thousand that the people didn't like. Then, Jesus showed up and told them something that blew their minds. Not only should they not fight back when a soldier made them carry his stuff, they should offer to carry it even farther! What?!

Jesus was teaching a lesson about love. When we love, we'll do things for other people even if it doesn't help us, or if we don't like doing it. (This does not include hurtful behavior. If someone is ever hurting you, you do not need to go along with it. You should tell a trusted adult.) Love "goes the extra mile." Get it? Love does more than what's expected. Jesus loves us way more than we can imagine. How can His love inspire you to go the extra mile this week?

HOLY Qs!

- *What's a healthy or helpful way I can use my spare time?*

- *Is there anyone I'm struggling to get along with? What am I going to do about it?*

BLESSING

Go following the way of the Savior, walking in the truth of the King, and living the life of the Friend. May your thoughts, words, and actions reflect the love of Jesus.

LOVING FRIENDS IS EASY . . .

MATTHEW 5:38-48

Why do you love your friends? Check out verses 46 and 47. It's pretty easy to love our friends. They're our friends because we get along with them and we like the same stuff. We like hanging out. We play together really well. Friendships are awesome! We don't need much help loving our friends. That's easy. But loving enemies? That can be tough. Down through the years, God's people had begun to read some old laws in a way that seemed to give permission to mistreat their enemies.

Loving enemies is way harder than loving friends. Jesus didn't just preach about this; He lived it. When Jesus was being hung on the cross, He forgave the people who did it. He forgave them right there, while He was still in pain, not later after it was all over. We can look at Jesus's life for an example of how to love our enemies. His love makes it possible. Embrace God's love for you and anything is possible . . . even loving your enemies.

HOLY Qs!

- Have I been jealous, grumpy, or really hard on anyone? What can I do about it?

- How will I be a good friend and listener?

BLESSING

Go following the way of the Savior, walking in the truth of the King, and living the life of the Friend. May your thoughts, words, and actions reflect the love of Jesus.

Day 7
IT STARTS WITH PRAYER

MATTHEW 5:38-48

What do you pray about when you talk to God? This whole week has been about loving our enemies, and there's one really important part of this we need to talk about. Check out verse 44. We're given some very specific advice on how to love our enemies: pray for them. Let's talk about some ways to pray for the people we don't get along with very well.

Pray for their home and their family, that there would be peace among them. Pray for your own reactions to them, that you would meet their anger with peace. Pray for them to do well on tests, have great days at school, or for their team to have success. Pray that they'll experience Jesus, somehow. Pray that they'll be heard and understood. Pray that you and they no longer see each other as enemies, but that the Holy Spirit would start healing the hurt and anger. Now, pause and pray for someone you're not getting along with very well right now.

HOLY Qs!

- *What have I been enjoying about prayer recently?*
- *How can I be obedient to God this week?*

BLESSING

Go following the way of the Savior, walking in the truth of the King, and living the life of the Friend. May your thoughts, words, and actions reflect the love of Jesus.

WEEK 18 Day 1
THE LORD'S PRAYER

It's a new week in your life with Jesus! Use the *5 What's or Lectio Divina* to guide your reading today. Enjoy God's love for you!

MATTHEW 6:9-15 (NIV)

9 "This, then, is how you should pray:
"'Our Father in heaven,
hallowed be your name,
10 your kingdom come,
your will be done,
 on earth as it is in heaven.
11 Give us today our daily bread.
12 And forgive us our debts,
 as we also have forgiven our debtors.
13 And lead us not into temptation,
 but deliver us from the evil one.'
14 For if you forgive other people when they sin against you, your heavenly Father will also forgive you. 15 But if you do not forgive others their sins, your Father will not forgive your sins."

Day 2
WHERE'S THE FOCUS?

MATTHEW 6:9-15

If you met someone who had never prayed before, what guidance would you give them? Jesus's disciples knew that prayer was talking with God, but they wanted to learn more about *how* to pray. Right before our Scripture starts, Jesus explains some right and wrong praying styles. For example, avoid being like the hypocrites who love to be seen praying. Hypocrites are people who *say* they believe one thing, but then *do* another. Praying in front of people is not bad, but praying just to show off is. The right way to pray puts the focus on God, not on us.

Even though Jesus opens with some ways not to pray, He makes it pretty clear in His life of prayer that there are many right ways to pray. God is really open to our conversations. He wants us to talk to Him. You can pray anywhere at any time. When and where do you pray? How do you focus on Him when you pray?

HOLY Qs!

- *Have my words matched my actions? Does who I say I am and how I act line up?*

- *How can I be honest and trustworthy this week?*

BLESSING

Go following the way of the Savior, walking in the truth of the King, and living the life of the Friend. May your thoughts, words, and actions reflect the love of Jesus.

THE LORD'S PRAYER

MATTHEW 6:9-15

Jesus models how to pray in verses 9-13. We call this the Lord's Prayer. We don't have to pray this exact prayer word-for-word every time. It's an example. It is a pattern to follow. It reminds us that there is more to praying than listing a bunch of things we need from God. We are missing out on a deep connection to God if we leave out the other important parts of prayer. A good reminder is to follow ACTS: Adoration (big word for praise), Confession (admitting our sins), Thanksgiving (giving thanks), Supplication (sharing our requests).

Have you memorized the Lord's Prayer? If not, give it a try. If so, how much can you say without looking? It's a great prayer to know and will help you develop good praying habits. Saying the prayer all together with a group of people is a powerful experience. What a great way to communicate with God! Finish your devotion time today praying that prayer.

HOLY Qs!

- What have I been enjoying about prayer recently?

- How can I be obedient to God this week?

BLESSING

Go following the way of the Savior, walking in the truth of the King, and living the life of the Friend. May your thoughts, words, and actions reflect the love of Jesus.

Day 4
KINGDOM-BRINGER

MATTHEW 6:9-15

How do you usually start a prayer? Jesus begins His prayer with, "Our Father." We are blessed with a Heavenly Father who loves and cares for us. God is like the perfect father. "Our Father" was both a familiar way to talk to God (like family) and a respectful way to talk to Him (like a King).

In verse 10, Jesus talks about God's kingdom coming. This isn't about some distant future, a faraway heaven. It's a prayer that asks the great King of the world to bring His kingdom among us, so the world will look the way He wants it to look. But if we're going to ask that, we have to be willing to accept our role in it. We are bringers of the kingdom. As God's love changes our life into a holy life, God's kingdom fills this world. This prayer is a big deal. We're basically praying, "God, I want to help bring Your kingdom. I want what You want." Are you ready to pray that prayer?

HOLY Qs!

- How can God's love give me confidence today?
- What's a healthy or helpful way I can use my spare time?

BLESSING

Go following the way of the Savior, walking in the truth of the King, and living the life of the Friend. May your thoughts, words, and actions reflect the love of Jesus.

Day 5
FOOD FOR TODAY

MATTHEW 6:9-15

Why do you think verse 11 mentions God giving us the food we need for *today*? Some of us have enough food in our refrigerator and pantry to feed us for weeks. We often forget what it is like to have to trust God to provide food for us each day. There are people who are hungry and can't afford to buy all of the food they need. In Exodus 16, God sent enough food each day to feed His people. They couldn't collect extra. They had to rely on Him to send food the next day, too. When we ask God to give us the food we need, we know He is the one who provides for us.

But, how does God provide? God often provides through other people. He wants everyone to have food. In other words, we can share with those in need. Look around you and across the world. What are some ways you and your family can help feed others?

HOLY Qs!

- *How will I be a good friend and listener?*
- *How can the way I spend my money reflect my relationship with Jesus?*

BLESSING

Go following the way of the Savior, walking in the truth of the King, and living the life of the Friend. May your thoughts, words, and actions reflect the love of Jesus.

Day 6
HE FORGIVES. WE FORGIVE.

MATTHEW 6:9-15

Why do teachers repeat themselves? There is one topic in the Lord's Prayer that is mentioned in verse 12, and then in verses 14 and 15. Forgiveness. Not only do we need to be forgiven, but we also need to forgive others. None of us are perfect. We've all messed up. The good news? Our Savior, Jesus, forgives us. We just have to ask. But don't stop there. We also need to forgive those who hurt us. This can sometimes be challenging. If someone hurts us, we may want to ignore them or be angry. However, God calls us to forgive them like He forgave us.

Can you think of any sins you need to confess? You can ask for forgiveness right now. Is there anyone who has hurt you? Pray that they will ask forgiveness. Anyone you need to forgive? If so, ask God for strength to forgive. Forgiving a person doesn't mean you think what they did was okay. It means you're going to let go of the anger over what they did. How do you think forgiveness can change a person?

HOLY Qs!

- *Is anything in my life really hard right now? Am I talking to God about it? Who else can I talk to?*

- *Have I been jealous, grumpy, or really hard on anyone? What can I do about it?*

BLESSING

Go following the way of the Savior, walking in the truth of the King, and living the life of the Friend. May your thoughts, words, and actions reflect the love of Jesus.

RAFTING THROUGH TEMPTATION

MATTHEW 6:9-15

Imagine sitting on a raft in the river. You could use paddles to steer the raft in the direction you want to go. Or you could yield (give in) to the river's current and let it take you wherever it wanted. Giving in to temptation leads in the wrong direction. Temptation is thinking about doing the wrong thing. By itself, it isn't sin. We are all tempted sometimes. Even Jesus was tempted. But if we yield to temptation, that means we give in to it. Our Scripture this week reminds us to pray for strength and protection to choose what is right. God shows the way through temptation.

What are some temptations you face? Whenever you are tempted to do wrong, look for God's way out. He makes you stronger. Prayer keeps us close to God. When we're close to God, it's easier to see our way around temptation.

HOLY Qs!

- *How does what I learned from Scripture inspire my thoughts and actions?*

- *What can I do to make wise choices this week?*

BLESSING

Go following the way of the Savior, walking in the truth of the King, and living the life of the Friend. May your thoughts, words, and actions reflect the love of Jesus.

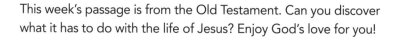

WEEK 19 Day 1
A PRAYER

This week's passage is from the Old Testament. Can you discover what it has to do with the life of Jesus? Enjoy God's love for you!

PSALM 71:1-6

¹ O Lᴏʀᴅ, I have come to you for protection;
don't let me be disgraced.
² Save me and rescue me,
for you do what is right.
Turn your ear to listen to me,
and set me free.
³ Be my rock of safety
where I can always hide.
Give the order to save me,
for you are my rock and my fortress.
⁴ My God, rescue me from the power of the wicked,
from the clutches of cruel oppressors.
⁵ O Lord, you alone are my hope.
I've trusted you, O Lᴏʀᴅ, from childhood.
⁶ Yes, you have been with me from birth;
from my mother's womb you have cared for me.
No wonder I am always praising you!

WHAT'S A PSALM?

PSALM 71:1-6

What's your favorite song? Do you know all the words? The Psalms (the "p" is silent) are a collection of favorite songs of the Jewish people. But they aren't just songs—they're prayers. Singing prayers? Yep. Many different people wrote the Psalms over hundreds of years. Over time, lots of other people heard and used these prayer songs to help their own talks with God. These prayer poems became songs that God's people sang and prayed together in worship, in their homes, and while they traveled.

When we read the Psalms, we are reading the prayer songs that Jesus memorized, prayed, and sang himself. So it's not surprising that Jesus's prayers used words from the Psalms, too. When He taught His disciples to pray, He followed the pattern and tradition of the Psalms. The Psalms can help us pray, too. They remind us it's okay to pray with our feelings. We can be angry, sad, joyful, or scared when we talk to God. And we can always ask for God's help. What words help you pray?

HOLY Qs!

- *What habits help me spend time getting to know God through Scripture?*

BLESSING

Go following the way of the Savior, walking in the truth of the King, and living the life of the Friend. May your thoughts, words, and actions reflect the love of Jesus.

Day 3
GOD THE ROCK

PSALM 71:1-6

Where do you feel the most safe? The person who wrote Psalm 71 (called the *psalmist*) was looking for a safe place. He or she saw trouble up ahead, and was asking God to help. The psalmist calls God a "rock of safety," and "my rock and my fortress." If you are in a flat land, a rocky mountain is a very safe place, a place that is high up and hard to get to. A fort made of rock could also be a strong and secure place to hide, a place that cannot be shaken or torn down.

Do you think God actually turns into a mountain or a fort? No, of course not. But the psalmist says that being with God is like being hidden away in a safe place. God is the One who cannot be shaken or torn down. Being with God is the safest place we can be. So if you were writing a prayer like Psalm 71, what would you call God? How would you describe God?

HOLY Qs!

- *How can God's love give me confidence today?*
- *What can I do to make wise choices this week?*

BLESSING

Go following the way of the Savior, walking in the truth of the King, and living the life of the Friend. May your thoughts, words, and actions reflect the love of Jesus.

GOD THE RIGHTEOUS

PSALM 71:1-6

Do you know what the word "righteous" means? In verse 2 it says, "Save me and rescue me, for you do what is right." But in other translations it says, "In your righteousness, rescue me." When we say God is righteous, it means that God always does what is right, good, and loving. God cares for people, treats people well, and helps us treat one another well. When we talk about God's justice or holiness, this is what we mean.

The psalmist knows who God is and what God is like. He doesn't say, "Save me and rescue me, for I always do what is right." No! He says, "Save me and rescue me, for you do what is right." We don't ask God to help us because we've earned His help. We ask God to help us because God is righteous, holy, just, and always loving. God will always care, and He will always do what is right. Can you think of any other words you would use for someone who always does what is right?

HOLY Qs!

- *What have I been enjoying about prayer recently?*

- *How can I learn from others this week?*

BLESSING

Go following the way of the Savior, walking in the truth of the King, and living the life of the Friend. May your thoughts, words, and actions reflect the love of Jesus.

Day 5
GOD THE RESCUER

PSALM 71:1-6

Ever been rescued? What's a movie or story where someone gets rescued? When someone is rescued it means he or she is taken away from danger. There are many stories in Scripture about times that God rescued a person or a group of people. But not every rescue looks the same. Sometimes God stops a dangerous situation. Sometimes He uses another person to bring rescue. Sometimes God lets us know we're not alone when it feels dangerous. Some-times the rescue happens right away. Other times the rescue feels like it takes for-ev-er.

Sometimes we know what we need to be rescued from. But other times we learn that what we thought was dangerous wasn't really dangerous at all. Or, what we thought was good for us was actually dangerous. But God knows all these things. When we ask God to rescue us, we also trust Him to do it the way He knows best. Is there something you want to ask God to rescue you, or someone else, from?

HOLY Qs!

- *Is anything in my life really hard right now? Am I talking to God about it? Who else can I talk to?*
- *What's a healthy or helpful way I can use my spare time?*

BLESSING

Go following the way of the Savior, walking in the truth of the King, and living the life of the Friend. May your thoughts, words, and actions reflect the love of Jesus.

Day 6
GOD THE LISTENER

PSALM 71:1-6

We've all had someone say they were listening, when really they weren't. So, how can you tell if someone is really listening to you? The psalmist says, "Turn your ear to listen to me." One time a three-year-old told her mom, "Listen to me with your eyes!" Pretty. Funny. But she really meant, "Turn your face to me so I know you are listening." The mom was looking at her phone, and needed that reminder. Do you ever want to tell God to listen to you with His eyes?

Sometimes when God doesn't answer us quickly, it might feel like God isn't listening. But Jesus said that God hears us all the time. And He said that God even knows what we need before we ask for it (Matthew 6:8)! God sees you, knows you, and listens to you because God is with you. But God invites us to listen too. We can't always hear God with our ears, but we can know God is speaking. What are some ways you can listen to God, even if you can't hear God speak? What helps you know He's listening?

HOLY Qs!

- *How will I be a good friend and listener?*
- *Is there anyone I'm struggling to get along with? What am I going to do about it?*

BLESSING

Go following the way of the Savior, walking in the truth of the King, and living the life of the Friend. May your thoughts, words, and actions reflect the love of Jesus.

Day 7
GOD THE TRUSTED

PSALM 71:1-6

Who are the adults and friends you trust the most? We learn to trust people when they do what they say they will do. We trust people when they listen to us and try to understand our feelings. People we trust keep their promises. And if they mess up, they apologize. And if we have a choice, we will always ask the people we trust for help. But there are people we have learned not to trust, too. No one wants to ask someone they don't trust for help, because the help probably won't come.

The Psalms are full of people asking God for help, just like Psalm 71. For thousands of years people have asked God for help because they have learned to trust God. The Psalms tell us that God can be trusted. But God doesn't just want you to believe what they say. God wants to show you that you can trust Him. During your life with Jesus, what stories or memories have shown you God can be trusted?

HOLY Qs!

- *Have my words matched my actions? Does who I say I am and how I act line up?*
- *What am I thankful for? How can I show how thankful I am this week?*

BLESSING

Go following the way of the Savior, walking in the truth of the King, and living the life of the Friend. May your thoughts, words, and actions reflect the love of Jesus.

WEEK 20 Day 1
FRUIT OF THE SPIRIT

It's a new week in your life with Jesus! Use the *5 What's or Lectio Divina* to guide your reading today. Enjoy God's love for you!

GALATIANS 5:22-23 (NIV)

22 But the fruit of the Spirit is love, joy, peace, forbearance, kindness, goodness, faithfulness, 23 gentleness and self-control. Against such things there is no law.

GALATIANS 5:22-23 (NLT)

22 But the Holy Spirit produces this kind of fruit in our lives: love, joy, peace, patience, kindness, goodness, faithfulness, 23 gentleness, and self-control. There is no law against these things!

Day 2
DIFFERENT VERSIONS

GALATIANS 5:22-23

Where did you get the Bible you have right now? Did you know it has 66 books? Written by over 40 authors. From the first book written to the last book written was over 1500 years. Amazing! These books were written by the poor, rich, young, old, powerful, and weak. There were kings and even people of different parts of the world who wrote these books. All this writing has been translated from its original language into different versions of the Bible. This doesn't mean the truth of what God is saying has been changed. But it does mean that as people translated Scripture, they used different methods.

Looking at different versions helps us see the same verse or story in different ways that might be super helpful as we learn about who Jesus is. What are some differences you see in the versions of our passage for this week?

HOLY Qs!

- *What habits help me spend time getting to know God through Scripture?*

- *How can I be obedient to God this week?*

BLESSING

Go following the way of the Savior, walking in the truth of the King, and living the life of the Friend. May your thoughts, words, and actions reflect the love of Jesus.

THE SPIRIT GROWS

GALATIANS 5:22-23

What's your favorite kind of fresh fruit? Jesus says the things that we say and do, and even the way we do them, is like fruit growing from a tree. An apple tree grows apples. The Spirit grows the fruit of the Spirit in followers of Jesus. People who are filled with the love of Jesus will grow love, joy, peace, patience, kindness, goodness, faithfulness, gentleness, and self-control.

This means that the thoughts you have, the way you see people, talk to people, and treat people, and even what you do when someone hurts you, will show more and more of these fruits as Jesus grows them in your life. We don't create these fruits on our own. Instead, we submit to Him and let Him change us. Let Him love us. Then, our lives start to grow this fruit.

HOLY Qs!

- *Have my words matched my actions? Does who I say I am and how I act line up?*

- *How can I keep from letting things like popularity or friends determine how I act?*

BLESSING

Go following the way of the Savior, walking in the truth of the King, and living the life of the Friend. May your thoughts, words, and actions reflect the love of Jesus.

Day 4
FRUIT OR FRUITS

GALATIANS 5:22-23

List as many fruits as you can in 10 seconds. Challenge your family. You'll list a lot of fruit. Of course, they're all different. Grown from different trees. Often in different parts of the world. Now check out verse 22. Notice it says "this kind of fruit" rather than "these kinds of fruits." Wait, that kind of makes it sound like it's all one fruit . . .

We don't get to pick and choose what fruits we'll allow the Spirit to develop in our lives. We don't say, "Okay, God, you can help me with my patience, but I am NOT gonna get any better at self-control." Instead, if we open ourselves up to the Spirit leading us, we will develop all the fruit in the list, not just a couple of them. While we may be naturally better at some of them, they're all important and God can develop all of them in our lives. So, this week, work on memorizing the whole list. After all, it's the "fruit" of the Spirit, not the "fruits."

HOLY Qs!

- God cares about our whole life, not just the spiritual parts. What healthy habits do I need to work on?

- How can I learn from others this week?

BLESSING

Go following the way of the Savior, walking in the truth of the King, and living the life of the Friend. May your thoughts, words, and actions reflect the love of Jesus.

FRUIT STRUGGLES

GALATIANS 5:22-23

While it's true that we can't pick and choose which fruit of the Spirit we'll have in our lives, sometimes some come more naturally to us than others. Where do you see fruit growing in your life? Where do you see yourself struggling?

This is not an exercise to beat ourselves up. Rather, it's helpful to know what we're struggling with because it helps us pray. It makes us aware of how God is showing up in our lives. Areas where we struggle are opportunities for God to do mighty works in us. Maybe kindness and gentleness is something you need to ask Jesus to really help you with. Maybe you've been wrestling with being joyful. Maybe there's a relationship that needs peace in it. Take some time to pray over each word today and ask God to help His fruit grow in you.

HOLY Qs!

- Is anything in my life really hard right now? Am I talking to God about it? Who else can I talk to?

- How does my relationship with Jesus impact my daily life in real ways?

BLESSING

Go following the way of the Savior, walking in the truth of the King, and living the life of the Friend. May your thoughts, words, and actions reflect the love of Jesus.

Day 6
PATIENTLY WAITING

GALATIANS 5:22-23

What's something you've had to wait a long time for? What did you do to pass the time? Did you ever feel impatient?

Check out verse 22. What does patience have to do with showing God's love? Whether it's waiting in a line at an amusement park or waiting on your mom to finish shopping, having patience is tough. But think of this: Has anyone ever been impatient with you? How did that make you feel? One reason the Holy Spirit grows patience in our lives is to help us treat others with respect and care. You don't have to fight to be first in line. You don't have to always get the first dish of ice cream. You'll notice that as you become more patient, you'll become more and more aware of the people around you. You'll get to see what Jesus sees and how you can love others well.

HOLY Qs!

- How will I be a good friend and listener?
- Have I been jealous, grumpy, or really hard on anyone? What can I do about it?

BLESSING
Go following the way of the Savior, walking in the truth of the King, and living the life of the Friend. May your thoughts, words, and actions reflect the love of Jesus.

LIMITLESS

GALATIANS 5:22-23

If you brought home freshly baked cookies how many would you be allowed to eat? Is there a limit? It's good to have a limit on things. Too much of even a good thing, like freshly baked cookies, can be bad for us. But verse 23 tells us there's no law or limit on one thing. Guess what it is.

Verse 23 tells us that there is no law or limit on the fruit of the Spirit. What?! No limit?! They are always good and always perfect. Nothing can stop them. When we live in the power of God, we have this unlimited supply of His love. It cannot be defeated or stopped. He is limitless. We can trust that no matter what comes our way, God's love is always working in us. How does it make you feel to know that God's love and His fruit are limitless in you?

HOLY Qs!

- What am I thankful for? How can I show how thankful I am this week?
- When good things happen, how do I give God the credit?

BLESSING

Go following the way of the Savior, walking in the truth of the King, and living the life of the Friend. May your thoughts, words, and actions reflect the love of Jesus.

WEEK 21 Day 1
THE WOMAN AT THE WELL

JOHN 4:21-30

(Leading up to this story, in verses 1-20, Jesus passes through Samaria on a journey back to Galilee. He sits at a well and asks a Samaritan woman for a drink. Then He tells her things about herself He (a stranger) wouldn't know, and offers her "living water." She wonders if He's a prophet, and asks Him about the proper place to worship God. Now you're all caught up.)

[21] Jesus replied, "Believe me, dear woman, the time is coming when it will no longer matter whether you worship the Father on this mountain or in Jerusalem. [22] You Samaritans know very little about the one you worship, while we Jews know all about him, for salvation comes through the Jews. [23] But the time is coming—indeed it's here now—when true worshipers will worship the Father in spirit and in truth. The Father is looking for those who will worship him that way. [24] For God is Spirit, so those who worship him must worship in spirit and in truth."
[25] The woman said, "I know the Messiah is coming—the one who is called Christ. When he comes, he will explain everything to us."
[26] Then Jesus told her, "I AM the Messiah!"
[27] Just then his disciples came back. They were shocked to find him talking to a woman, but none of them had the nerve to ask, "What do you want with her?" or "Why are you talking to her?"
[28] The woman left her water jar beside the well and ran back to the village, telling everyone, [29] "Come and see a man who told me everything I ever did! Could he possibly be the Messiah?"
[30] So the people came streaming from the village to see him.

HE TALKED TO WHO?

JOHN 4:21-30

Jesus is up to it again. Name another time when Jesus did something totally unexpected. Well, here He is talking to a Samaritan (the Jews didn't get along with them) woman (not respected among men) who is a known sinner (look up verses 17-18) right out in the open! Jesus often seems to spend time with people who make everyone else ask, "What in the world is He thinking?!" It's bad enough He chose to even travel *through* Samaria. Most Jews traveled all the way around it. But now He's *hanging out* with Samaritans?

There are other stories, even highlighted in this devotion book, of Jesus hanging out with unexpected people. Jesus cared for people His society didn't respect—like sinners, Samaritans, and women. He knew they were created equally in God's image, but choosing to treat them with kindness made a lot of people mad. Do you ever see people who are treated poorly? As you live your life with Jesus, what could your response be?

HOLY Qs!

- *Who in my life needs to hear about Jesus? How can they hear it from me?*

- *How can God's love give me confidence today?*

BLESSING

Go following the way of the Savior, walking in the truth of the King, and living the life of the Friend. May your thoughts, words, and actions reflect the love of Jesus.

Day 3
A GRAND PLAN, PART 1

JOHN 4:21-30

Ok. Put your detective hat on. You have a job to do. The story of Jesus being the Messiah and saving the world goes waaaay back. Check out Genesis 12:3. God is talking to Abram (who becomes Abraham) and gives some pretty big news: the entire world would be blessed through Abraham's family. How would God bless the world through Abraham's family? Well, check out Matthew 1. See that list of names? It starts with Abraham and goes through generation after generation. And who is at the bottom of the list in verse 16? Is your mind not blown?!

Look at verse 22 of our passage this week. "Salvation comes through the Jews." Jesus is pointing out His place in the stories of Abraham and of God's people. It's been about Jesus all this time! Before you do anything else today, pause and pray, giving thanks for Jesus and for His role in your life already. Tune in tomorrow for Part 2.

HOLY Qs!

- *When good things happen, how do I give God the credit?*
- *How does my relationship with Jesus impact my daily life in real ways?*

BLESSING

Go following the way of the Savior, walking in the truth of the King, and living the life of the Friend. May your thoughts, words, and actions reflect the love of Jesus.

A GRAND PLAN, PART 2

JOHN 4:21-30

This is Part 2 from yesterday. What's something you've planned for way in advance? Maybe a party or a trip? God's prevenient grace (check out Day 1 for a refresher) has been at work preparing the way for Jesus to come and save the world since Genesis. That's a lot of planning. Salvation, a right relationship with God, can only come through Jesus. After God's prevenient grace makes a way, God's saving grace brings us into that relationship with Him.

People get to know Jesus in all kinds of different ways. In the Bible, someone might meet Him at a well, or from up in a tree, or on a mountainside. Today, people might get to know Jesus when they come to church for the first time, when they have a relationship with a Christian friend, when trusted adults teach them about Jesus, or when they reach out to Jesus through prayer. How did you get to know Jesus? How are you still getting to know Jesus?

HOLY Qs!

- *What have I been enjoying about prayer recently?*

- *What habits help me spend time getting to know God through Scripture?*

BLESSING

Go following the way of the Savior, walking in the truth of the King, and living the life of the Friend. May your thoughts, words, and actions reflect the love of Jesus.

Day 5
ANYWHERE WORSHIP

JOHN 4:21-30

What makes worshiping God in a church special? What do you love about your church? The Samaritans and the Jews had different ideas of where the proper temple was to worship God. A temple or church building is a special place to worship and learn about God. Worshiping there can be very meaningful, but check out verse 21. Jesus made it clear to this woman that it wasn't going to matter where she went to worship. The Holy Spirit, God on earth, was going to be given freely to the whole world. Being in God's presence could happen anywhere!

You can worship God anywhere you are, anytime of day. In your room, at school, outside, inside; it doesn't matter. While it's great to gather with other worshipers like you do at church, you can keep worshiping God even when you aren't there. What are your favorite ways to connect with God? Drawing? Writing? Praying? Being outside? Singing? How do those things help you connect with Him?

HOLY Qs!

- How does what I learned from Scripture inspire my thoughts and actions?

- Have my words matched my actions? Does who I say I am and how I act line up?

BLESSING

Go following the way of the Savior, walking in the truth of the King, and living the life of the Friend. May your thoughts, words, and actions reflect the love of Jesus.

FROM WHERE TO HOW

JOHN 4:21-30

If you look up verse 20 in this week's passage, you'd see that the Samaritan woman asks Jesus where her people should worship. Jesus answers her, but then quickly moves from *where* to worship to *how* to worship. Think of something you know a lot about. Basketball. Reading. Something else? Now, practice explaining it to someone. What did you focus on more, where or how? Sure you can read in a library, but that's not *how* to read. You can play basketball in a gym, but that's not *how* to play basketball.

Jesus wasn't super concerned about the place the woman needed to worship. He was concerned with how. And what did He say? (Check out verses 23-24.) When we really worship, the Holy Spirit is with us, guiding us, teaching us, loving us. And when we worship, we don't want to be fake or just pretend to worship. We want to be real and honest with God. How can you be honest and real in your worship this week?

HOLY Qs!

- *How have I been trustworthy recently?*
- *God cares about our whole life, not just the spiritual parts. What healthy habits do I need to work on?*

BLESSING

Go following the way of the Savior, walking in the truth of the King, and living the life of the Friend. May your thoughts, words, and actions reflect the love of Jesus.

Day 7
TELL YOUR STORY

JOHN 4:21-30

Can you think of a time you learned something in an unexpected way? Or learned from an unexpected person? Jesus used unexpected people to make an impact on other people quite often. This story is no different. He used a Samaritan woman. Remember, Jews and Samaritans were not friendly to each other. Women were not respected like men were. Jesus, however, saw equal value in Jews, Samaritans, women, and men. He saw them as people and as leaders.

Check out verses 29-30. Not only did this woman listen to Jesus, she got others to come listen to Him. Now, look up verses 39-41. Many people became believers that day because of the woman's story. Jesus chose this woman to minister to the Samaritans. In the same way, Jesus continues to choose women and men to serve Him, to be leaders, to be ministers, and to spread His good news to the world. She just had to tell her story. How do you tell your "life with Jesus" story?

HOLY Qs!

- What am I thankful for? How can I show how thankful I am this week?

- How will I be a good friend and listener?

BLESSING

Go following the way of the Savior, walking in the truth of the King, and living the life of the Friend. May your thoughts, words, and actions reflect the love of Jesus.

WEEK 22 Day 1
SEED PARABLES

It's a new week in your life with Jesus! Use the *5 What's or Lectio Divina* to guide your reading today. Enjoy God's love for you!

MARK 4:26-34

26 Jesus also said, "The Kingdom of God is like a farmer who scatters seed on the ground. 27 Night and day, while he's asleep or awake, the seed sprouts and grows, but he does not understand how it happens. 28 The earth produces the crops on its own. First a leaf blade pushes through, then the heads of wheat are formed, and finally the grain ripens. 29 And as soon as the grain is ready, the farmer comes and harvests it with a sickle, for the harvest time has come."

30 Jesus said, "How can I describe the Kingdom of God? What story should I use to illustrate it? 31 It is like a mustard seed planted in the ground. It is the smallest of all seeds, 32 but it becomes the largest of all garden plants; it grows long branches, and birds can make nests in its shade."

33 Jesus used many similar stories and illustrations to teach the people as much as they could understand. 34 In fact, in his public ministry he never taught without using parables; but afterward, when he was alone with his disciples, he explained everything to them.

Day 2
PARABLE FAN

MARK 4:26-34

What's a story you know that teaches a lesson? Jesus used those a lot. They're called parables (PAIR-uh-bulls): simple stories used to explain a spiritual lesson. Jesus knew that lessons learned in the form of a story were easier to remember. He also knew His disciples would need to really think about the parable in order to understand His message. He wanted them to think deeply and ask questions. Why? Because pretty soon they would be sharing the message and answering questions. He knew He would not always be around to do the teaching.

Jesus could have just given us a list of right and wrong, and then given a quiz to test our memory. But He knew people learn better when they have a story to think about. Plus, Jesus isn't a huge fan of tests (Matthew 4:7). The challenge of figuring out a parable helps us discover and remember what it teaches. The more we take the time to understand His parables, the wiser and closer to Him we'll grow.

HOLY Qs!

- *What habits help me spend time getting to know God through Scripture?*
- *How can I be obedient to God this week?*

BLESSING

Go following the way of the Savior, walking in the truth of the King, and living the life of the Friend. May your thoughts, words, and actions reflect the love of Jesus.

Day 3
PLANTING SEEDS

MARK 4:26-34

What kinds of seeds, flowers, or veggies have you tried to plant? Did they grow as fast as you thought they would? The two parables in our Scripture have many things in common. They are parables about the kingdom of God, and they use seeds and growth as examples. Jesus told these parables to encourage us to keep telling others about Him, even when we don't see results. The kingdom of God doesn't always grow the way we think it should. The parables can help us understand our part in how God's kingdom will grow.

Have you ever tried sharing about Jesus with your friends, but they didn't seem interested? Have you prayed for people, but not seen the results you hoped for? Have you invited someone to church, but been turned down? Don't be discouraged. You are planting seeds. The plants may not grow as fast as you would like. You might not see your friends become Christians. But keep letting God work through you. One day God may surprise you with a great harvest.

HOLY Qs!

- *How will I be a good friend and listener?*
- *Who in my life needs to hear about Jesus? How can they hear it from me?*

BLESSING

Go following the way of the Savior, walking in the truth of the King, and living the life of the Friend. May your thoughts, words, and actions reflect the love of Jesus.

153

Day 4

GOD MAKES IT GROW

MARK 4:26-34

What do you think you would discover if you could cut open a seed and study it under a microscope? All of the information a seed needs to become a plant is stored right inside. If we plant a tomato seed, it sprouts a plant, grows more tomatoes, and produces more seeds. We can water the plant, but we can't control all that is going on to make it grow. Verses 26-29 tells the parable of the growing seed. The farmer plants the seeds, but the earth makes the plants grow. The same is true with the gospel. We can plant the seeds (spread the good news). We might even get to water the seeds with encouragement and love, but God will make His kingdom grow.

Have you ever heard someone share how they became a Christian? Some stories make it obvious that God was putting the right people and events together at just the right time. Pray today that you will be faithful to plant seeds and trusting enough to let God do His work.

HOLY Qs!

- *When good things happen, how do I give God the credit?*
- *What am I thankful for? How can I show how thankful I am this week?*

BLESSING

Go following the way of the Savior, walking in the truth of the King, and living the life of the Friend. May your thoughts, words, and actions reflect the love of Jesus.

ITTY BITTY MUSTARD SEED

MARK 4:26-34

The second parable Jesus shares in this Scripture is about the kingdom of God. What is He trying to tell us by comparing it to a mustard seed? A mustard seed is tiny but grows into the largest of all garden plants. When Jesus told this story to the disciples, they were probably feeling small and not very important. After all, Jesus was just getting started. Hardly anyone in the world knew about Him. He started with a really small group of followers. They likely were afraid people wouldn't listen to their message. Jesus wanted them to know they weren't on their own. Through Him, their message would grow and be heard. The church is what it is today because the disciples spread the message of Jesus.

Do you ever feel tiny like a mustard seed? Do you sometimes feel overlooked and unheard? God changed the world through fishermen, and He can work through you, too. Your age, gender, race, or family income do not matter. How can you stay connected to Jesus, so you will grow into your full potential?

HOLY Qs!

- *How can God's love give me confidence today?*

- *How does what I learned from Scripture inspire my thoughts and actions?*

BLESSING

Go following the way of the Savior, walking in the truth of the King, and living the life of the Friend. May your thoughts, words, and actions reflect the love of Jesus.

Day 6
SMALL TO BIG

MARK 4:26-34

What is the biggest tree you have ever seen? Try to imagine how long it has been growing. Some Sequoia trees can grow over 350 feet tall and live for thousands of years. That's a big, old tree! There are trees alive today that were around when Jesus was telling His parables. It is hard to imagine that something so big that has lasted so long grew from one tiny seed.

Have you ever thought about how your little acts of kindness can grow into something huge? When you are kind to people, with God's love guiding your words and actions, you are showing people Jesus. Your kindness could cause a chain reaction of kindness. Kindness inspires others to be kind too. It could also make someone curious about Christians. "Why are they always so kind to me?" You might never know exactly how big your small act can grow. What are some ways you could plant kindness this week?

HOLY Qs!

- *Have my words matched my actions? Does who I say I am and how I act line up?*
- *What's a healthy or helpful way I can use my spare time?*

BLESSING

Go following the way of the Savior, walking in the truth of the King, and living the life of the Friend. May your thoughts, words, and actions reflect the love of Jesus.

Day 7
GOOD TIMING

MARK 4:26-34

Have you ever walked through a corn maze or stood beside a field of corn? How tall did it grow? A good farmer knows right when to pick the corn. If it's picked too soon, the kernels are too hard. If it's picked too late, the corn is chewy and doesn't taste good. God knows the best time for Jesus to come to earth a second time. He has a plan for all of His people. He knows what is best for each individual and for all of us as a whole.

Do you wish Jesus would come again soon, or wait until much later? People have been trying to guess for many years when He will return. We don't have to worry about His timing because He knows what is best. When Jesus comes again, all that is wrong will be made right. God's love is constantly working in us and in the world, preparing His kingdom. How do you see God preparing His kingdom?

HOLY Qs!

- *What can I do to make wise choices this week?*

- *How does my relationship with Jesus impact my daily life in real ways?*

BLESSING

Go following the way of the Savior, walking in the truth of the King, and living the life of the Friend. May your thoughts, words, and actions reflect the love of Jesus.

WEEK 23 Day 1
WOMEN WHO SUPPORTED JESUS

It's a new week in your life with Jesus! Use the *5 What's or Lectio Divina* to guide your reading today. Enjoy God's love for you!

LUKE 8:1-3

¹ Soon afterward Jesus began a tour of the nearby towns and villages, preaching and announcing the Good News about the Kingdom of God. He took his twelve disciples with him, ² along with some women who had been cured of evil spirits and diseases. Among them were Mary Magdalene, from whom he had cast out seven demons; ³ Joanna, the wife of Chuza, Herod's business manager; Susanna; and many others who were contributing from their own resources to support Jesus and his disciples.

GIRLS ALLOWED

LUKE 8:1-3

Do you think there are some things only boys should do? Or, can boys and girls do all the same things? In Jesus's culture, there were a lot of things that only boys and men could do. Women weren't supposed to talk to or be friends with men outside their family. Women and girls were supposed to stay home to cook, clean, and take care of children. Men were supposed to have jobs, learn about Scripture, and lead their communities.

But just like we saw with the woman of Samaria in John 4 (Week 21), Jesus had very different ideas than the people around Him. Jesus was friends with Mary, Joanna, Susanna, and other women. He invited them to travel with Him and the disciples. And it was the women who were helping to pay for things!

Jesus didn't just let them tag along behind. These women were leading the way, showing others how to follow Jesus. Who are some girls or women you know who are good examples of following Jesus?

HOLY Qs!

- How will I be a good friend and listener?

- Have I been jealous, grumpy, or really hard on anyone? What can I do about it?

BLESSING

Go following the way of the Savior, walking in the truth of the King, and living the life of the Friend. May your thoughts, words, and actions reflect the love of Jesus.

Day 3
SO NOT NORMAL

LUKE 8:1-3

Have you ever thought about why some things are in the Bible? Luke and all of the Gospel writers had a big job to do. They wanted to describe Jesus's life, but they couldn't include *everything*. So we know that what they included are the most important parts of Jesus's life. Why would Luke write about Joanna, Mary, Susanna, and the other women? Was this really that important?

These details could have been easily forgotten. But they tell us something very important about who Jesus is. The way He included and respected women was not normal back then. In many places of the world, it's still not normal. This reminds us that Jesus is not "normal." But He is showing us what *should* be normal! Jesus shows us that it is *right* to treat men and women equally.

Can you think of some other things Jesus has done that aren't "normal"? Are there times Jesus has asked you to do what was right, even if it wasn't "normal" or popular?

HOLY Qs!

- *How can I keep from letting things like popularity or friends determine how I act?*

- *How can God's love give me confidence today?*

BLESSING

Go following the way of the Savior, walking in the truth of the King, and living the life of the Friend. May your thoughts, words, and actions reflect the love of Jesus.

Day 4
WHAT WE HAVE

LUKE 8:1-3

Sometimes it can feel like we don't have enough money, enough education, or enough power to really do much to make a difference in the world around us. But can you imagine what advice Mary Magdalene, Joanna, or Susanna might give us?

Because they were women, they were often told they didn't have enough. But something about Jesus changed their minds. Joanna's husband worked for Herod, the king. She decided to use what she owned to help Jesus's message get to others. Mary had been set free by Jesus, and she decided to give her whole life to helping others be set free. Susanna also decided that she was going to use her own money to help Jesus and His disciples. Women didn't usually have their own money back then. So these decisions were very generous and courageous.

We don't all have the same things. But we can give what we have, and trust that Jesus will use it well. What do *you* have, and how can you give it to Jesus?

HOLY Qs!

- *How can the way I spend my money reflect my relationship with Jesus?*

- *What am I thankful for? How can I show how thankful I am this week?*

BLESSING

Go following the way of the Savior, walking in the truth of the King, and living the life of the Friend. May your thoughts, words, and actions reflect the love of Jesus.

Day 5
ALL ARE INVITED

LUKE 8:1-3

When you have a party, how do you decide who to invite? The Jewish teachers and priests in Jesus's day had an idea about who would get invited into God's kingdom. They said only healthy, Jewish men would get an invitation to that party. But sick people, women, and non-Jewish people couldn't come.

It is through Jesus that we're invited to God's party. So who did the invitation go to? These verses of Luke 8 show us that women are definitely invited. And it teaches us that God's kingdom is a place where men and women can learn and work side by side. But the invitation is even bigger than that. Other stories of Jesus tell us that all people—sick, poor, healthy, rich, from different cultures—are invited!

Sometimes people who follow Jesus still forget this. Sometimes we decide who God should invite to the party, and who should be left out. When this happens, we need Jesus to remind us that He invited us *all* to join His kingdom. How can you help others know that Jesus invites everyone?

HOLY Qs!

- *When good things happen, how do I give God the credit?*
- *How can I learn from others this week?*

BLESSING

Go following the way of the Savior, walking in the truth of the King, and living the life of the Friend. May your thoughts, words, and actions reflect the love of Jesus.

FAMILY HISTORY

LUKE 8:1-3

Do you know any stories about your ancestors? Ancestors are family members who lived before us, like great-great-great grandparents. Matthew records a list of Jesus's ancestors in Matthew 1. But there's something unusual about the names there. Jewish family histories usually only included the men's names. But in Jesus's family history, five women are included: Tamar, Rahab, Ruth, Bathsheba, and His mother Mary. You can find the stories of these women in Genesis 38, Joshua 2, the book of Ruth, and 2 Samuel 11-12.

These women were strong, obedient, and trusted God in very difficult times. Jesus knew His family history. When Jesus chose to respect and include women, He wasn't doing anything new. He was doing what God had always done. Tamar, Rahab, Ruth, Bathsheba, and Mary trusted God. They were important parts of the story that led to Jesus coming to earth. They helped to build a family of many generations, including Jesus. Find a story in the Bible about a woman trusting God. Why do you think it's important?

HOLY Qs!

- *What's a healthy or helpful way I can use my spare time?*

- *Who in my life needs to hear about Jesus? How can they hear it from me?*

BLESSING

Go following the way of the Savior, walking in the truth of the King, and living the life of the Friend. May your thoughts, words, and actions reflect the love of Jesus.

Day 7
GOING STRONG

LUKE 8:1-3

Do you know any women pastors? If we don't see any women preaching or leading, it might be hard to imagine it is something women can do. But God's work of including women didn't end with Jesus. Even though we don't know a lot about them, we know that there were many women who led the church from the very beginning.

Paul was the great missionary who preached and started churches in many countries. Paul's ministry came many years after Jesus and His crew traveled from town to town in Luke 8:1-3. In his letter to the church in Rome, Paul speaks highly of several women ministers (in Romans 16). Phoebe was a church leader of her town. Priscilla and her husband Aquila pastored a church in their home. Junia spent time in jail for following and preaching about Jesus. Paul also greets and thanks other women friends— Mary, Julia, Tryphena, Tryphosa, and many others.

From its earliest days, Jesus's church has been led by men and women in partnership together. This is the beautiful way of God's kingdom. Where do you see men and women leading together?

HOLY Qs!

- *How can I be honest and trustworthy this week?*

- *What can I do to make wise choices this week?*

BLESSING

Go following the way of the Savior, walking in the truth of the King, and living the life of the Friend. May your thoughts, words, and actions reflect the love of Jesus.

WEEK 24 Day 1
HANNAH'S PRAYER

This week's passage is from the Old Testament. Can you discover what it has to do with the life of Jesus? Enjoy God's love for you!

1 SAMUEL 2:1-2

1 Then Hannah prayed:
"My heart rejoices in the LORD!
The LORD has made me strong.
Now I have an answer for my enemies;
I rejoice because you rescued me.
2 No one is holy like the LORD!
There is no one besides you;
there is no Rock like our God."

Day 2

GOD DID IT

1 SAMUEL 2:1-2

What's something you've really wanted but couldn't get on your own? Hannah would understand how you feel. She couldn't have children. She wanted to have a baby so badly with her husband, El-kanah. But it never happened. People even made fun of her. Hannah went to the temple and cried and prayed.

Then, God did something amazing. He gave Hannah a baby. It was time to rejoice! She finally got what she wanted. She was so excited, it would have been easy to jump in and get totally wrapped up in life with her baby, Samuel. Instead, Hannah took the time to give credit and praise to God. God did it! She knew God had blessed her with Samuel. The love God showed her filled her so much that she just had to answer with the prayer of praise we see in these verses. What has happened in your life that you want to praise God for? If you wrote a prayer of praise, what would it say?

HOLY Qs!

- When good things happen, how do I give God the credit?

- Is there anyone I'm struggling to get along with? What am I going to do about it?

BLESSING

Go following the way of the Savior, walking in the truth of the King, and living the life of the Friend. May your thoughts, words, and actions reflect the love of Jesus.

Day 3

IT'S KIND OF LIKE . . .

1 SAMUEL 2:1-2

Read the first verse. What's the first word that starts with the letter "r"? Rejoices. What do you think that means? Rejoicing is kind of like when you're laughing with a friend and having a good time. It's kind of like when you are laying out in your yard and looking at the clouds, and feel really peaceful. It's kind of like when you've won the championship game and you're celebrating on the field with your team. It's even like that hug from someone who makes you feel safe and loved. It's all those feelings wrapped into one! That's what Hannah was feeling.

As followers of Jesus we will find ourselves in moments like Hannah, rejoicing in the love and goodness of God! Not everything in our Christian walk will be rejoicing. Like Hannah, you'll have struggles. But your life with Jesus will bring you lots of opportunities to rejoice. How can you rejoice today?

HOLY Qs!

- *What am I thankful for? How can I show how thankful I am this week?*

- *What have I been enjoying about prayer recently?*

BLESSING

Go following the way of the Savior, walking in the truth of the King, and living the life of the Friend. May your thoughts, words, and actions reflect the love of Jesus.

Day 4
STRONG

1 SAMUEL 2:1-2

Think of the word "strong." What are three things that come to mind? Maybe a weight lifter with muscles? How about a huge monster truck? Or maybe a bear or a lion? Here's a fact about strength: *Strength comes in our weakness.* Say whaaaat?

It's true! Check out verse 1. Hannah is speaking of strength. Who does she say her strength has come from? She was weak and hurting. Life wasn't going well, and she couldn't do anything about it. Not one thing. Then the Lord came and gave her strength. He does the same for you and me. That doesn't mean He gives us muscles.

(Well, unless you're Samson . . .) The Lord gave her strength to deal with what was going on in her life. What could it look like in your own life to get strength from God? What do you need His strength to help you with?

HOLY Qs!

- *How does my relationship with Jesus impact my daily life in real ways?*

- *What's a healthy or helpful way I can use my spare time?*

BLESSING

Go following the way of the Savior, walking in the truth of the King, and living the life of the Friend. May your thoughts, words, and actions reflect the love of Jesus.

REALLY BAD SPOT

1 SAMUEL 2:1-2

Have you ever had to be rescued or saved? Or do you know someone who has? What's a story of rescue you know, even if it's from a movie, book, or TV show? Rescue gets a person out of a bad situation and brings them back where they belong. Check out the end of verse 1. Hannah's story is a rescue story.

We needed to be rescued too. We were in a bad situation. Sin had separated us from being close to God. Sin puts us in a really bad spot. When we are separated from God we are separated from life the way it was meant to be. We are separated from being in a relationship with God. That's a bad situation. And there's nothing you and I can do about it. But Jesus rescued us from the power of sin. Now, life with Jesus brings us back into a relationship with God. It's right where we belong. Check out page vii to read a little more about this. He has given us true life! How can you say thank you to your Rescuer today?

HOLY Qs!

- *Is anything in my life really hard right now? Am I talking to God about it? Who else can I talk to?*

- *Have my words matched my actions? Does who I say I am and how I act line up?*

BLESSING

Go following the way of the Savior, walking in the truth of the King, and living the life of the Friend. May your thoughts, words, and actions reflect the love of Jesus.

Day 6
HOLY

1 SAMUEL 2:1-2

Name a time you made a mistake or a poor decision. It's okay. We've all done it. It's not fun to think about now, but we are in a world full of imperfect people who make mistakes. But not God. Check out verse 2. What's that word "holy" mean?

When this verse says that God is holy and there are none like Him it's saying that He is perfect in all He does. Always. He never makes a mistake. He is entirely set apart from sin and selfishness. God = holy = perfect = awesome. He loves you perfectly. His plans are perfect. He won't make a mistake. When it doesn't make sense to you, trust our holy, loving God. His plans involve making us holy, too. A life with Jesus is a holy life. Each day won't be perfect, but God is working in us each day. Leave your mistakes in the past. God's holiness is all we need for today and tomorrow. How does His holiness help your life with Jesus?

HOLY Qs!

- *How can I be obedient to God this week?*
- *God cares about our whole life, not just the spiritual parts. What healthy habits do I need to work on?*

BLESSING

Go following the way of the Savior, walking in the truth of the King, and living the life of the Friend. May your thoughts, words, and actions reflect the love of Jesus.

Day 7
QUITTING TIME?

1 SAMUEL 2:1-2

What's a time you just wanted to quit something? Hannah's prayer gives us some really good truth to live by. Hannah knew that she couldn't face life and its many challenges without the Lord. She kept following God. She never quit. We don't really know how long this particular challenge of hers lasted, but we know that she kept following God. She sang to Him. She rejoiced in Him. She praised Him. She kept going.

You know, God loves you like He loved Hannah. He's here for you like He was there for her. Hannah's prayer celebrates her relationship with God. She experienced great joy with her baby, Samuel, because she trusted God and didn't quit. She ended up dedicating her little boy to God so that he would be used by God to do great things. Learn from Hannah's example. Don't quit. Keep following God, enjoy your life with Jesus, and celebrate the great things along the way.

HOLY Qs!

- How can God's love give me confidence today?
- What habits help me spend time getting to know God through Scripture?

BLESSING

Go following the way of the Savior, walking in the truth of the King, and living the life of the Friend. May your thoughts, words, and actions reflect the love of Jesus.

WEEK 25 Day 1
NAOMI'S THANKFULNESS

This week's passage is from the Old Testament. Can you discover what it has to do with the life of Jesus? Enjoy God's love for you!

RUTH 4:14-17

(How'd we get here? Naomi was Ruth's mother-in-law. Both their husbands died, making them widows, and they went home to Judah where Naomi grew up. In that time, if you were a widow, you were very poor and powerless. In Judah, Ruth met Boaz, a good man who married her and redeemed their family. Ruth and Boaz had a baby, and that's where our story picks up. If you want to read the whole story— and it's a good one— just read the four chapters of the Book of Ruth!)

[14] Then the women of the town said to Naomi, "Praise the LORD, who has now provided a redeemer for your family! May this child be famous in Israel. [15] May he restore your youth and care for you in your old age. For he is the son of your daughter-in-law who loves you and has been better to you than seven sons!"
[16] Naomi took the baby and cuddled him to her breast. And she cared for him as if he were her own. [17] The neighbor women said, "Now at last Naomi has a son again!" And they named him Obed. He became the father of Jesse and the grandfather of David.

YOU'VE GOT A FRIEND

RUTH 4:14-17

Why is it important to have Christian friends? In the full story for this week (not just the short passage, but the whole book of Ruth), Ruth offers amazing friendship by staying with Naomi, and in return Naomi leads her to her new home and her new faith. Ruth isn't from Naomi's homeland. Naomi is an Israelite, a Jew, one of God's chosen people. Ruth becomes part of the Israelites through this friendship. By choosing to follow Naomi, she entered into a life centered around worshiping God.

Our Christian friends are important in our lives because they influence us to make good choices. Christian friends will pray with us and for us. Christian friends can give us advice. Christian friends understand our faith and what it means to live for Jesus each day. These relationships are so important. Who are your Christian friends? How do they help your life with Jesus?

HOLY Qs!

- *How can I be honest and trustworthy this week?*
- *What can I do to make wise choices this week?*

BLESSING

Go following the way of the Savior, walking in the truth of the King, and living the life of the Friend. May your thoughts, words, and actions reflect the love of Jesus.

173

Day 3
IMPORTANT THINGS

RUTH 4:14-17

Think about the other people living in your home. Name something that's really important to each of them. When Naomi and Ruth's husbands died, Naomi gave Ruth the option of staying behind in her homeland and marrying someone new. This meant that Ruth wouldn't have to be a widow. (Being a widow was a pretty hard life.) Plus, it was Ruth's home, so she was familiar with it. It seems like a no-brainer to stick around.

But Ruth chose her friendship with Naomi. Look up Ruth 1:16-17. Wowza! Ruth was super committed to staying with and caring for Naomi. Sometimes, that's what friendship is. We take whatever is important to our friends and we make that thing really important to us. It may have very little to do with us, but because it matters to them, we make it matter to us. Their big deal becomes our big deal. What's important to your friends? How can those things become important to you, too?

HOLY Qs!

- *How will I be a good friend and listener?*
- *Have I been jealous, grumpy, or really hard on anyone? What can I do about it?*

BLESSING

Go following the way of the Savior, walking in the truth of the King, and living the life of the Friend. May your thoughts, words, and actions reflect the love of Jesus.

A PERFECT SEVEN

RUTH 4:14-17

What's something you wish you could have seven of? Seven pizzas? Seven cats? Seven tickets to a baseball game? In the Bible, the number "seven" gets used quite a bit. However, it doesn't always mean the *actual* number seven. In the Bible, seven often represents perfection, or completeness. If everything was just right, just how it should be, the best possible situation, it might be expressed with the number seven.

Check out verse 15. God has been so good to Naomi, and the whole town recognizes it. The way Boaz has taken care of her family and given them hope for a future is even better than what seven sons would have brought her. In other words, it's more perfect than perfect! God made Naomi's story complete with her new grandson. What are some ways you still see God making things good and right in the world?

HOLY Qs!

- *When good things happen, how do I give God the credit?*

BLESSING

Go following the way of the Savior, walking in the truth of the King, and living the life of the Friend. May your thoughts, words, and actions reflect the love of Jesus.

Day 5
AN UNCERTAIN FUTURE

RUTH 4:14-17

What's something hard you've had to deal with in your life? Naomi and Ruth's story is a tough one. They dealt with death, sadness, and a very uncertain future. There are people today dealing with very similar things. Maybe you're dealing with them or you know someone who is. Even though they faced so much grief, Naomi never turned her back on God. Instead, she led Ruth to her homeland so God could be Ruth's God, too!

When we're dealing with yucky stuff in our life, it's pretty easy to blame God, or at least to turn away from God. It can be hard to pray. It can be hard to worship. Jesus understands what it's like to go through really, really difficult days. We also have a Bible full of stories of God coming through for people, helping them through their hardest times in ways they never expected. If you ask around in your family or church, you could probably hear other people's stories about this, too. How have you seen God's goodness when things have been hard?

HOLY Qs!

- Is anything in my life really hard right now? Am I talking to God about it? Who else can I talk to?

BLESSING

Go following the way of the Savior, walking in the truth of the King, and living the life of the Friend. May your thoughts, words, and actions reflect the love of Jesus.

HE MAKES IT RIGHT

RUTH 4:14-17

If you had to own a piece of land, where would it be? Near a beach or near a mountain? In the cold or in the heat? An important part of the story of Ruth and Naomi actually has to do with buying some land. To redeem (take care of, make right) their family, one of their relatives has to buy Naomi's husband's land. Part of that also means that he would marry Ruth. Yes, it sounds weird, but this was the custom of the day.

Later in Scripture, the Israelites didn't have land to call their own. They didn't have a king to lead and protect them. They felt lost like Naomi and Ruth. Then, Jesus came. Out of His love, He did what was necessary to redeem (take care of, make right) God's people so that their story could continue. Both stories were redeemed by a son. Jesus takes what is lost, broken, and incomplete and makes it right again. What do you need Jesus to make right in your life? What's He already made right?

HOLY Qs!

- *How can God's love give me confidence today?*

- *Have my words matched my actions? Does who I say I am and how I act line up?*

BLESSING

Go following the way of the Savior, walking in the truth of the King, and living the life of the Friend. May your thoughts, words, and actions reflect the love of Jesus.

Day 7
REEEEALLLY GREAT

RUTH 4:14-17

The book of Ruth is an interesting choice to include in the Bible. It doesn't tell the story of the Israelites and their promised land. It doesn't tell too much about their laws, or their prophets, or their kings. Really, you could read almost the whole book (which is really short) and come up to the end and wonder, "Why did I just read that? Sure, it's a great story of friendship and loyalty, but what does it have to do with anything else in the Bible?"

Now check out verse 17. Whoa. We're seeing some connection. Not only is Ruth a great story of friendship and redemption, but Ruth is King David's great-grandmother. And, remember, Jesus is part of King David's royal line. Ruth is Jesus's great-great-reeeeallly-greee-aaat grandmother. Ruth's story has a special place in the story of God's people. God is always at work in ways we might not be thinking about. How can we pay careful attention to see God working in our life story?

HOLY Qs!

- *What am I thankful for? How can I show how thankful I am this week?*
- *How can the way I spend my money reflect my relationship with Jesus?*

BLESSING

Go following the way of the Savior, walking in the truth of the King, and living the life of the Friend. May your thoughts, words, and actions reflect the love of Jesus.

WEEK 26 Day 1
JESUS CALMS THE STORM

It's a new week in your life with Jesus! Use the *5 What's or Lectio Divina* to guide your reading today. Enjoy God's love for you!

MATTHEW 8:23-27

²³ Then Jesus got into the boat and started across the lake with his disciples. ²⁴ Suddenly, a fierce storm struck the lake, with waves breaking into the boat. But Jesus was sleeping. ²⁵ The disciples went and woke him up, shouting, "Lord, save us! We're going to drown!"

²⁶ Jesus responded, "Why are you afraid? You have so little faith!" Then he got up and rebuked the wind and waves, and suddenly there was a great calm.

²⁷ The disciples were amazed. "Who is this man?" they asked. "Even the winds and waves obey him!"

Day 2
STORMS WILL COME

MATTHEW 8:23-27

Do you like storms? What's the best part? What's the worst part? In this week's story, the disciples followed Jesus onto a boat and started to cross a lake. Suddenly, a storm struck. The disciples were experienced fishermen and would usually be able to tell if a storm was coming. This storm was unexpected and so fierce that the waves splashed into the boat. The disciples thought they were going to drown. This storm came when the disciples were following Jesus. They were doing the right thing, yet the storm still crashed into them.

In the Bible, storms and rough water can represent hard times in life. Have you ever gone through a hard time? Even when you follow Jesus, challenging times will come. Being a Christian won't protect you from going through difficult stuff. How can God use hard times to help you grow stronger and closer to Him?

HOLY Qs!

- How can I be obedient to God this week?

- Is anything in my life really hard right now? Am I talking to God about it? Who else can I talk to?

BLESSING

Go following the way of the Savior, walking in the truth of the King, and living the life of the Friend. May your thoughts, words, and actions reflect the love of Jesus.

STORMY PEACE

MATTHEW 8:23-27

Where is the strangest place you have fallen asleep? Jesus fell asleep on a boat during an angry storm! Waves crashed. Wind howled. Rain drenched. His disciples were panicking all around Him, yet He slept in perfect peace. How could He sleep during such a stressful time? He was probably tired from teaching all day, but more importantly, He wasn't worried about the situation. He knew whose power He really trusted.

When you go through a storm or challenging time, does it sometimes seem like Jesus is asleep? Have you asked Him for help, but felt like He wasn't listening? It may feel like He's asleep if you're not hearing what you want to hear, but Jesus is right there with you in hard times, just like He was with the disciples. He may be quiet for a time. Maybe it's to see if you will trust Him. What will it take for you to have the peace of Christ even in hard times?

HOLY Qs!

- God cares about our whole life, not just the spiritual parts. What healthy habits do I need to work on?

- How does my relationship with Jesus impact my daily life in real ways?

BLESSING

Go following the way of the Savior, walking in the truth of the King, and living the life of the Friend. May your thoughts, words, and actions reflect the love of Jesus.

Day 4
BE HONEST

MATTHEW 8:23-27

Think of a recent time when you were scared. What did you do? When the disciples were afraid on the boat, they woke Jesus up and said, "Lord, save us! We're going to drown!" They called Him "Lord" which showed they knew He was God's Son and He had authority and power. They told Him what they needed. But look at verse 25. They shouted! They knew that if He didn't help them, they were lost. Crying out to Jesus was the best thing they could do during the storm.

Crying out to Jesus is the right response in hard times. He isn't afraid of your emotions. You can be confused, or angry, or doubtful, or just plain scared and it won't bother Jesus. You don't have to pretend everything is perfect when you pray. Be real and honest. He knows what you're really thinking and feeling anyway. So you might as well tell Him. Pray today, and be really, really honest with God.

HOLY Qs!

- *How does what I learned from Scripture inspire my thoughts and actions?*

- *What have I been enjoying about prayer recently?*

BLESSING

Go following the way of the Savior, walking in the truth of the King, and living the life of the Friend. May your thoughts, words, and actions reflect the love of Jesus.

Day 5
WAY MORE

MATTHEW 8:23-27

What's another story you can think of where God showed control over wind, waves, or storms? Check out: Exodus 14:21-22, Genesis 7:4, Exodus 9:23. And that's not all of them. In other words, this isn't the first time we've seen God's power control the weather. These other stories would have been famous to the Jews who were in the boat with Jesus. For Him to get up and control the weather wouldn't just have been a neat trick. It was way more.

Jesus made a statement when He displayed His power that day. He was God right there in front of them! He commanded the power of the God of the universe. Slowly, Jesus was revealing to His disciples, through both His teaching and His actions, who He was. Have you ever had something happen, or heard something, and you were absolutely sure it was God? If not, it's okay. God will show you His power and make himself known to you. Keep praying. Stay close to Him.

HOLY Qs!

- *How can God's love give me confidence today?*

- *What can I do to make wise choices this week?*

BLESSING

Go following the way of the Savior, walking in the truth of the King, and living the life of the Friend. May your thoughts, words, and actions reflect the love of Jesus.

Day 6
ALL WAVES

MATTHEW 8:23-27

What images come to your mind when you think of waves? Do waves help you relax or make you nervous? Read Mark 4:1, 35-41. This is a different version of the story. Verse 1 tells us about what happened earlier in the day. Jesus sat in a boat teaching the crowd who rested on the shore. The waves gently rocked the boat. Their rhythm and repetition was soothing. After Jesus and the disciples started to cross the lake, a fierce storm struck. The waves suddenly became violent and crashed into the boat. Relaxation was quickly replaced with distress. It wasn't until Jesus spoke to the wind and waves that the calm was restored.

Jesus is with you when the waves are calm and when they are crashing. When life is good, Jesus is there. When life is hard, Jesus is there. When life is good, we can praise Him. When life is hard, we can praise Him. What are some ways to praise Him in good times and hard times?

HOLY Qs!

- *What's a healthy or helpful way I can use my spare time?*

- *Have I been jealous, grumpy, or really hard on anyone? What can I do about it?*

BLESSING

Go following the way of the Savior, walking in the truth of the King, and living the life of the Friend. May your thoughts, words, and actions reflect the love of Jesus.

Day 7
SUPERPOWERS

MATTHEW 8:23-27

If you could have any super power, what would it be? There have been several fictional characters in movies or comics who had control over the wind or water. Jesus can control both, and He's no comic book character. He's real! After Jesus calmed the storm, the disciples were amazed. "Who is this man?" they asked. Even the wind and waves obey Him; why would we ever be afraid of anything that comes our way?

You can be confident that your challenges are no match for Jesus's power. This means we can trust He has the power we need to make it through anything. A life with Jesus doesn't mean there won't be storms. It means that Jesus is with us and gives us the power to make it through the storms. Maybe someone you know needs this reminder. Think for a moment about what someone else might be going through. How can you remind them who Jesus is for them?

HOLY Qs!

- *What habits help me spend time getting to know God through Scripture?*
- *When good things happen, how do I give God the credit?*

BLESSING

Go following the way of the Savior, walking in the truth of the King, and living the life of the Friend. May your thoughts, words, and actions reflect the love of Jesus.

WEEK 27 Day 1
JESUS SENDS THE TWELVE

It's a new week in your life with Jesus! Use the *5 What's or Lectio Divina* to guide your reading today. Enjoy God's love for you!

LUKE 9:1-6

¹ One day Jesus called together his twelve disciples and gave them power and authority to cast out all demons and to heal all diseases. ² Then he sent them out to tell everyone about the Kingdom of God and to heal the sick. ³ "Take nothing for your journey," he instructed them. "Don't take a walking stick, a traveler's bag, food, money, or even a change of clothes. ⁴ Wherever you go, stay in the same house until you leave town. ⁵ And if a town refuses to welcome you, shake its dust from your feet as you leave to show that you have abandoned those people to their fate."
⁶ So they began their circuit of the villages, preaching the Good News and healing the sick.

Day 2
SUPER WORK

LUKE 9:1-6

Does your favorite superhero work alone, or with a team? Many of the heroes in popular stories do all the rescuing alone. It proves how powerful they are, because they don't need anyone else. But Jesus is different. He proves His power by working with and through people who have less power than He does.

Jesus had been preaching that the kingdom of God was near. He had been healing people and silencing demons. This was something no one else could do. But then He shared His mission with His disciples. How do you think they felt? Surprised? Afraid? Nervous?

In Week 11 we learned that a disciple learns to become like the teacher. Jesus had been preparing His disciples for this the whole time. Jesus shared His power with them so that they could do what He did. Jesus didn't work alone then, and He doesn't work alone now. Jesus invites all of us into His mission. He shares His power so that we can do His work. How is Jesus sharing His work with you?

HOLY Qs!

- *What have I been enjoying about prayer recently?*

- *How can I be obedient to God this week?*

BLESSING

Go following the way of the Savior, walking in the truth of the King, and living the life of the Friend. May your thoughts, words, and actions reflect the love of Jesus.

Day 3
GROWING MORE

LUKE 9:1-6

What does it mean to be dependent and independent? Dependent means needing someone else. Independent means doing stuff without needing someone else. As we get older, we naturally grow to become more *independent*. That means we can do more things for ourselves. Jesus's kingdom is kind of opposite. In our lives with Jesus, we grow more and more *dependent* on God. That means we rely on God more and more.

So when Jesus sent His disciples out with nothing, it was on purpose. He wanted them to learn that God could take care of them. He didn't want them to rely on their own good planning or skills or money. He wanted them to rely on what God could do.

You don't have to have a perfect plan or lots of money, or be grown up to follow Jesus. If you can trust God to take care of you, you can follow Jesus! What's something that you are trusting God for right now?

HOLY Qs!

- *What have I been enjoying about prayer recently?*
- *How can I learn from others this week?*

BLESSING

Go following the way of the Savior, walking in the truth of the King, and living the life of the Friend. May your thoughts, words, and actions reflect the love of Jesus.

Day 4
NICE SOCKS

LUKE 9:1-6

What do you have to do to prepare to have people over to your house? Make your bed? Make some cookies? Hang up your socks? This is hospitality. Helping others feel welcome. Hospitality is important in Jesus's kingdom. It's all about welcoming guests by being friendly and generous. Every culture practices hospitality differently, but it's important everywhere.

Jesus sent His disciples into new towns where they didn't know anyone. They were supposed to go knock on doors, and see if anyone would let them stay in their house. The disciples were depending on God, by depending on the hospitality of strangers. The strangers who showed hospitality were going to get some really good news. They were going to see people healed, maybe even in their own house.

Jesus asks us to be hospitable and generous, because He is. But many times, when we share hospitality we receive even better gifts than we give away. How can we show hospitality at home, at church, in school, on the soccer field, and at the lunch table?

HOLY Qs!

- How will I be a good friend and listener?
- How can I learn from others this week?

BLESSING

Go following the way of the Savior, walking in the truth of the King, and living the life of the Friend. May your thoughts, words, and actions reflect the love of Jesus.

Day 5
SURPRISE!

LUKE 9:1-6

Name a time you were surprised by a visitor. The people in the towns of Galilee must have been really surprised when the disciples came. These towns were very small. They were far out in the country, away from the cities and main roads. Not many people walked all the way to a tiny village where they didn't know anyone.

But then Jesus's disciples showed up—surprise! Imagine if you lived in one of those towns, and you heard that God's kingdom was coming right there. And then you saw God's kingdom come when your neighbors got healed. What a great surprise!

Jesus still sends disciples to preach about God's kingdom. He sends people all over the world, to huge cities and tiny villages. Who was sent to you? If your family has known Jesus for a long time, ask your parents or grandparents how they first heard about Jesus. How did your own life with Jesus get started? If you're new to a life with Jesus, maybe page vii can help.

HOLY Qs!

- How can the way I spend my money reflect my relationship with Jesus?

- Is there anyone I'm struggling to get along with? What am I going to do about it?

BLESSING

Go following the way of the Savior, walking in the truth of the King, and living the life of the Friend. May your thoughts, words, and actions reflect the love of Jesus.

Day 6
SHAKE THE DUST

LUKE 9:1-6

What do you do when someone tells you "No"? Do you just walk away? Or do you try to change their mind? Most of us want to convince others to do what we want, especially when it's something we think is really important.

But when Jesus sent the disciples into the towns, He told them not to do that. Instead, if a stranger told them no, they were just supposed to "shake the dust" and walk away. This might sound rude, but it's actually very respectful. From the beginning, God has given humans the ability to make our own choices. Jesus doesn't argue with us to prove He is right. And He didn't ask His disciples to do that, either.

When Jesus sent out His disciples, He didn't tell them to make people change. He just asked them to be obedient and to be dependent on God. We can ask God to change us, and to change others too. How does this idea change *you*?

HOLY Qs!

- *How can I be honest and trustworthy this week?*
- *What's a healthy or helpful way I can use my spare time?*

BLESSING

Go following the way of the Savior, walking in the truth of the King, and living the life of the Friend. May your thoughts, words, and actions reflect the love of Jesus.

191

Day 7
PRACTICE ISN'T PERFECT

LUKE 9:1-6

What kinds of things do you practice? Maybe you go to soccer or basketball practice. Maybe you practice piano, violin, or trumpet. You may even be practicing to learn a new language. We learn through practice. And when we practice, we don't have to get it perfect. We learn how to do something by doing it. And eventually we get better and better.

We can practice life with Jesus, too. When Jesus sent His disciples into the towns, they weren't ready to do everything by themselves yet. There was a lot Jesus still needed to teach them. But they were ready to start practicing. They practiced preaching the good news like they heard Jesus preach it. They practiced praying for and healing people. And most of all, they practiced depending on God.

The disciples never got it perfect, and neither will we. Jesus is the only perfect one. But every day we practice listening to and depending on Jesus, we will be more and more like Him. What things are you practicing in your life with Jesus?

HOLY Qs!

- *What habits help me spend time getting to know God through Scripture?*
- *Who in my life needs to hear about Jesus? How can they hear it from me?*

BLESSING

Go following the way of the Savior, walking in the truth of the King, and living the life of the Friend. May your thoughts, words, and actions reflect the love of Jesus.

JESUS FEEDS 5,000

It's a new week in your life with Jesus! Use the *5 What's or Lectio Divina* to guide your reading today. Enjoy God's love for you!

MATTHEW 14:13-21

[13] As soon as Jesus heard the news, he left in a boat to a remote area to be alone. But the crowds heard where he was headed and followed on foot from many towns. [14] Jesus saw the huge crowd as he stepped from the boat, and he had compassion on them and healed their sick.

[15] That evening the disciples came to him and said, "This is a remote place, and it's already getting late. Send the crowds away so they can go to the villages and buy food for themselves."

[16] But Jesus said, "That isn't necessary—you feed them."

[17] "But we have only five loaves of bread and two fish!" they answered.

[18] "Bring them here," he said. [19] Then he told the people to sit down on the grass. Jesus took the five loaves and two fish, looked up toward heaven, and blessed them. Then, breaking the loaves into pieces, he gave the bread to the disciples, who distributed it to th' people. [20] They all ate as much as they wanted, and afterward, th' disciples picked up twelve baskets of leftovers. [21] About 5,000 men were fed that day, in addition to all the women and children!

Day 2
JESUS FEELS SADNESS TOO

MATTHEW 14:13-21

Something just happened. That's what the first few words of this Scripture tell us. When Jesus heard the news, He went on a boat to spend some time alone. What happened? This story takes place right after Jesus found out that one of His good friends and important supporters died. John the Baptist was Jesus's cousin and had done very important work in preparing the way for Jesus. Jesus was human, and had real human emotions.

Have you ever lost someone? Jesus knows how you feel. He knows the pain of loss. He is close to you. You can share your hurt and pain with Him. He understands. Sadness is okay. You are not alone. Jesus living a human life means He understands the things we go through most days. The feelings. The joy. The hurt. He isn't some far-off God, sitting on a throne telling people what to do. He's a God who came as a real person to live and die. In that way, He knows you so well.

HOLY Qs!

- *How can God's love give me confidence today?*
- *How does what I learned from Scripture inspire my thoughts and actions?*

BLESSING

Go following the way of the Savior, walking in the truth of the King, and living the life of the Friend. May your thoughts, words, and actions reflect the love of Jesus.

Day 3
LET'S GRUB

MATTHEW 14:13-21

What's the difference between need and want? What do you *want* to have in your life? What do you *need* to have to live? Was food on your list? If not, re-write your list. You need food. Fruits. Veggies. Protein. Maybe even the occasional cookie. Your body needs food to be healthy. It's woven into who we are deep down. If we don't have food ready for us to eat, we will go after food until we get some or die trying.

This story of Jesus providing a ridiculous amount of food to a giant crowd points to something very simple: Jesus cares about our needs. Jesus cared for this crowd's basic need: to eat. He didn't just meet them with important spiritual truths. He fed their hungry stomachs. A life with Jesus doesn't mean ignoring your own basic needs or the needs of others. Take care of yourself. Stay healthy. Help others do the same. How do you keep your own body and brain healthy? How can you help others in the same way?

HOLY Qs!

- *What am I thankful for? How can I show how thankful I am this week?*

- *God cares about our whole life, not just the spiritual parts. What healthy habits do I need to work on?*

BLESSING

Go following the way of the Savior, walking in the truth of the King, and living the life of the Friend. May your thoughts, words, and actions reflect the love of Jesus.

Day 4
WHAT DO YOU SEE?

MATTHEW 14:13-21

If you were in charge of meals for today, what would you make for yourself? What if you were feeding a whole crowd? In verses 15-17, the disciples gathered what they had and quickly realized they didn't have enough to feed the crowd. Not even close. Five loaves of bread and two fish. That's it. That's all they could see.

Jesus saw so much more. Jesus creates so much more. Like the disciples, we often feel like we have too little to make a difference. We might look at who we are and not see much there. ("I can't even drive. I can't even make toast yet. How can I make a difference?") We see only the little we have or can do. Jesus, on the other hand, sees so much more. He sees the best version of you. Some people saw a few pieces of bread and fish. Jesus saw a giant feast. He can take what we give Him and do more than we ever imagined!

HOLY Qs!

- *What have I been enjoying about prayer recently?*

- *Who in my life needs to hear about Jesus? How can they hear it from me?*

BLESSING

Go following the way of the Savior, walking in the truth of the King, and living the life of the Friend. May your thoughts, words, and actions reflect the love of Jesus.

WHO HE REALLY WAS

MATTHEW 14:13-21

Jesus is a miracle worker, for sure. But He isn't ONLY a miracle worker. He wasn't just on earth to heal and feed. Sure, He spent a lot of His time that way, but ultimately He came as Messiah and Savior. He came to reveal who God is.

Jesus's miracles weren't just some neat tricks. They pointed to who He really was: the Son of God. He wanted people to believe in Him and follow Him. If they had just gone home for some food, they probably would've found some grub, but they would have missed the way better plan Jesus had. He was feeding people, yes. But He was doing way more. He was revealing who He was. Let's remember, sometimes God challenges us to really trust Him. Trusting Him, and then seeing the results, is one way God reveals himself to us. What are some ways you can trust God this week?

HOLY Qs!

- *How does my relationship with Jesus impact my daily life in real ways?*

- *What habits help me spend time getting to know God through Scripture?*

BLESSING

Go following the way of the Savior, walking in the truth of the King, and living the life of the Friend. May your thoughts, words, and actions reflect the love of Jesus.

Day 6
BLESS IT

MATTHEW 14:13-21

Do you pray before eating? Why do you think we do this? Jesus set an example for us by pausing to bless the food before eating. A traditional Jewish prayer of blessing and thanks over the food would sound something like this (try it out loud): "Blessed are you, O Lord our God, King of the universe, who brings food from the earth." What does your before-food prayer sound like?

This prayer was a way to stop during the day and remember that life itself was given by God. Things like food and water come from Him. He is the Creator of the universe and is far more loving and powerful than we could ever imagine. He is far wiser than we could ever know. We can rely on Him. What are you thankful for? You'll be amazed at how your relationship grows deeper with God when you live a thankful life. Take a few moments and thank Him for the things on your list.

HOLY Qs!

- *When good things happen, how do I give God the credit?*

- *Have I been jealous, grumpy, or really hard on anyone? What can I do about it?*

BLESSING

Go following the way of the Savior, walking in the truth of the King, and living the life of the Friend. May your thoughts, words, and actions reflect the love of Jesus.

PARTNERS IN JOY

MATTHEW 14:13-21

Imagine for a moment you're one of the disciples standing close to Jesus. He blesses the food and hands you a basket. There's only a loaf of bread and one fish in it. He tells you to go take it to the people. You're confused because there isn't enough. But you do it. And as you tear the bread to give it to the first person, you look down and see more bread. Every time you give a fish, there's another in the basket. What do you think you'd be feeling?

Jesus was performing a miracle, but He let the disciples be a part of it. They got to be the ones that took the food around and showed people how there was enough for everyone. Can you imagine the joy they felt? The excitement? Jesus also wants to do amazing things through you. He wants you to share in the joy of helping others. And like the disciples, when you jump in and help, you'll be glad He partnered with you to change the world.

HOLY Qs!

- *How can I be obedient to God this week?*
- *How can the way I spend my money reflect my relationship with Jesus?*

BLESSING

Go following the way of the Savior, walking in the truth of the King, and living the life of the Friend. May your thoughts, words, and actions reflect the love of Jesus.

WEEK 29 Day 1
JESUS HEALS A DEAF MAN

It's a new week in your life with Jesus! Use the *5 What's or Lectio Divina* to guide your reading today. Enjoy God's love for you!

MARK 7:31-37

[31] Jesus left Tyre and went up to Sidon before going back to the Sea of Galilee and the region of the Ten Towns. [32] A deaf man with a speech impediment was brought to him, and the people begged Jesus to lay his hands on the man to heal him.

[33] Jesus led him away from the crowd so they could be alone. He put his fingers into the man's ears. Then, spitting on his own fingers, he touched the man's tongue. [34] Looking up to heaven, he sighed and said, "Ephphatha," which means, "Be opened!" [35] Instantly the man could hear perfectly, and his tongue was freed so he could speak plainly!

[36] Jesus told the crowd not to tell anyone, but the more he told them not to, the more they spread the news. [37] They were completely amazed and said again and again, "Everything he does is wonderful. He even makes the deaf to hear and gives speech to those who cannot speak."

Day 2
PRAY, FRIEND, PRAY

MARK 7:31-37

If you could hear your closest friend's prayers today, what do you think they would be saying to Jesus? We explored Christian friendship back when we took a look at Ruth and Naomi's story (Week 25). This week's passage of healing isn't usually one that gets used to talk about friendship. But check out verse 32. The man may not have seen Jesus if it wasn't for the people who brought him to Jesus. They begged Jesus to heal him. *Begged!* They didn't just politely ask, "Jesus, if you have a moment, and sorry to bother you, but if you wouldn't mind a quick healing . . ." Begging is desperate. They cared about their friend.

Do you ever bring your friends' concerns to Jesus in prayer? Do you know what they care about? What they're celebrating or worried about? How their life with Jesus is going? Let's learn from this week's passage and bring our friends' prayers to Jesus like they're our own prayers. And if you don't know what your friends are praying about, how could you find out?

HOLY Qs!

- *How will I be a good friend and listener?*
- *What have I been enjoying about prayer recently?*

BLESSING

Go following the way of the Savior, walking in the truth of the King, and living the life of the Friend. May your thoughts, words, and actions reflect the love of Jesus.

Day 3

AIR-UH-MAY-ICK

MARK 7:31-37

Can you speak another language? What can you say? Did you know the Bible was written in a different language? The writers of the Bible—depending on when and where they lived—spoke Hebrew, Greek, or Aramaic (air-uh-MAY-ick). The Bible was written over a span of 1500 years. Then, over 1000 years ago, some Christians, led by the Holy Spirit, took all the letters and stories written down and put them together as one whole book of Scriptures.

Check out verse 34. Can you pronounce the word *Ephphatha?* It's okay if you can't. It's an Aramaic word. Sometimes Mark liked to capture the exact words Jesus spoke in His native language. The Scriptures have withstood thousands of years, lots of languages and translations, and traveled thousands of miles. Yet, here they are, right there for you to read, showing us who Jesus is and who we were created to be. What a powerful and amazing gift! Take time to say a prayer of thanks for the Bible today.

HOLY Qs!

- *How does what I learned from Scripture inspire my thoughts and actions?*

- *What habits help me spend time getting to know God through Scripture?*

BLESSING

Go following the way of the Savior, walking in the truth of the King, and living the life of the Friend. May your thoughts, words, and actions reflect the love of Jesus.

SPIT IN YOUR EYE?

If you could get rid of one part of going to the doctor, which part would you get rid of? (Is it getting a shot? That doesn't seem to be anyone's favorite.) What about if the doctor spit on his fingers and then touched your tongue? Would your answer change? Gross! Look at verse 33. This is kind of a weird way to heal someone, right? At least it would be for us.

But check this out: among rabbis and some other leaders, spitting was actually a sign of healing because sometimes healers used saliva in their process. This might have made the man actually feel safe with what Jesus was doing, because he would have recognized that Jesus was intent on healing. Remember, the man couldn't hear Jesus talk, but he could see Jesus spit! It's not the only time Jesus did something like this. In John 9, He used spit to heal a blind man. Jesus sometimes used ways of healing that were modern for that time period. How can Jesus use modern ways of healing now?

HOLY Qs!

- *When good things happen, how do I give God the credit?*

BLESSING

Go following the way of the Savior, walking in the truth of the King, and living the life of the Friend. May your thoughts, words, and actions reflect the love of Jesus.

203

Day 5
ALONE TIME

MARK 7:31-37

What's something you like to do when you're alone? Some people really look forward to their alone time, while others would rather be with other people pretty much all the time. Either way, there are great benefits to being alone with Jesus. Check out verse 33. Why didn't Jesus just do what He was going to do right there with the whole crowd around?

Sometimes we need to be alone with Jesus so we can give Him our full attention. Alone doesn't just mean not having other people around. It also means turning off distractions so you can focus on your time with Him. Turn off screens. Go someplace quiet, or ask your family to give you some space. Plan to read Scripture, or read this devotion. Spend a little time in prayer, speaking and listening. It's a healthy part of your spiritual life to take time to be alone with Jesus often. Make it a habit in your life with Jesus. What can your alone-with-Jesus habit look like? Where? When? How often? What will you do?

HOLY Qs!

- *How can I be obedient to God this week?*
- *God cares about our whole life, not just the spiritual parts. What healthy habits do I need to work on?*

BLESSING

Go following the way of the Savior, walking in the truth of the King, and living the life of the Friend. May your thoughts, words, and actions reflect the love of Jesus.

WAIT. THERE'S MORE.

MARK 7:31-37

Let's say someone asked you, "What's the best part of being a Christian?" What would your answer be? Jesus called Christians to go into the world and spread the good news of His love. But check out verse 36. Why would Jesus tell people not to say anything? Doesn't He want us talking about His awesomeness? If you know a guy who can heal deaf people, wouldn't you want to tell everyone? Obviously.

Jesus was getting to be known as a healer and miracle worker. However, that's not the only thing He was sent to do. He had the power to just stay in one place and heal every person of everything wrong until everybody was fixed up like new, but Jesus was sent to earth as a human with a different mission. He was the Messiah, the One who would come and bring His people true freedom. There's more than just the good news of Jesus healing—there's Jesus saving. Jesus saves. What does that mean to you?

HOLY Qs!

- *What am I thankful for? How can I show how thankful I am this week?*

- *What's a healthy or helpful way I can use my spare time?*

BLESSING

Go following the way of the Savior, walking in the truth of the King, and living the life of the Friend. May your thoughts, words, and actions reflect the love of Jesus.

Day 7
A STORY WORTH TELLING

MARK 7:31-37

Have you ever known what was going to happen before it actually did? How did you know? Take a minute to look up Isaiah 35:5. That Scripture was written hundreds of years before Jesus. And it's about Jesus! And look how right it is. Before Jesus's grandparents' grandparents were ever born, Isaiah, the prophet, talked about the Messiah helping the deaf to hear. Just like in our passage this week.

There is no doubt that Jesus really is the Messiah. He really is the One who came to change the whole world. Isaiah prophesied a Savior and a King. Then, Jesus came and filled those roles, and He also chose to be a perfect Friend. Isaiah listened to God and told the story of Jesus years before. Now you can listen and tell His story to your friends today! If you'd like to know more about Jesus as your Savior, King, and Friend, or if you'd like to learn how to talk about Him to others, turn to page vii.

HOLY Qs!

- *Who in my life needs to hear about Jesus? How can they hear it from me?*

- *How can I learn from others this week?*

BLESSING

Go following the way of the Savior, walking in the truth of the King, and living the life of the Friend. May your thoughts, words, and actions reflect the love of Jesus.

WEEK 30 Day 1
GREATEST IN THE KINGDOM

It's a new week in your life with Jesus! Use the *5 What's or Lectio Divina* to guide your reading today. Enjoy God's love for you!

LUKE 9:46-48

⁴⁶ Then his disciples began arguing about which of them was the greatest. ⁴⁷ But Jesus knew their thoughts, so he brought a little child to his side. ⁴⁸ Then he said to them, "Anyone who welcomes a little child like this on my behalf welcomes me, and anyone who welcomes me also welcomes my Father who sent me. Whoever is the least among you is the greatest."

Day 2
PRIDEFUL FIGHT

LUKE 9:46-48

What is the strangest argument you've ever had with your friends? (Is vanilla really a flavor? How old is too old to go trick-or-treating?) The disciples had a strange argument. They argued about which one of them was the greatest. To fully understand their argument, we need to back up a little bit. Jesus had just led Peter, James, and John up on a high mountain for a really special time of prayer. They probably felt like they were special. Meanwhile, the other disciples were having trouble casting a demon out of a boy. They were likely feeling defeated. They also probably wondered why Peter, James, and John were given special treatment. Pride started an argument.

Pride is when you're way too worried about what others think of you, or you're too caught up in what you think of yourself. Pride comes when we put ourselves before others, even Jesus. We make ourselves the most important thing. The disciples were having a prideful argument. What can we do so pride doesn't take over in our lives?

HOLY Qs!

- *Have I been jealous, grumpy, or really hard on anyone? What can I do about it?*
- *Is there anyone I'm struggling to get along with? What am I going to do about it?*

BLESSING

Go following the way of the Savior, walking in the truth of the King, and living the life of the Friend. May your thoughts, words, and actions reflect the love of Jesus.

THE COMPARISON GAME

LUKE 9:46-48

What's a skill you don't have that you wish you did? Do you ever look at people who have that skill and compare yourself to them? The disciples wanted to determine which of them was the greatest. Who had known Jesus the longest? Who had healed the most sick people in Jesus's name? Who did Jesus stand next to the most? Questions like that. Not a healthy way to spend your time, disciples.

We're all created by God, and we all have certain gifts given to us that we can use in our lives with Jesus. We have no reason for comparisons. Instead of comparing ourselves to others, let's embrace God's love for us. He created us. Jesus can use us, just how we are, to expand His kingdom. Your gifts aren't better or worse than anyone else's. What's important is that you use those gifts for Jesus. Be humble and use your gifts to encourage others. That is kingdom greatness. In what ways has God gifted you?

HOLY Qs!

- *How will I be a good friend and listener?*
- *When good things happen, how do I give God the credit?*

BLESSING

Go following the way of the Savior, walking in the truth of the King, and living the life of the Friend. May your thoughts, words, and actions reflect the love of Jesus.

Day 4
OVER AND OVER

LUKE 9:46-48

How many times have you had an adult tell you to clean your room? You probably meant to pick up those socks and toys, but it is easy to forget. We don't always learn our lesson the first time. The disciples meant well, but they had to be told repeatedly not to argue about who was the greatest. They argued about it during the Last Supper (Luke 22:24). They argued about it in our Scripture for this week. Jesus knew their thoughts. He saw them struggling with pride, but He did not give up on them. He continued to teach them and encouraged them to grow.

We all make mistakes. We all struggle with selfishness. Jesus is patient and will continue to help you grow. Be patient. Keep growing. Keep exploring Scripture. Keep loving. Keep learning!

HOLY Qs!

- What habits help me spend time getting to know God through Scripture?

- What can I do to make wise choices this week?

BLESSING

Go following the way of the Savior, walking in the truth of the King, and living the life of the Friend. May your thoughts, words, and actions reflect the love of Jesus.

YOU ARE GREAT

LUKE 9:46-48

What's the best part about being a kid (and not being an adult yet)? During Jesus's days on earth, children didn't get a lot of respect. They couldn't earn money to help their family, and children under 12 couldn't be taught the Torah (the five books at the beginning of the Bible). So they didn't get a ton of attention. That had to hurt. Children were given very little respect, yet Jesus asked a child to stand at His side. He said a child was the greatest among them. Jesus was always showing love to people everyone else didn't treat well. That really surprised the disciples.

Do you ever feel like you are not very important? Do you think people look down on you because of your age? Jesus thinks you're awesome. He loves how old you are. He loves how tall you are. He loves your personality. What do you think you, as a kid, can teach the world around you?

HOLY Qs!

- *How can God's love give me confidence today?*

- *What am I thankful for? How can I show how thankful I am this week?*

BLESSING

Go following the way of the Savior, walking in the truth of the King, and living the life of the Friend. May your thoughts, words, and actions reflect the love of Jesus.

Day 6
NOT SO POPULAR

LUKE 9:46-48

What does it take to be popular? Popularity often depends on who your friends are. Jesus was not concerned with popularity. He gave a child a place at His side, showing honor to someone the people around Him often ignored. He sometimes ate with tax collectors and other unpopular people. He reminded us that popularity doesn't matter. Jesus welcomed the unpopular into His presence. He even said that welcoming a child (or a person not so popular) was like welcoming Him.

It's natural to want to hang with the popular kids. Or to be one of the popular kids. There's nothing wrong with being popular, unless you have to treat people poorly to get or keep your popularity. We must learn from Jesus, by looking at the kinds of friends He chose to have, and how He treated even the most unpopular. Who is someone that needs your Jesus-like love and attention this week?

HOLY Qs!

- *How can I keep from letting things like popularity or friends determine how I act?*
- *How can I learn from others this week?*

BLESSING

Go following the way of the Savior, walking in the truth of the King, and living the life of the Friend. May your thoughts, words, and actions reflect the love of Jesus.

WHO IS GREAT?

LUKE 9:46-48

Name a famous person you like. Why are they famous? Great singing? Great cooking? Or maybe they're a great leader, like a president or a king. When the question of greatness became a problem with the disciples, Jesus asked a child to stand beside Him. Jesus said it was the least (least popular, least expected) among them who would someday be the greatest. Why do you think that is?

Greatness in the kingdom doesn't look much like greatness in the world. Being an awesome singer or basketball player or president isn't kingdom-greatness. These things aren't bad, but Jesus cares about other things. Showing kindness. Being humble. Practicing compassion. Jesus showed us these things. He lived them. Then, in this passage, Jesus was like, "Forget everything you thought you knew about being great. With me, greatness is very different." How can being least lead to being great? What qualities of kingdom-greatness do you need Jesus to really help you with this week?

HOLY Qs!

- Have my words matched my actions? Does who I say I am and how I act line up?
- How can I be honest and trustworthy this week?

BLESSING

Go following the way of the Savior, walking in the truth of the King, and living the life of the Friend. May your thoughts, words, and actions reflect the love of Jesus.

WEEK 31 Day 1
LOST SHEEP

It's a new week in your life with Jesus! Use the *5 What's or Lectio Divina* to guide your reading today. Enjoy God's love for you!

LUKE 15:4-7

4 "If a man has a hundred sheep and one of them gets lost, what will he do? Won't he leave the ninety-nine others in the wilderness and go to search for the one that is lost until he finds it? 5 And when he has found it, he will joyfully carry it home on his shoulders. 6 When he arrives, he will call together his friends and neighbors, saying, 'Rejoice with me because I have found my lost sheep.' 7 In the same way, there is more joy in heaven over one lost sinner who repents and returns to God than over ninety-nine others who are righteous and haven't strayed away!"

MASTER TEACHER

LUKE 15:4-7

Here are some theology words: pneumatology, hamartiology, atonement, apologetics, exegesis. Which ones can you pronounce? Know what any of them mean? Imagine if this book was written using words like these to teach us more about who Jesus is. You probably wouldn't last very long reading it. Most of us wouldn't. Why? Because this book is for kids and most kids haven't had a chance to learn words like these yet. (Probably most adults, too.)

Jesus understood things like this. He knew how to teach people in ways they would understand. He tells this week's story about a sheep because shepherding was a pretty common thing among the people He was teaching. A shepherding story would have made them go, "Oh, sheep! I totally get what He's saying!" Jesus was a master teacher. Now, 2000 years later, there might not be quite as many shepherds reading this. That's why we have Sunday school teachers, pastors, and books like this, to help us connect with the great Teacher. How do stories help you grow in your life with Jesus?

HOLY Qs!

- *How does my relationship with Jesus impact my daily life in real ways?*

- *How can I learn from others this week?*

BLESSING

Go following the way of the Savior, walking in the truth of the King, and living the life of the Friend. May your thoughts, words, and actions reflect the love of Jesus.

Day 3
LIONS, BEARS, AND CROSSES

LUKE 15:4-7

Here's another famous shepherding story. Look up 1 Samuel 17:34-35. It's a story about David. David's story is often connected to Jesus's story. For one, David was also a shepherd and also risked his life to go after a lost sheep. He fought lions and bears. HE FOUGHT LIONS AND BEARS! Are you kidding? David was incredible. He was willing to put himself in danger in order to save his sheep.

Fast forward to Jesus. How did Jesus put himself in danger in order to save us? We are often compared to sheep in the Bible. Jesus is called the Shepherd. (Remember yesterday's devotion? Shepherding was a big deal back then.) Like David, Jesus put himself in harm's way for us. For Jesus, it wasn't a lion or bear. He faced Roman soldiers and a cross. But He was willing to do it. He was also willing to go even further. Jesus died to save us. What a great Shepherd! How else is Jesus like a Shepherd in your life?

HOLY Qs!

- What can I do to make wise choices this week?
- When good things happen, how do I give God the credit?

BLESSING

Go following the way of the Savior, walking in the truth of the King, and living the life of the Friend. May your thoughts, words, and actions reflect the love of Jesus.

IT'S A LOVE STORY

LUKE 15:4-7

Ever felt like someone else was getting all the attention? How did you handle it? Sometimes people read this week's passage and go, "Yeah, but what about the other 99 sheep? That was pretty reckless of Jesus to leave them alone." Jesus used shepherding stories to teach people about a life with Him. This story was not meant to be a lesson on how to shepherd real sheep in all their fuzzy glory. This was a story used to teach people about God's love. It was a story about our life with Him.

He was explaining to everyone how much He loves us. He loves us so much that He comes after us, even if we run away from His love. The shepherd in this story loved those other 99 sheep too. That's why He was their shepherd. But that one sheep was lost and needed help. Jesus's love is so huge that He will come and find us if we are lost . How do you feel about Jesus, knowing His love for you is that big and that bold?

HOLY Qs!

- *What have I been enjoying about prayer recently?*

BLESSING

Go following the way of the Savior, walking in the truth of the King, and living the life of the Friend. May your thoughts, words, and actions reflect the love of Jesus.

Day 5
SHOULDER RIDE

LUKE 15:4-7

When's the last time you had a piggyback ride? Riding on some-one's shoulders is usually pretty full of joy. It's silly. It's fun. Check out verse 5. The shepherd doesn't shout at the sheep for getting lost. He doesn't put a leash on it and drag it back to the others. He scoops it up and joyfully carries it on His shoulders, so glad to have found His lost little buddy.

Sometimes, when people get far from God, they don't want God to come after them. They feel embarrassed. They think God will love them less because of the mistakes they made. They're afraid of the punishment they'll receive. This is a great story to help people see that, no matter how lost they are, Jesus is ready to scoop them up with love and welcome them back. If you've made mistakes, Jesus doesn't love you less. Even if you turn away from Jesus, His love is still there. He can't wait to carry you back into a relationship with Him. Let yourself feel God's love for you each day!

HOLY Qs!

- *How can I be obedient to God this week?*
- *How does what I learned from Scripture inspire my thoughts and actions?*

BLESSING

Go following the way of the Savior, walking in the truth of the King, and living the life of the Friend. May your thoughts, words, and actions reflect the love of Jesus.

Day 6
PARTY TIME

LUKE 15:4-7

What's something you, your family, your friends, or your church get together to celebrate? Check out verse 6. The shepherd returns with the sheep and calls everyone. "Let's have a party! I got my sheep back. Let's make some punch, grill some hot dogs, and play pin the tail on the . . . sheep? Weird. Anyway, let's celebrate!"

It's important to celebrate life with the people around us. Birthdays. Graduations. New homes. New babies. The church is good at celebrating. But the biggest celebration—the one that extends all the way to heaven—happens when someone begins a relationship with Jesus. How can you join in the celebration? Ask your pastor what your church does to celebrate new believers, people who have just started a life with Jesus. Do you have ideas for ways to celebrate? We know heaven is rejoicing; let's join in too!

HOLY Qs!

- *How will I be a good friend and listener?*
- *How can the way I spend my money reflect my relationship with Jesus?*

BLESSING

Go following the way of the Savior, walking in the truth of the King, and living the life of the Friend. May your thoughts, words, and actions reflect the love of Jesus.

Day 7
NO BONUS POINTS

LUKE 15:4-7

Are you a Christian? Already in a relationship with Jesus? Check out verse 7. Does that sound kind of harsh to you? Maybe you can't remember a time when you weren't a Christian. Maybe you've been following Jesus your whole life. Where's your party? Don't worry. You are being celebrated for sure. But Jesus may have been trying to get the attention of a few specific people listening to this story.

Jesus was telling this story to some Pharisees who were very unhappy with Him. Jesus hung out with sinners and the Pharisees didn't like that. These Pharisees saw themselves as the most righteous, the closest to God. This story from Jesus made clear to the Pharisees that they wouldn't get bonus points. Jesus loves everyone equally. God's love reaches everyone. So when one of the sinners Jesus hung out with believed in Him, that party in heaven just got louder. No matter how long you've been a follower of Jesus, you are being celebrated. Your life with Jesus might not be new, but celebrate today anyway!

HOLY Qs!

- *What am I thankful for? How can I show how thankful I am this week?*

BLESSING

Go following the way of the Savior, walking in the truth of the King, and living the life of the Friend. May your thoughts, words, and actions reflect the love of Jesus.

WEEK 32 Day 1
TRANSFIGURATION

It's a new week in your life with Jesus! Use the 5 What's or *Lectio Divina* to guide your reading today. Enjoy God's love for you!

MATTHEW 17:1-9

[1] Six days later Jesus took Peter and the two brothers, James and John, and led them up a high mountain to be alone. [2] As the men watched, Jesus' appearance was transformed so that his face shone like the sun, and his clothes became as white as light. [3] Suddenly, Moses and Elijah appeared and began talking with Jesus.
[4] Peter exclaimed, "Lord, it's wonderful for us to be here! If you want, I'll make three shelters as memorials—one for you, one for Moses, and one for Elijah."
[5] But even as he spoke, a bright cloud overshadowed them, and a voice from the cloud said, "This is my dearly loved Son, who brings me great joy. Listen to him." [6] The disciples were terrified and fell face down on the ground.
[7] Then Jesus came over and touched them. "Get up," he said. "Don't be afraid." [8] And when they looked up, Moses and Elijah were gone, and they saw only Jesus.
[9] As they went back down the mountain, Jesus commanded them, "Don't tell anyone what you have seen until the Son of Man has been raised from the dead."

Day 2
SEE HIM

MATTHEW 17:1-9

What are some things that have changed in appearance since you first saw them? Peter, James, and John saw changes in Jesus's appearance in this week's story of the transfiguration. Transfiguration (trans-fig-yur-AY-shun) is a word we don't use often. It means to change in appearance or shape. The passage says that Jesus's appearance was transformed. His face shone like the sun and His clothes became white as light. His glory was made known to some of His disciples. This means they could finally see Him as more than just a man. They saw Him as God's Son.

How do you see Jesus? Has your life with Jesus transformed the way you see Him? Jesus is more than a great teacher or leader or super nice guy. He is God's Son. He lived life perfectly. He shows us perfect love. He broke the power of sin forever. He connects us with God. He's a friend, but He's even more. He's your Savior. He's your King. And, He's your Friend. Find out more on page vii.

HOLY Qs!

- *How can I be honest and trustworthy this week?*
- *How does my relationship with Jesus impact my daily life in real ways?*

BLESSING

Go following the way of the Savior, walking in the truth of the King, and living the life of the Friend. May your thoughts, words, and actions reflect the love of Jesus.

222

Day 3
ADVENTURE TIME

MATTHEW 17:1-9

Picture a mountain you've been on, or one you've seen in pictures. Jesus took Peter, James, and John on a trip up a high mountain. Maybe it looked similar to the one you're thinking of. The disciples often had an exciting time when they were with Jesus. He told great stories and challenged them to think hard. He healed people and performed miracles. But up on this mountain, they were in for a treat. They were able to see Jesus in a new way. They saw Moses and Elijah, heroes of the faith. They actually heard God talk about His Son. What an adventure!

Following Jesus can still be an exciting adventure. You'll be called into situations you weren't expecting. You'll be led into things that might seem a little scary. You'll see God work in mighty and mysterious ways. He'll challenge the way you think and how you see others. A life with Jesus will not be boring. What gets you excited about following Jesus?

HOLY Qs!

- *How does what I learned from Scripture inspire my thoughts and actions?*
- *When good things happen, how do I give God the credit?*

BLESSING

Go following the way of the Savior, walking in the truth of the King, and living the life of the Friend. May your thoughts, words, and actions reflect the love of Jesus.

Day 4
THAT'S PRETTY IMPORTANT

MATTHEW 17:1-9

If you could meet any person from history, who would it be? Peter, James, and John met two heroes from the past while they were on the mountain. Moses led the Israelites out of Egypt. He received the Ten Commandments from God. Elijah was an incredible prophet. Even when a wicked queen tried to kill him, he kept on preaching. Peter wanted to make shelters for Jesus, Moses, and Elijah. Maybe it was to honor them or to convince them to stay. Even though Moses and Elijah were impressive, Jesus was the one deserving honor and praise. In fact, that's why Moses and Elijah were there.

These "famous people" showing up next to Jesus proved to the disciples just how important Jesus really was. To make it even clearer, God spoke out loud and declared how much He loved Jesus. What sorts of things have you seen or experienced that have changed the way you see Jesus?

HOLY Qs!

- *What habits help me spend time getting to know God through Scripture?*
- *How can the way I spend my money reflect my relationship with Jesus?*

BLESSING

Go following the way of the Savior, walking in the truth of the King, and living the life of the Friend. May your thoughts, words, and actions reflect the love of Jesus.

STOP AND LISTEN

MATTHEW 17:1-9

What's a time you had to listen to something very carefully so you didn't miss anything important? God wanted to make sure Peter, James, and John were listening to Jesus. He told them that Jesus was His dearly loved Son, who brought Him joy. He then specifically said, "Listen to Him." God knew Jesus would be joining Him in heaven soon. He wanted to make sure the disciples truly believed who Jesus was and would listen to everything Jesus said before He left.

Life can get very busy and loud. There aren't many times when we stop and just focus on listening. Sometimes it is hard to hear what Jesus has to say. Can you imagine if God got your attention with a cloud and spoke directly to you like He did on the mountain? What are some ways God might try to get your attention? Do you ever set aside time to be with God? (You do if you're reading this devotion!) How can you try to listen to Jesus this week?

HOLY Qs!

- *How will I be a good friend and listener?*

- *What have I been enjoying about prayer recently?*

BLESSING

Go following the way of the Savior, walking in the truth of the King, and living the life of the Friend. May your thoughts, words, and actions reflect the love of Jesus.

Day 6
A DIFFERENT KIND OF FEAR

MATTHEW 17:1-9

What frightens you? Earthquakes? Darkness? Eating brussels sprouts? The bright cloud overhead and God's booming voice frightened Peter, James, and John. They were so scared that they dropped facedown on the ground. Jesus came over and told them not to be afraid. If there had been any doubt in their minds that Jesus was truly the Messiah, it had now been chased away. There was no denying God's powerful words. They knew Jesus was the One they had been waiting for and the One they needed.

You might have heard people talk about "fearing God" before. This doesn't mean fear like being afraid of darkness or earthquakes. Fearing God means respecting God's awesomeness. It means being humble in God's presence. God is powerful. God is King. God is Creator of the world. Jesus even defeated death, the thing that many people fear the most! God is God and we are not. It's a good thing to recognize that awesome power. What gets you excited about God's awesomeness?

HOLY Qs!

- *How can God's love give me confidence today?*

- *Is anything in my life really hard right now? Am I talking to God about it? Who else can I talk to?*

BLESSING

Go following the way of the Savior, walking in the truth of the King, and living the life of the Friend. May your thoughts, words, and actions reflect the love of Jesus.

SECRET TIME IS OVER

MATTHEW 17:1-9

When you hear really exciting news, what does it make you want to do? Once Peter, James, and John recovered from the shock of all they saw on the mountain, they were probably bursting with excitement and wanted to tell everyone what they had experienced. Check out verse 9. What did Jesus tell them to do? He knew people would struggle to understand or accept who He was at the time.

Today, we get to tell the whole story of Jesus to the world. We do it with our words ("Let me tell you this amazing story") and with our actions (living like Jesus so people know who He is). If you believe the good news, then like the disciples, you'll want to tell others about a life with Jesus. Secret time is over. Let's spread the word. How can you spread the news with your words this week? With your actions?

HOLY Qs!

- *Who in my life needs to hear about Jesus? How can they hear it from me?*

- *How can I be obedient to God this week?*

BLESSING

Go following the way of the Savior, walking in the truth of the King, and living the life of the Friend. May your thoughts, words, and actions reflect the love of Jesus.

WEEK 33 Day 1
SERVING OTHERS

It's a new week in your life with Jesus! Use the *5 What's or Lectio Divina* to guide your reading today. Enjoy God's love for you!

MATTHEW 20:25-34

25 But Jesus called them together and said, "You know that the rulers in this world lord it over their people, and officials flaunt their authority over those under them. 26 But among you it will be different. Whoever wants to be a leader among you must be your servant, 27 and whoever wants to be first among you must become your slave. 28 For even the Son of Man came not to be served but to serve others and to give his life as a ransom for many."

29 As Jesus and the disciples left the town of Jericho, a large crowd followed behind. 30 Two blind men were sitting beside the road. When they heard that Jesus was coming that way, they began shouting, "Lord, Son of David, have mercy on us!"

31 "Be quiet!" the crowd yelled at them.
But they only shouted louder, "Lord, Son of David, have mercy on us!"

32 When Jesus heard them, he stopped and called, "What do you want me to do for you?"

33 "Lord," they said, "we want to see!" 34 Jesus felt sorry for them and touched their eyes. Instantly they could see! Then they followed him.

Day 2

A NEW WAY TO LEAD

MATTHEW 20:25-34

Who are some leaders that you know? A leader is a person with power, or authority, in other peoples' lives. Maybe you thought of your parents or grandparents, political leaders, teachers, pastors, or coaches.

The Scripture for this week includes the end of a conversation Jesus had with His disciples about leadership. It started because two of the disciples asked for more power than the other disciples. Jesus told them that being a leader in Jesus's kingdom was different than they thought.

Jesus explained there is an "old way" of leading people and a "new way." In the old way, leaders think they are better than the people who follow them. Leaders can be demanding, and use their power to get what they want. But in the new way of Jesus's kingdom, leaders care more about their followers than they care about themselves. Leaders use their power to do what is best for others. Can you think of a leader who leads in Jesus's new way?

HOLY Qs!

- *How does what I learned from Scripture inspire my thoughts and actions?*
- *Is there anyone I'm struggling to get along with? What am I going to do about it?*

BLESSING

Go following the way of the Savior, walking in the truth of the King, and living the life of the Friend. May your thoughts, words, and actions reflect the love of Jesus.

Day 3
A NEW WAY TO USE POWER

MATTHEW 20:25-34

If you could choose a superpower, what would it be? What would you do with it? Jesus doesn't just have a superpower, Jesus is *all-powerful*. But the way He uses His power is kind of surprising. In our story this week, Jesus uses His power to heal two blind men. The only money they had was from begging on the street. They were some of the poorest people in their community. Many people even thought that blind people were not as good as everyone else. They had zero power.

Jesus was not rich, but people thought He was important, and they listened to what He said. He had the power of being popular, the power of teaching, and the power of miracles. And Jesus is the very best at leading in the "new way" He taught His disciples. He used all these powers to do what is best for others, like when He healed the two blind men. What power do you have, and how can you use it for others?

HOLY Qs!

- *How can I keep from letting things like popularity or friends determine how I act?*
- *What can I do to make wise choices this week?*

BLESSING

Go following the way of the Savior, walking in the truth of the King, and living the life of the Friend. May your thoughts, words, and actions reflect the love of Jesus.

THE NO SHUSH-ING ZONE

MATTHEW 20:25-34

Ever been "shushed"? Ever gotten the *stink eye?* Maybe someone said, "hush!" or "be quiet!" when you were trying to talk. Or, they just gave you *the look* without having to say anything at all. Sometimes we need to be reminded that we should be quiet or respectful. But it can also feel like what we have to say isn't important. And that can hurt.

When the blind men called out to Jesus, they got shushed. Maybe the crowd thought Jesus was too busy. Or maybe they were embarrassed by the poor, raggedy blind men sitting outside their town. But whatever their reason, Jesus disagreed. He heard the blind men, stopped what He was doing, and went to them. He started a conversation with them, and did what they asked Him to do. His actions proved that they were important.

Jesus wants all people to know that they are heard, seen, and valued. He doesn't want anyone to be blocked out or shushed up. How do you feel knowing Jesus is always listening?

HOLY Qs!

- *How can God's love give me confidence today?*
- *How can I learn from others this week?*

BLESSING

Go following the way of the Savior, walking in the truth of the King, and living the life of the Friend. May your thoughts, words, and actions reflect the love of Jesus.

Day 5
WHO SERVES WHO?

MATTHEW 20:25-34

What do you think of when you hear the word "serve"? Is it a waiter bringing you food at a restaurant? If you look in the dictionary, the word *serve* means "to perform duties or services for another person." Kings, presidents, and all kinds of powerful people have people that do things for them—making food, cleaning the house, driving them around. Even when these people are paid, we usually think of the person *serving* as less important than the one *being* served.

But Jesus says this is part of the "old way" of thinking. Jesus is certainly the most important, but He said His job was to serve other people—not have them serve Him. Imagine if you saw the president of your country washing clothes or cooking food for the citizens of your country. What would you think? Have you seen any important or powerful people serve you or others? How did that make you feel?

HOLY Qs!

- Is anything in my life really hard right now? Am I talking to God about it? Who else can I talk to?

- What's a healthy or helpful way I can use my spare time?

BLESSING

Go following the way of the Savior, walking in the truth of the King, and living the life of the Friend. May your thoughts, words, and actions reflect the love of Jesus.

WHAT DO YOU WANT?

MATTHEW 20:25-34

What's something you've really wanted recently? What did you do to get it? Sometimes we can just get what we want on our own. It's easy. Other times we need to ask someone's help to get it. That's not always so easy. Like if we're afraid to ask for something. Maybe it's too expensive, or too hard to get, or we feel embarrassed asking for it. Look back at what happened in this week's story in verses 32 and 33. Jesus invited the blind men to ask for what they wanted. Does this seem strange to you? Shouldn't Jesus just know what they wanted? Well, He did *know*; but that's not why He asked.

It takes courage and trust to ask for what we want. The blind men trusted that Jesus could make them see. They showed courage in asking Jesus to heal them. They asked out loud, in front of everybody. Yikes. Can you imagine Jesus coming to you and asking, "What do you want me to do for you?" How would you answer?

HOLY Qs!

- *What am I thankful for? How can I show how thankful I am this week?*
- *How can the way I spend my money reflect my relationship with Jesus?*

BLESSING

Go following the way of the Savior, walking in the truth of the King, and living the life of the Friend. May your thoughts, words, and actions reflect the love of Jesus.

Day 7
SERVING LIKE JESUS

MATTHEW 20:25-34

Who do you know that loves, serves, and leads like Jesus? How'd they get to be that way? Ask them. You'll probably hear them tell you about someone *they* know who served, loved, and led them like Jesus. When we follow Jesus, people around us start to notice.

It's kind of like dominoes that fall in a chain reaction. First, Jesus serves someone like He did the blind men in our story. Then, the men followed Him. They could see and they wanted to follow Jesus. They noticed how He loved, served, and led the disciples. Jesus made their lives better. For the blind men, more than their sight was changed. The person who is loved by Jesus is changed forever.

This is what a life with Jesus is like. The love of Jesus and the leadership of Jesus change us forever. Then, as we love, serve, and lead others like Jesus does for us, their lives are changed too. How can *you* serve, love, and lead like Jesus?

HOLY Qs!

- *Have my words matched my actions? Does who I say I am and how I act line up?*
- *Who in my life needs to hear about Jesus? How can they hear it from me?*

BLESSING

Go following the way of the Savior, walking in the truth of the King, and living the life of the Friend. May your thoughts, words, and actions reflect the love of Jesus.

WEEK 34 Day 1
THE COMING OF THE KINGDOM

It's a new week in your life with Jesus! Use the *5 What's or Lectio Divina* to guide your reading today. Enjoy God's love for you!

LUKE 17:20-21

20 One day the Pharisees asked Jesus, "When will the Kingdom of God come?"
Jesus replied, "The Kingdom of God can't be detected by visible signs. 21 You won't be able to say, 'Here it is!' or 'It's over there!' For the Kingdom of God is already among you."

Day 2
LEARNING STUFF IS COOL

LUKE 17:20-21

What kid do you know that knows all the answers in church? She has Scripture memorized. He remembers all the disciple's names. Maybe it's you. This week's story, like many stories in the Gospels, leads off with the Pharisees asking Jesus a few questions. The Pharisees were the experts in the law: the Old Testament (before it was called that). They really knew their stuff. They weren't exactly sold on Jesus being who He said He was, so they were always asking questions to try to trick Him.

The thing about the Pharisees—they weren't exactly known for their willingness to learn. We can look at the Pharisees and say, "Wow! It would be so cool to study hard and learn as much as they did!" But, we still want to be willing to learn new things. Consider it a gift that we have Jesus in the Gospels, other important biblical authors, Sunday school teachers, parents, grandparents, pastors, and others who can continue to teach us in our faith. You can always be ready to listen and learn more.

HOLY Qs!

- How can I learn from others this week?
- How does my relationship with Jesus impact my daily life in real ways?

BLESSING

Go following the way of the Savior, walking in the truth of the King, and living the life of the Friend. May your thoughts, words, and actions reflect the love of Jesus.

MY KIND OF KINGDOM

LUKE 17:20-21

Check out verse 20. The Pharisees were really asking, "When is the messiah going to come and start to rule like the king he's supposed to be?!" Remember, the Pharisees and other Jews had been waiting for a long time for their Savior to show up. And they wanted him to fight. Picture a conquering warrior king. What's he wearing? What's he riding? What's he holding? That's kind of what the Jewish people were picturing.

The kingdom of God they were talking about was when this messiah would do some heavy conquering, and they'd be back on top like the old days. Jesus, however, had a different idea in mind with the kingdom. Really, our ideas of how we want Jesus to show up don't always look like how He actually works. It's good to pray with total honesty. Maybe you're praying for healing, or for a bad situation to end. Don't stop! Jesus loves you and He's listening. Like the kingdom the Pharisees wanted, Jesus may not fix things exactly how you're thinking, but however He shows up, He'll do it out of love!

HOLY Qs!

- *What have I been enjoying about prayer recently?*
- *When good things happen, how do I give God the credit?*

BLESSING

Go following the way of the Savior, walking in the truth of the King, and living the life of the Friend. May your thoughts, words, and actions reflect the love of Jesus.

Day 4

ALL THE FRENCH FRIES YOU CAN EAT (PROBABLY)

LUKE 17:20-21

One way the phrase "kingdom of God" gets used is in talking about heaven. What do you know about heaven? What's exciting about it? What's confusing about it? Heaven gets talked about a lot in Christian circles. There are songs and movies about it. Heaven is a pretty big deal.

Living forever, after all—where everything is perfect—sounds awesome. In the next few days, we're going to talk about heaven meeting earth and what that looks like in our lives right now. Today, it's okay to take a moment and look toward the future. God has promised an amazing, perfect life forever with Jesus, where everything is right. Heaven is good news. While we can't let the future good news keep us from the present good news (more on that tomorrow) we can still definitely celebrate the future. Living in God's love, loving Jesus as Savior, King, and Friend, means also living forever with God. What about heaven makes you want to celebrate?

HOLY Qs!

- Who in my life needs to hear about Jesus? How can they hear it from me?

- How can the way I spend my money reflect my relationship with Jesus?

BLESSING

Go following the way of the Savior, walking in the truth of the King, and living the life of the Friend. May your thoughts, words, and actions reflect the love of Jesus.

WAIT, NOW? LIKE, RIGHT NOW?

LUKE 17:20-21

Check out verse 21. The kingdom is already among you. Remember, the Pharisees liked to ask questions to try to trip Jesus up. The question in verse 20 could almost be re-written to say, "We know YOU'RE not the one we're waiting for, crazy guy from Nazareth, so when WILL the kingdom actually get started?" Jesus lets them know they didn't trip Him up one bit. "The kingdom of God is here. I'm here."

Rather than sitting and waiting on a future kingdom to show up, followers of Jesus started believing that the kingdom had come 2000 years ago. Someday, it will be fully complete. Everything will be right, like it was meant to be. But here's some really good news: It's already started. The kingdom isn't all the way here, but it started showing up when Jesus showed up. Because Jesus came to make things right, the world started getting a little bit more like heaven. So Christians don't just celebrate the heaven of someday. We get the great joy of celebrating the heaven that has already started! (More on this tomorrow.)

HOLY Qs!

- *What am I thankful for? How can I show how thankful I am this week?*
- *How does what I learned from Scripture inspire my thoughts and actions?*

BLESSING

Go following the way of the Savior, walking in the truth of the King, and living the life of the Friend. May your thoughts, words, and actions reflect the love of Jesus.

Day 6
HEAVEN-BRINGER, PART 1

LUKE 17:20-21

It's time to celebrate what Jesus is doing through you in the world right now. What good have you done in the world in the last week? Think about your relationships with your parents, siblings, and friends at school, opportunities to serve, and whatever else. Who did you help? Who did you serve? Who did you care for? Who did you teach?

You know what, Christian? You're a heaven-bringer! That's right. Remember yesterday when we talked about heaven already starting? You're a part of that. Whenever God does good in the world through His people, heaven meets earth. When people are healed, when people are loved, when people are cared for, those are little pieces of heaven right here among us. Why? Because in heaven, everyone is healed, everyone is loved, and everyone is cared for. We're getting glimpses of how heaven will be, when everything is perfect. It starts right now. How can you bring more glimpses of heaven to earth this week?

HOLY Qs!

- God cares about our whole life, not just the spiritual parts. What healthy habits do I need to work on?

- Is anything in my life really hard right now? Am I talking to God about it? Who else can I talk to?

BLESSING

Go following the way of the Savior, walking in the truth of the King, and living the life of the Friend. May your thoughts, words, and actions reflect the love of Jesus.

HEAVEN-BRINGER, PART 2

LUKE 17:20-21

So heaven-bringing is about what we do for others that show them what heaven will be like. Heaven-bringing is also about being close to God. People were created to have a close, intimate relationship with God, their Creator. Since heaven is about making all things right and perfect, having that relationship with God brings a little more heaven to earth.

When you worship God, when you pray, when you spend time with God, when you gather with your church family, when you listen, when you obey, when you tell other people about the good news of Jesus, all of these things bring little glimpses of heaven to earth. So, when you do for others in the name of Jesus, or when you worship Him, you are being a heaven-bring-er and kingdom builder! The kingdom of God is expanding—getting bigger and bigger in the world—because of you! Hopefully that gets you excited. It's God's mission in the world. He invites you to join in that mission, as a Christian, to keep on bringing more and more heaven to earth.

HOLY Qs!

- *How can God's love give me confidence today?*
- *What can I do to make wise choices this week?*

BLESSING

Go following the way of the Savior, walking in the truth of the King, and living the life of the Friend. May your thoughts, words, and actions reflect the love of Jesus.

WEEK 35 Day 1
JESUS BLESSES THE CHILDREN

It's a new week in your life with Jesus! Use the *5 What's or Lectio Divina* to guide your reading today. Enjoy God's love for you!

LUKE 18:15-17

15 One day some parents brought their little children to Jesus so he could touch and bless them. But when the disciples saw this, they scolded the parents for bothering him.
16 Then Jesus called for the children and said to the disciples, "Let the children come to me. Don't stop them! For the Kingdom of God belongs to those who are like these children. 17 I tell you the truth, anyone who doesn't receive the Kingdom of God like a child will never enter it."

THEY BROUGHT YOU HERE

LUKE 18:15-17

What's something you've been taught to do by someone in your house? Life skills? Building skills? Sewing skills? Money skills? It's kind of weird to think about, but from the moment you're born, the people raising you are teaching you not to need them anymore. They're teaching you to live on your own. Of course, you'll always need their relationship, but there are lots of things you don't need them to do for you anymore. Like when you were a baby you needed them to feed you and change your diaper. Now, you can probably do that yourself! (Or you may not wear a diaper anymore.)

Christian family members and mentors are also teaching you to have your own relationship with Jesus. Maybe they gave you this book. Maybe they pray with you. Check out verse 15. Those parents brought their kids to Jesus. Nowadays, Christian families do the same. They're bringing you to Jesus so that you'll get stronger and stronger in that relationship. Someday, if you have kids, you'll bring them to Jesus the same way. Thank those people for bringing you to Jesus today!

HOLY Qs!

- *How does what I learned from Scripture inspire my thoughts and actions?*
- *What can I do to make wise choices this week?*

BLESSING

Go following the way of the Savior, walking in the truth of the King, and living the life of the Friend. May your thoughts, words, and actions reflect the love of Jesus.

Day 3
THE GROWN-UPS

LUKE 18:15-17

Who else teaches you about Jesus, besides your family? Or maybe you don't have Christian parents, so all of your Christian mentors are outside of your house. Or maybe you don't live with your parents, but you live with Christian foster parents, grandparents, or other family. Maybe you have Sunday school teachers who are loving and investing in your relationship with Jesus. You won't fully understand just yet, but someday you are going to be really, really thankful for the way they helped shape you.

Like the disciples in this story, not every Christian adult around you is great with kids. The disciples tried to shoo the kids and parents away. They didn't think kids were important enough to be with Jesus at that moment. The disciples weren't bad people. They just didn't understand. Even though they may not have been kid people, we can still learn a lot from the disciples as they grew in their faith. How can you learn about faith from watching the grown-ups in your life?

HOLY Qs!

- *How can I keep from letting things like popularity or friends determine how I act?*

BLESSING

Go following the way of the Savior, walking in the truth of the King, and living the life of the Friend. May your thoughts, words, and actions reflect the love of Jesus.

Day 4
WHADDYA KNOW?

LUKE 18:15-17

What do you know a lot about that your parents don't know? Is it a TV show, science topic, game, art, or type of dance? Now, what do your parents know a lot about that you don't know? (Hint: It's probably a lot.) Adults have been around longer, so they know more stuff. They've experienced more life.

Check out verse 16. Jesus wasn't about to stop those kids from getting to Him. Getting to Jesus, their Savior, King and Friend, had nothing to do with who a person was. The disciples didn't understand this yet. In their culture, Jewish men were the only religious leaders. Women? Children? Don't even think about it.

Jesus, however, didn't care that they were kids. He didn't care how much they knew or didn't know. He didn't care where they were from. Kids have the same access to Jesus that adults do, no matter how much knowledge they have packed away. Being close to Jesus is not about where you're from, what you know, or what you've done. It's about a relationship. He just really wants to be with you.

HOLY Qs!

- How does my relationship with Jesus impact my daily life in real ways?
- What's a healthy or helpful way I can use my spare time?

BLESSING

Go following the way of the Savior, walking in the truth of the King, and living the life of the Friend. May your thoughts, words, and actions reflect the love of Jesus.

Day 5
KINGDOM WORK

LUKE 18:15-17

What comes to mind when you hear the word "kingdom"? What do you see? Check out verses 16-17. The word "kingdom" gets used a lot by Jesus in this and other passages around the Bible. After all, the people were waiting for a new King to show up. Jesus wasn't shying away from His role as the Messiah; He was just a very different type of king than they were expecting.

Did you know you're already living in Jesus's kingdom? It's not just a far off kingdom that's waiting for us when we die. The kingdom of God is being brought right here to earth. There is a King who leads it (Jesus) and people who help it grow and flourish (Christians). Someday the kingdom will be complete and perfect. We call that heaven. But the process has already started. As we worship God, allow the Holy Spirit to work in us, and show kindness and love to others, a little more kingdom shows up in the world. God's bringing the kingdom now! How can you help God build the kingdom?

HOLY Qs!

- What have I been enjoying about prayer recently?
- How can God's love give me confidence today?

BLESSING

Go following the way of the Savior, walking in the truth of the King, and living the life of the Friend. May your thoughts, words, and actions reflect the love of Jesus.

Day 6
FOLLOW THAT KID

LUKE 18:15-17

Ever heard an adult talk about how great it was to be a kid? What do they mean by that? Well, Jesus talks about it, too. Check out verse 17. He's talking to adults here, and He wants them to be more like kids. What do you think He means? Why does He want the adults He's teaching to "receive the kingdom of God like a child"?

You're the kid, and there's an adult writing this, so it might be weird to be told what it's like to be . . . you, but here it goes. As a kid, you are curious. You ask lots of questions. You trust the people who love you. You're willing to believe in the amazing things Jesus did. Adults need to be more like kids to really understand Jesus. They need to trust. They need to be curious. They need to believe. Finally, adults need to remember that they have more to learn. This helps them to be wide open to learn from Jesus. How can you inspire the adults in your life to follow Jesus like a kid?

HOLY Qs!

- *What am I thankful for? How can I show how thankful I am this week?*

BLESSING

Go following the way of the Savior, walking in the truth of the King, and living the life of the Friend. May your thoughts, words, and actions reflect the love of Jesus.

Day 7
WHODDYA KNOW?

LUKE 18:15-17

What do you think it takes to become a citizen of another country? Ask around. It's not easy. Check out the end of verse 17. Jesus talks about entering the kingdom. Is entering the kingdom like entering another country? What do you think it takes to enter God's kingdom?

If you go to another country, you have to follow their rules. If you want to be a citizen, you might have to take a test that shows you understand their history and way of life. You have to fill out a lot of paperwork, and say the right things.

To enter into God's kingdom, you just have to do one thing: have a loving relationship with Jesus. He becomes your Savior, King, and Friend. You don't have to have to take a test or memorize a bunch of biblical history. Entering the kingdom is not about what you do, it's about who you know. Then, the things you do, you do because of your loving relationship with Jesus.

HOLY Qs!

- *What habits help me spend time getting to know God through Scripture?*
- *Have my words matched my actions? Does who I say I am and how I act line up?*

BLESSING

Go following the way of the Savior, walking in the truth of the King, and living the life of the Friend. May your thoughts, words, and actions reflect the love of Jesus.

WEEK 36 Day 1
JESUS IS THE MESSIAH

It's a new week in your life with Jesus! Use the *5 What's or Lectio Divina* to guide your reading today. Enjoy God's love for you!

JOHN 10:24-30

24 The people surrounded him and asked, "How long are you going to keep us in suspense? If you are the Messiah, tell us plainly."
25 Jesus replied, "I have already told you, and you don't believe me. The proof is the work I do in my Father's name. 26 But you don't believe me because you are not my sheep. 27 My sheep listen to my voice; I know them, and they follow me. 28 I give them eternal life, and they will never perish. No one can snatch them away from me, 29 for my Father has given them to me, and he is more powerful than anyone else. No one can snatch them from the Father's hand. 30 The Father and I are one."

Day 2
NOT THE DAY TO DIE

JOHN 10:24-30

Think of a time someone tried to start an argument. How did you respond? In this passage, Jesus was in a tricky situation. He was in the temple surrounded by Jewish leaders. They said, "If you are the Messiah, tell us plainly." Jesus was wise. He knew there were times He could tell people directly that He was God's Son. This was not one of those times. He knew a direct answer at this moment could result in the people killing Him (that's in verse 31). Jesus knew He had more to do before His death. This was not the day to die.

There are times when you have to choose your words carefully. Stand up for what you believe in, but think about the best way to reach someone. Sometimes it is best to say nothing at all. Knowing which option to choose takes wisdom. What are some different places and situations you've had to use wisdom when talking about your faith?

HOLY Qs!

- How does what I learned from Scripture inspire my thoughts and actions?

- How can I be obedient to God this week?

BLESSING

Go following the way of the Savior, walking in the truth of the King, and living the life of the Friend. May your thoughts, words, and actions reflect the love of Jesus.

ACTIONS SPEAK

JOHN 10:24-30

Who are some people you can watch work and quickly tell what their job is? (For example, if you see someone hammering on a roof, you can quickly tell they work in construction.) When a crowd wanted Jesus to tell them if He was the Messiah, He told them that the proof was in the work He did in His Father's name. The Jewish leaders saw and heard about many of the miracles Jesus performed. They knew that He healed people. They knew He had fed 5,000 people and had raised Lazarus from the dead. They saw Him teach people about God and fulfill prophecies. His actions showed He was the Messiah to everyone who was willing to really pay attention.

Our actions reveal who we really are. What do your actions say about you? Do you treat people with respect? Are you patient and helpful? Do you try to be generous? Are you consistent in how you act—regardless of whether you are at home or at school? When people see you, who do they think you are?

HOLY Qs!

- *Have my words matched my actions? Does who I say I am and how I act line up?*

- *Who in my life needs to hear about Jesus? How can they hear it from me?*

BLESSING

Go following the way of the Savior, walking in the truth of the King, and living the life of the Friend. May your thoughts, words, and actions reflect the love of Jesus.

Day 4
HIS VOICE

JOHN 10:24-30

Whose voice could you hear in a crowd and immediately know who it was? In verse 27, Jesus talks about His sheep listening to His voice and following Him. Several times in the Bible, Jesus calls himself the Good Shepherd and calls His believers sheep. Shepherds lead their flock to food, water, and shelter. Sheep know the voice of their shepherd and fully trust and follow him. The more time we spend with Jesus, our Good Shepherd, the easier we will be able to hear His voice and follow.

Jesus rarely speaks to us with a direct voice from heaven. So how can you recognize His voice? You can read the Bible so you're familiar with who Jesus is and what He says. You can pray for understanding and wisdom, and allow time for Him to respond. He may direct your thoughts to His answer as you listen. You can also talk to other Christians you trust. In what ways will you listen for Jesus to speak this week?

HOLY Qs!

- *What habits help me spend time getting to know God through Scripture?*
- *What have I been enjoying about prayer recently?*

BLESSING

Go following the way of the Savior, walking in the truth of the King, and living the life of the Friend. May your thoughts, words, and actions reflect the love of Jesus.

ETERNAL LIFE

JOHN 10:24-30

What do you think life will be like in 100 years? How about in 1,000 years? How about 1,000,000 years? Does your head hurt yet? Now try imagining eternity, where there is no end to time. Mind-blowing, right? Check out verse 28. Jesus says He gives His sheep (Christians) eternal life, and they will never perish or die. Choosing to live a life with Jesus now means getting to live with Jesus forever.

What do you imagine heaven will be like? We don't know all the answers about heaven, but we do know that it will be perfect. There won't be sin, pain, or death. It will be the world as God intended it: perfect. Heaven starts now, though. Glimpses of heaven come to this world a little at a time through God's people, as we live in God's love and spread that love to the people around us. Heaven isn't just someday, far away. It's here now. Your life with Jesus is part of eternity! Look around. Where do you see "heaven on earth" happening around you?

HOLY Qs!

- *How will I be a good friend and listener?*
- *What am I thankful for? How can I show how thankful I am this week?*

BLESSING

Go following the way of the Savior, walking in the truth of the King, and living the life of the Friend. May your thoughts, words, and actions reflect the love of Jesus.

Day 6
POWER HANDS

JOHN 10:24-30

What's something or someone you think of as powerful? Check out verse 29. God is more powerful than anyone or anything. Look at Romans 8:38-39. This is a good Scripture to help us understand our story this week. Lots of things in this world seem powerful, but none of them are more powerful than God's love for us. Nothing can separate us from God. Sure, we can make selfish decisions, or tell God we don't want anything to do with Him. But that doesn't cut off His love for us. His love is just too powerful.

Following Jesus means living in God's powerful love. He offers us that power. Power to stand up to temptation, so it can't separate us from God. Power to be courageous in scary times, because fear can't separate us either. God's powerful love is the most powerful thing to ever exist. How do you feel God's power in your life with Jesus? How do you feel His love?

HOLY Qs!

- How can God's love give me confidence today?

- Is anything in my life really hard right now? Am I talking to God about it? Who else can I talk to?

BLESSING

Go following the way of the Savior, walking in the truth of the King, and living the life of the Friend. May your thoughts, words, and actions reflect the love of Jesus.

THE WONDERS OF WISDOM

JOHN 10:24-30

Describe something you know a lot about. Math? Computers? Triple chocolate cake? Explain it as simply and plainly as possible, so anyone could understand. Check out verse 24. They just wanted a straight answer. Can you blame them? "Just tell us, plainly, no weird word pictures or interesting sayings—are you the Messiah?" During your life with Jesus, you might often find yourself being like the people Jesus encounters. Don't you sometimes just want Jesus to come out and answer you? Wouldn't it be nice if you said, "Jesus, should I pick A or B," and He was like, "Pick A! I have spoken!"

The Bible requires wisdom for us to read and understand it. It's not just full of straight answers to every single question we have. Wisdom helps us listen well, really take our time, and understand things because we care enough to figure them out. Life with Jesus is guided by wisdom. So, where does wisdom come from? How can you get more of it?

HOLY Qs!

- *God cares about our whole life, not just the spiritual parts. What healthy habits do I need to work on?*

- *When good things happen, how do I give God the credit?*

BLESSING

Go following the way of the Savior, walking in the truth of the King, and living the life of the Friend. May your thoughts, words, and actions reflect the love of Jesus.

RAISING OF LAZARUS

JOHN 11:32-44 (NIV)

32 When Mary reached the place where Jesus was and saw him, she fell at his feet and said, "Lord, if you had been here, my brother would not have died."
33 When Jesus saw her weeping, and the Jews who had come along with her also weeping, he was deeply moved in spirit and troubled. 34 "Where have you laid him?" he asked.
"Come and see, Lord," they replied.
35 Jesus wept.
36 Then the Jews said, "See how he loved him!"
37 But some of them said, "Could not he who opened the eyes of the blind man have kept this man from dying?"
38 Jesus, once more deeply moved, came to the tomb. It was a cave with a stone laid across the entrance. 39 "Take away the stone," he said.
"But, Lord," said Martha, the sister of the dead man, "by this time there is a bad odor, for he has been there four days."
40 Then Jesus said, "Did I not tell you that if you believe, you will see the glory of God?"
41 So they took away the stone. Then Jesus looked up and said, "Father, I thank you that you have heard me. 42 I knew that you always hear me, but I said this for the benefit of the people standing here, that they may believe that you sent me."
43 When he had said this, Jesus called in a loud voice, "Lazarus, come out!" 44 The dead man came out, his hands and feet wrapped with strips of linen, and a cloth around his face.
Jesus said to them, "Take off the grave clothes and let him go."

Day 2
FRIEND OF MINE

The two sisters sent a message to Jesus telling him, "Lord, your dear friend is very sick." – John 11:3, NLT

What kinds of things do you tell your friends? Some of Jesus's best friends were a brother and two sisters—Lazarus, Mary, and Martha. They lived in a town called Bethany, near Jerusalem. When Lazarus got sick, Jesus was preaching in a different town. Mary and Martha knew Jesus would want to know, so they sent Him a message. And they were right. Jesus loved His friend Lazarus. He cared about him.

But Lazarus, Mary, and Martha are not Jesus's only friends. We are too! Remember that Jesus loves all of us as our Savior, King, and Friend. (You can read more about this on page vii.) As your Friend, Jesus cares about what's happening in your life just as much as He cared about His friend Lazarus. You can tell Him things. You know, like friends do. You can tell Him about your life and feelings. What do you want to share with your friend Jesus today?

HOLY Qs!

- *How will I be a good friend and listener?*
- *How can God's love give me confidence today?*

BLESSING

Go following the way of the Savior, walking in the truth of the King, and living the life of the Friend. May your thoughts, words, and actions reflect the love of Jesus.

Day 3
DISAPPOINTED

JOHN 11:32-44

Think of a time when things didn't turn out like you hoped. What happened? Look at the beginning of our story in verse 32. How do you think Mary was feeling? Mary and Martha hoped that Lazarus would get better. They wished that Jesus had come sooner to heal him. But Lazarus had already died. Jesus got there too late. They were sad, and disappointed. When Jesus came, Martha and Mary didn't hide their feelings from Him. They knew that Jesus had the power to heal their brother. And they couldn't understand why He didn't.

When you feel disappointed, do you talk about it? Sometimes it might be hard, because we don't want to make other people sad or upset. But Jesus is always safe. He will not be upset, even if you feel like He disappointed you. We don't always understand why Jesus doesn't do what we think should happen. But we can always know that Jesus, our Friend, loves us. Do you feel disappointed about anything right now?

HOLY Qs!

- *What can I do to make wise choices this week?*
- *Have my words matched my actions? Does who I say I am and how I act line up?*

BLESSING

Go following the way of the Savior, walking in the truth of the King, and living the life of the Friend. May your thoughts, words, and actions reflect the love of Jesus.

Day 4
GRIEF

JOHN 11:32-44

What makes you cry? Some people cry easily. Other people hardly ever cry. In all the stories in the Gospels, there's not a lot of talk about Jesus crying. And when it happened in this story, it wasn't just a little cry—Jesus wept. So what made Jesus so upset? (You can find clues in verses 34-38.)

The deep sadness we feel when someone dies is called *grief*. It's the feeling of losing something you can never get back. It's the feeling you get when things are not the way they should be. Jesus wept because He felt the grief of losing His friend, and He saw other peoples' grief.

Death was not part of God's original creation. But sin created sickness, brokenness, and death in everyone. This is why Jesus was grieving, too. He knows death is not the way things were sup-posed to be. Tomorrow we'll talk about Jesus's power over death. But even Jesus's power doesn't make grief go away. When we are grieving, we know Jesus under-stands. When you feel grief, who are some trusted adults you can talk to about it?

HOLY Qs!

- *Is anything in my life really hard right now? Am I talking to God about it? Who else can I talk to?*

- *How can I learn from others this week?*

BLESSING

Go following the way of the Savior, walking in the truth of the King, and living the life of the Friend. May your thoughts, words, and actions reflect the love of Jesus.

Day 5
RESURRECTION

JOHN 11:32-44

Ever heard a ghost story? There are some frightening tales out there. They're mostly just designed to get a good scare out of you. Lots of people just avoid them so scary images don't live in their head. Good plan. But when Jesus brought Lazarus back to life, it didn't happen like any of those stories. It's not a scary story, but a triumphant one. Oh, and this story is true.

Earlier in the story, Jesus tells Martha, "'I am the resurrection and the life. The one who believes in me will live, even though they die'" (John 11:25, NIV). "Resurrection" means the raising up of the dead. Jesus is the power of life, and can give life even after death! Lazarus wasn't *kind of* dead like in a fairy tale enchantment. He was all the way dead. But when Jesus called to Lazarus, He made him all the way alive again—body and spirit. And one day Jesus will do the same for all of us! What do you imagine resurrection will be like?

HOLY Qs!

- *What habits help me spend time getting to know God through Scripture?*

- *What am I thankful for? How can I show how thankful I am this week?*

BLESSING

Go following the way of the Savior, walking in the truth of the King, and living the life of the Friend. May your thoughts, words, and actions reflect the love of Jesus.

Day 6
NOT OUR WAY

JOHN 11:32-44

Have you ever predicted how a TV show, book, or movie was going to end? Sometimes it's easy to figure out what the people will do, and how it will all happen. But with Jesus, it isn't always that easy. In fact, we may have a lot of questions. Like: Why did Jesus wait two days before He came to visit Lazarus? If Jesus knew He was going to raise Lazarus from the dead, why did He weep? What other questions do you have about this story?

Jesus is OK with our questions. But not all our questions can be answered. The prophet Isaiah reminded us: "'My thoughts are nothing like your thoughts,' says the LORD. 'And my ways are far beyond anything you could imagine'" (Isaiah 55:8, NLT). With Jesus, there are mysteries we will never understand. But He invites us to trust that He is good, even if we don't understand.

What is something in your life that Jesus is asking you to trust Him with, even if you still have questions?

HOLY Qs!

- *How have I been trustworthy recently?*
- *When good things happen, how do I give God the credit?*

BLESSING

Go following the way of the Savior, walking in the truth of the King, and living the life of the Friend. May your thoughts, words, and actions reflect the love of Jesus.

Day 7
JUMP RIGHT IN

JOHN 11:32-44

Ever had a friend jump out and surprise you? How did you react? Jesus gave His friends a different sort of surprise when Lazarus walked out of that tomb. There were lots of superstitions about dead bodies back then. Bodies were wrapped tightly with strips of cloth and spices were put on them before they were buried. So, when Lazarus walked out of the tomb, the people watching had lots of reasons to freeze up or run away in fear. But what did Jesus do? He told them to unwrap Lazarus. It's like He wanted them to see this up close, to be part of the miracle, instead of just being spectators.

Jesus still does this. When He transforms peoples' bodies and spirits, He doesn't want us just standing around. He wants us to be part of the process so we can see and participate in His power up close. Jesus invites people into His mission all the time. Let's not be afraid to be part of a miracle. Jump right in! How can you jump in where God is working?

HOLY Qs!

- What's a healthy or helpful way I can use my spare time?

- Have I been jealous, grumpy, or really hard on anyone? What can I do about it?

BLESSING

Go following the way of the Savior, walking in the truth of the King, and living the life of the Friend. May your thoughts, words, and actions reflect the love of Jesus.

WEEK 38 Day 1
ZACCHAEUS

It's a new week in your life with Jesus! Use the *5 What's or Lectio Divina* to guide your reading today. Enjoy God's love for you!

LUKE 19:1-10

1 Jesus entered Jericho and made his way through the town. 2 There was a man there named Zacchaeus. He was the chief tax collector in the region, and he had become very rich. 3 He tried to get a look at Jesus, but he was too short to see over the crowd. 4 So he ran ahead and climbed a sycamore-fig tree beside the road, for Jesus was going to pass that way.
5 When Jesus came by, he looked up at Zacchaeus and called him by name. "Zacchaeus!" he said. "Quick, come down! I must be a guest in your home today."
6 Zacchaeus quickly climbed down and took Jesus to his house in great excitement and joy. 7 But the people were displeased. "He has gone to be the guest of a notorious sinner," they grumbled.
8 Meanwhile, Zacchaeus stood before the Lord and said, "I will give half my wealth to the poor, Lord, and if I have cheated people on their taxes, I will give them back four times as much!"
9 Jesus responded, "Salvation has come to this home today, for this man has shown himself to be a true son of Abraham. 10 For the Son of Man came to seek and save those who are lost."

Day 2
SAVIOR

LUKE 19:1-10

In verse 1 you'll see the name Jericho. Do you remember that Bible story? Yep. This is the same Jericho that was conquered by Joshua. Jericho was one of the last stops for Joshua and God's people before entering the promised land in the Old Testament. This is Jesus's last stop before entering Jerusalem where He was ultimately arrested and hung on the cross, which led to His resurrection and conquering of sin and death.

Joshua's name and Jesus's name both come from the same Hebrew word. Can you see where this is going? Joshua showed the power of God in the city of Jericho before getting to the promised land for God's people. Jesus was about to show the power of God at Jericho before bringing the true promise of salvation for all through the cross. Joshua's story, all those years before, was leading to Jesus's story. Like Jericho, Jesus was about to break down the walls, but not walls of stone. He was about to break down the walls of sin so that everyone could be saved and set free! What does it mean to be free from sin?

HOLY Qs!

- How does what I learned from Scripture inspire my thoughts and actions?
- How have I been trustworthy recently?

BLESSING

Go following the way of the Savior, walking in the truth of the King, and living the life of the Friend. May your thoughts, words, and actions reflect the love of Jesus.

NOT THAT PERSON

LUKE 19:1-10

Imagine having a job that makes you unpopular, like the person at the bouncy house who's in charge of telling people their time is over. Zacchaeus had one of these jobs. He was a tax collector. He was in charge of collecting money people owed the government. There was another reason he wasn't liked. He lied to people and collected more money than he needed to collect. Then he'd keep the extra money for himself. Lots of tax collectors did this.

Did the people like Zacchaeus? Nope. But Jesus loved him, just like He loves all of us. There is no one He doesn't love. Zacchaeus was arrogant, stole money, and worst of all, he had the power to get away with it. Do you know someone like Zacchaeus? Is there someone you think is mean, rude, or unfair? Sometimes, we have trouble seeing how Jesus could love these people. They seem so unlovable to us. How does the story of Zacchaeus change the way you think about them?

HOLY Qs!

- How can I be obedient to God this week?
- What's a healthy or helpful way I can use my spare time?

BLESSING

Go following the way of the Savior, walking in the truth of the King, and living the life of the Friend. May your thoughts, words, and actions reflect the love of Jesus.

Day 4
THAT'S DIFFERENT

LUKE 19:1-10

"Actions speak louder than words." Ever heard this? What's it mean? Jesus told Zacchaeus that He was coming to his house. In verse 8, we discover something amazing. Zacchaeus's life had been changed. He believed that Jesus was the Son of God. Not only that, but Zacchaeus also began to think of others. He gave all he stole back and then some. Zacchaeus's life changed that day. He didn't just believe differently, his actions were different.

When Jesus changes us, our actions change. Remember the fruit of the Spirit? (Check out Week 20 for a refresher.) Those things begin to show up in a life with Jesus. We see goodness in Zacchaeus the day he began a relationship with Jesus. We see his life start to change right away. He paid back what he stole, and even gave back a little more. How does your relationship with Jesus make you act differently?

HOLY Qs!

- *How can God's love give me confidence today?*
- *How can the way I spend my money reflect my relationship with Jesus?*

BLESSING

Go following the way of the Savior, walking in the truth of the King, and living the life of the Friend. May your thoughts, words, and actions reflect the love of Jesus.

A LITTLE EXTRA IS OKAY

LUKE 19:1-10

There were lots of times Jesus's decisions weren't very popular with other leaders. For example, people did not like his choice to visit Zacchaeus. Zacchaeus worked for the harsh and mean Roman empire that stole from them. Check out verse 7. They called him a "notorious sinner." In other words, people thought he was trouble.

Of all the people Jesus could have visited in Jericho, he chose Zacchaeus. What?! The crowd was furious. They didn't believe he was worthy of Jesus's attention. Some believed they were more worthy of Jesus's attention than Zacchaeus. It's a temptation to compare ourselves to others like this. We think, "Hey, they're getting special treatment. What about me?" Here's the thing, Jesus often gave more attention to the people who needed it most—the poor, the sick, the mistreated, the outsiders like Zacchaeus. That doesn't mean He loved the people in the crowd any less. He just knew Zacchaeus needed Him in that moment. Who can you think of that might need a little extra attention?

HOLY Qs!

- Have I been jealous, grumpy, or really hard on anyone? What can I do about it?

- Is there anyone I'm struggling to get along with? What am I going to do about it?

BLESSING

Go following the way of the Savior, walking in the truth of the King, and living the life of the Friend. May your thoughts, words, and actions reflect the love of Jesus.

Day 6
NOT SURE WHEN

LUKE 19:1-10

When did you become a Christian? When did you start your life with Jesus? When did Zacchaeus start his life with Jesus? Can you find the exact spot in the passage? You probably can't. Why? Because it doesn't exactly say. We don't see Zacchaeus pray a special prayer to be saved. We don't see his baptism. Maybe he gave his life to Jesus up in the tree? Maybe it happened as Jesus and Zacchaeus walked to his house. We don't know exactly when it happened. Maybe Zacchaeus doesn't even know. We just know it happened. Check out verses 8 and 9.

Here's what we do know exactly. Jesus said salvation had come to his home. His life changed. His actions changed. He was a new person. Some people know the exact moment they became a Christian. Others don't remember one specific moment. Either way, it's just as real. A life with Jesus changes us. When we're Christians, it shows up in our love and actions, even if we can't say exactly when it started.

HOLY Qs!

- *Who in my life needs to hear about Jesus? How can they hear it from me?*

- *Is anything in my life really hard right now? Am I talking to God about it? Who else can I talk to?*

BLESSING

Go following the way of the Savior, walking in the truth of the King, and living the life of the Friend. May your thoughts, words, and actions reflect the love of Jesus.

GET OUT OF THAT TREE

LUKE 19:1-10

Do you like climbing trees? What's your favorite place to climb? Now, imagine you are Zacchaeus up in a tree and Jesus just called you by name to come down. Would you move quickly and with joy and excitement? It's easy to say yes because we know how this story ends. But, what if we didn't know how it ended? Often in our lives with Jesus, He speaks and we are not so quick to respond. Sometimes we even respond with grumpy or unthankful thoughts, especially if we feel like He's calling us to do something we don't want to do.

Check out verse 6. We aren't going to respond to Jesus perfectly all the time, but this is a great way to respond to Jesus, and can even be transformed into a prayer we pray: "Jesus, help me to respond quickly with excitement and joy when you call me, no matter what I'm asked to do." What is Jesus calling you to do that makes you excited?

HOLY Qs!

- *What have I been enjoying about prayer recently?*
- *God cares about our whole life, not just the spiritual parts. What healthy habits do I need to work on?*

BLESSING

Go following the way of the Savior, walking in the truth of the King, and living the life of the Friend. May your thoughts, words, and actions reflect the love of Jesus.

WEEK 39 Day 1
THE GREATEST COMMANDMENT

It's a new week in your life with Jesus! Use the *5 What's or Lectio Divina* to guide your reading today. Enjoy God's love for you!

MATTHEW 22:34-40

³⁴ But when the Pharisees heard that he had silenced the Sadducees with his reply, they met together to question him again.
³⁵ One of them, an expert in religious law, tried to trap him with
this question: ³⁶ "Teacher, which is the most important commandment in the law of Moses?"
³⁷ Jesus replied, "'You must love the LORD your God with all your
heart, all your soul, and all your mind.' ³⁸ This is the first and
greatest commandment. ³⁹ A second is equally important: 'Love
your neighbor as yourself.' ⁴⁰ The entire law and all the demands
of the prophets are based on these two commandments."

JEALOUS MUCH?

MATTHEW 22:34-40

What does jealousy feel like? This passage has some people who were very jealous of Jesus. They were religious teachers from two different groups: the Pharisees (FAIR-uh-seas) and the Sadducees (SAD-you-seas). They were the most important religious people of the Jewish faith. So what was the problem? People were listening to Jesus instead of them, and many times Jesus pointed out what the Pharisees and Sadducees were doing wrong. Ouch. These groups disagreed about a lot of things, but they agreed on one thing for sure. They didn't like Jesus.

So they tried to mess Him up. They asked Him hard questions in front of the people He was teaching. If He answered wrong, they figured people would start to doubt what He was teaching. (Read more of their questions in Matthew 22:15-33.) Of course, Jesus answered every question perfectly. That just made the Pharisees and Sadducees even more angry and jealous. We all feel jealous sometimes. Jealousy can grow inside of us. It gets our thoughts all twisted up, and it can hurt the people around us. How can jealousy be harmful?

HOLY Qs!

- *Have I been jealous, grumpy, or really hard on anyone? What can I do about it?*

- *How can I keep from letting things like popularity or friends determine how I act?*

BLESSING

Go following the way of the Savior, walking in the truth of the King, and living the life of the Friend. May your thoughts, words, and actions reflect the love of Jesus.

Day 3
A WALL OR A PATH?

MATTHEW 22:34-40

Do you remember the Ten Commandments? (Flip back to Week 15 if you need a reminder.) The Pharisees taught that the Ten Commandments were like a big wall, keeping people away from the things God didn't like. They *really* didn't want to cross that wall, even by accident. So they made lots of their own rules so people didn't even get close to the wall. All these extra rules were like little fences all over the ground in front of the wall. When someone stepped in the wrong place and broke a rule, the Pharisees made sure everyone knew about it.

But when Jesus preached, He helped people think differently. The rules came from love. Following God's rules was like a *path* in their life with God. They showed how to love God and love others. The Pharisees wanted to prove they were good by keeping a lot of rules. It's like they forgot all about the love behind the rules. Sometimes we can forget that too. What rules in your life help you love God and others?

HOLY Qs!

- *How can I learn from others this week?*
- *How can I be obedient to God this week?*

BLESSING

Go following the way of the Savior, walking in the truth of the King, and living the life of the Friend. May your thoughts, words, and actions reflect the love of Jesus.

IT'S MOST IMPORTANT

MATTHEW 22:34-40

Which commandment would *you* say is most important? The Pharisees expected Jesus to choose one of the Ten Commandments. Then they could accuse Him of picking the wrong one. But Jesus didn't just choose one. Look again at Jesus's answer in verse 37. He was talking about the first three commandments that tell us how to live in relationship with God. (Flip back to Week 15 for more.) But He was also using the words from a famous part of Scripture called the Shema (shuh-MAH). (We'll talk more about that next week.) Jesus tells us that loving God with our whole selves is the most important thing about this new life with God.

God is not like anyone else. So a relationship with God is not like any other relationship. God wants to be included in every part of our life. We don't just love God when we're at church, or when we're reading the Bible. What do you think it looks like to love God with all your heart, your mind, and your soul?

HOLY Qs!

- *How can God's love give me confidence today?*
- *What have I been enjoying about prayer recently?*

BLESSING

Go following the way of the Savior, walking in the truth of the King, and living the life of the Friend. May your thoughts, words, and actions reflect the love of Jesus.

Day 5
LIVING IN LOVE

MATTHEW 22:34-40

Do you remember what Commandments 5-10 talk about? (Look back at Week 15 to check.) These are the commandments that teach us how to be good neighbors. So when Jesus talked about loving your neighbor as yourself—He was talking about these commandments. He was telling us they are all connected to each other.

When we let God's love fill us—when we really let ourselves feel His love—our whole life is affected. We're living in the middle of His love. God's love fills and guides our decisions, our actions, and our words. So our decisions, actions, and words begin to look like love! Jesus said that loving our neighbors is one of the most important things in our life with God. Loving God and loving others always go together. It's like a big way we love God is by loving others. How do you feel God's love? How does God's love for you help you love others?

HOLY Qs!

- *Have my words matched my actions? Does who I say I am and how I act line up?*
- *How will I be a good friend and listener?*

BLESSING

Go following the way of the Savior, walking in the truth of the King, and living the life of the Friend. May your thoughts, words, and actions reflect the love of Jesus.

Day 6
LOVING SELF

MATTHEW 22:34-40

What are some things we do to take care of ourselves? We pay attention to when we're hungry and thirsty. If we stub a toe, we might wrap it with a bandage. We sleep when we're tired, and we play when we want to have fun. When we feel sad, we talk to someone we trust. These are all ways that we love ourselves. We treat our bodies and our feelings with respect and care.

When Jesus says to "love your neighbor as yourself," this is what He's talking about. Jesus doesn't tell us to stop caring for or loving ourselves. He just says, love others the same as you love yourself. If you want to feel safe, happy, and loved, know that people around you want to feel the same way. Jesus says it another way in Matthew 7:12—treat others the way you want to be treated. What do you think is the hardest thing about loving others this way? When has someone loved you like this?

HOLY Qs!

- *God cares about our whole life, not just the spiritual parts. What healthy habits do I need to work on?*

- *Is anything in my life really hard right now? Am I talking to God about it? Who else can I talk to?*

BLESSING

Go following the way of the Savior, walking in the truth of the King, and living the life of the Friend. May your thoughts, words, and actions reflect the love of Jesus.

Day 7

MOST IMPORTANT THING. AGAIN.

MATTHEW 22:34-40

Look at verse 36. Do you remember why the Pharisees asked Jesus this question? Jesus had been teaching about life with God in a very different way than the Pharisees or Sadducees understood it. The Pharisees liked rules. They even made up extra rules, but this made them love the rules more than they actually loved God.

When the Pharisees asked their question, Jesus knew they were focused on the wrong thing. That's why He didn't pick one commandment with His answer. Instead, He summed up all the commandments and showed them how to really follow the commandments: Love God with everything and love others. All the commandments work together in this new life with God. They have one purpose.

The Pharisees thought Jesus was destroying the Law (the commandments). But Jesus said He was *fulfilling* the Law (Matthew 5:17). That means He came to show us what a life with God *really* looks like. Jesus makes it even more clear how to live our lives with God. How does this passage help you understand a life with Jesus?

HOLY Qs!

- *What am I thankful for? How can I show how thankful I am this week?*

- *How does my relationship with Jesus impact my daily life in real ways?*

BLESSING

Go following the way of the Savior, walking in the truth of the King, and living the life of the Friend. May your thoughts, words, and actions reflect the love of Jesus.

WEEK 40 Day 1
SHEMA

This week's passage is from the Old Testament. Can you discover what it has to do with the life of Jesus? Enjoy God's love for you!

DEUTERONOMY 6:4-9

⁴ Listen, O Israel! The LORD is our God, the LORD alone. ⁵ And you must love the LORD your God with all your heart, all your soul, and all your strength. ⁶ And you must commit yourselves wholeheartedly to these commands that I am giving you today. ⁷ Repeat them again and again to your children. Talk about them when you are at home and when you are on the road, when you are going to bed and when you are getting up. ⁸ Tie them to your hands and wear them on your forehead as reminders. ⁹ Write them on the doorposts of your house and on your gates.

Day 2
HEAR EVERY DAY

DEUTERONOMY 6:4-9

This passage of Scripture is called the Shema (shuh-MAH). Shema means "Hear, O Israel." Or, in our version here, "Listen, O Israel." This became a very important passage and prayer in the Jewish faith, and remains one to this day. Look at verse 7. Repeat it at bedtime and in the morning. Some people of faith really took this to heart. They said this prayerful Scripture every night before bed, and every morning when waking up.

There's a lot to be learned by focusing on the Shema. What if you had a passage of Scripture you thought was so important that you decided to make it part of your daily routine, saying it every morning and night? What would happen? That Scripture would become a part of you. It would inspire you. You'd never forget it. You'd remember it when hard times happened, when you were confused, or when you were fighting temptation. What verse of Scripture is so powerful to you that it's worth making a huge part of your life? (It might even be this one.)

HOLY Qs!

- *What habits help me spend time getting to know God through Scripture?*

BLESSING

Go following the way of the Savior, walking in the truth of the King, and living the life of the Friend. May your thoughts, words, and actions reflect the love of Jesus.

WHOLEHEARTEDLY, PART 1

DEUTERONOMY 6:4-9

Would you rather do a physical or mental challenge? Put it this way. Would you rather be in a running race or a math challenge? There's no wrong answer. We're all built to enjoy different things. Thinking about those differences, remember last week when we talked about the greatest commandment? It sounded a lot like the Shema, with one little difference. Matthew 22:37 says to love the Lord with all your heart, soul, and *mind*. Verse 5 this week says heart, soul, and *strength*. Wonder why?

There are several different theories on this little change. Perhaps the ancient Israelites would choose a physical challenge (a running race), and the people Jesus were teaching would pick the mind challenge (a math challenge). Some say it's just because the words didn't translate exactly right from Hebrew (what the ancient Israelites spoke) to Aramaic (what Jesus spoke) to Greek (what the New Testament was written in). No matter why, both passages mean the same thing: Love God with every part of who you are. How do you love God with every part of who you are?

HOLY Qs!

- *God cares about our whole life, not just the spiritual parts. What healthy habits do I need to work on?*

- *How can God's love give me confidence today?*

BLESSING

Go following the way of the Savior, walking in the truth of the King, and living the life of the Friend. May your thoughts, words, and actions reflect the love of Jesus.

Day 4
WHOLEHEARTEDLY, PART 2

DEUTERONOMY 6:4-9

What do you love to do? Just looooove to do. Can't get enough. Sports? Crafting? Binge-watching? Check out verse 6. There's a word in there—wholeheartedly—that needs our attention. We talked yesterday about the difference between mind and strength—how both mean giving our whole selves to Jesus. But what does it mean to give your whole self to Jesus?

This means your school self, your home self, your church self, your playing-outside-with-friends self. It means loving Jesus and letting Him be King of your ideas, actions, words, attitudes, and choices. It means totally loving the One who created you. This isn't easy. It takes work. It takes a community of people helping to teach and guide you. It takes prayer for strength and wisdom. Jesus does so much with what we give Him. The more we see this, the more freely we'll give Him every part of who we are. Is there an area of your life you have trouble letting Jesus in, letting Him lead?

HOLY Qs!

- What have I been enjoying about prayer recently?
- How can I be obedient to God this week?

BLESSING

Go following the way of the Savior, walking in the truth of the King, and living the life of the Friend. May your thoughts, words, and actions reflect the love of Jesus.

FOLLOW THE LEADER

DEUTERONOMY 6:4-9

What does your family like to do together? Go on walks? Watch movies? Make dinner? What's your family's thing? Check out verse 7. This is addressing parents, but since this book is for kids and their families, let's talk from the kid's side of things. How do you, as the kid, help your family love and follow Jesus?

Usually, we let our parents do the leading. But what if our parents aren't Christian? Or what if you have a deep desire to really grow your life with Jesus, but other people in your house aren't feeling that same desire? Kids can be spiritual leaders, too. Sometimes, parents need kids to remind them what's important. Kids can set examples of prayer, Scripture reading, kindness in their words and actions, and wisdom in their decision-making. If they let you, you can be an inspiration for someone! How can you lead your household in their relationships with Jesus?

HOLY Qs!

- *Have my words matched my actions? Does who I say I am and how I act line up?*

BLESSING

Go following the way of the Savior, walking in the truth of the King, and living the life of the Friend. May your thoughts, words, and actions reflect the love of Jesus.

Day 6
EVERYWHERE. ALWAYS.

DEUTERONOMY 6:4-9

Following Jesus is a full-time commitment. It becomes what our life is about. That doesn't mean we can't do stuff like play soccer or learn a sweet clarinet solo. It just means that, no matter what we're doing, we're living in God's love and spreading it to the people around us. Check out verse 7. It's pretty clear that a relationship with Jesus is not just a church thing.

At home. On the road. Going to bed. Getting up. In other words—everywhere, always. That's what Moses, the one who is speaking the words of the Shema, wants us to remember. Loving God with our heart, soul, and strength is something that goes with us. It's something Christian parents are supposed to remind their kids about, teaching them and modeling faith for them. It's something Christian kids can model to their friends. There's nowhere we can be where the love of Jesus can't be with us. Is there a place in your life that reeeeally needs the love of Jesus now?

HOLY Qs!

- Who in my life needs to hear about Jesus? How can they hear it from me?
- How will I be a good friend and listener?

BLESSING

Go following the way of the Savior, walking in the truth of the King, and living the life of the Friend. May your thoughts, words, and actions reflect the love of Jesus.

WRISTS, FOREHEADS, AND DOORPOSTS

DEUTERONOMY 6:4-9

How do you remember when you have something important to do? Check out verses 8 and 9. Moses is referring to some ancient practices that served as both personal and social reminders of what was important. You don't literally need to attach anything to your forehead. (Also, you'd better check before you go nailing things to the front door.) It's not so much *how* you remind yourself and the world. Instead, it's important that you *do* remind yourself and the world of God's love.

Wrists and foreheads: What are some ways to help yourself grow closer to Jesus each day? (Hint: You might be reading one right now.) Doorposts: What ways will people know that you and/ or your family are Christians? You don't have to put out a big banner. Instead, the world will know because of the way you live. Sure, you could get a t-shirt that says, "I'm a Christian." But that wouldn't have near the impact as showing who Jesus is through your attitudes and actions. What are your "wrists, foreheads, and doorposts" that remind yourself and show the world that you love God?

HOLY Qs!

- *What can I do to make wise choices this week?*

- *Have I been jealous, grumpy, or really hard on anyone? What can I do about it?*

BLESSING

Go following the way of the Savior, walking in the truth of the King, and living the life of the Friend. May your thoughts, words, and actions reflect the love of Jesus.

WEEK 41 Day 1
LOVE IS . . .

It's a new week in your life with Jesus! Use the *5 What's or Lectio Divina* to guide your reading today. Enjoy God's love for you!

1 CORINTHIANS 13:4-7

[4] Love is patient and kind. Love is not jealous or boastful or proud [5] or rude. It does not demand its own way. It is not irritable, and it keeps no record of being wronged. [6] It does not rejoice about injustice but rejoices whenever the truth wins out. [7] Love never gives up, never loses faith, is always hopeful, and endures through every circumstance.

Day 2
LET'S LOVE

1 CORINTHIANS 13:4-7

If you could write a letter to your whole church, what would it say? The books 1 and 2 Corinthians (pronounced First and Second Core-INTH-ee-ans) are letters written by Paul to the church in Corinth. In this part of the letter, he spends a lot of time on love. When you read the verses for this week you will notice it starts with two things love *does*, being patient and kind, followed by eight things love *doesn't* do. It looks like the church in Corinth was having a hard time loving each other, so Paul was trying to help them understand what love really is.

This letter gets used a lot in weddings. People love to talk about love at weddings. There's another place this letter gets used. Devotional books! To get started this week, read through the passage slowly and think about each of the words used to describe love. What examples from your life come to mind as you read each one? Pray this Scripture today, and ask God to help you love well.

HOLY Qs!

- *Have my words matched my actions? Does who I say I am and how I act line up?*

- *How will I be a good friend and listener?*

BLESSING

Go following the way of the Savior, walking in the truth of the King, and living the life of the Friend. May your thoughts, words, and actions reflect the love of Jesus.

Day 3
PATIENCE

1 CORINTHIANS 13:4-7

Think of a time you lost your patience. What about a time someone lost their patience with you? Patience isn't easy. Toddlers are really bad at it. But really, all ages struggle with it. Patience is calmly waiting for something without getting upset. You may be waiting for something to happen or waiting for a situation to change that's taking a while. Patience can also be about waiting for somebody's bad attitude to get better. This is what it means to be patient with others.

Patience says, "I'm okay. God's got this. I don't need to be in charge. I can wait." There were plenty of people in Corinth with ancestors who waited for years in the desert, or waited for years in captivity, or waited for years for the Messiah to come. They knew about patience, they just weren't usually very good at it. This was a reminder that they could love each other by being patient with each other. Take some time to pray for patience today.

HOLY Qs!

- What am I thankful for? How can I show how thankful I am this week?
- What have I been enjoying about prayer recently?

BLESSING

Go following the way of the Savior, walking in the truth of the King, and living the life of the Friend. May your thoughts, words, and actions reflect the love of Jesus.

Day 4
KINDNESS

1 CORINTHIANS 13:4-7

Think of a time someone was kind to you. What did they do? Kindness is more of an action. It's something you say, show, or do for someone that helps them or makes them happy. It can be a warm smile that helps someone feel noticed. It can be cleaning your sister's room as a surprise so she doesn't have to do it herself. Kindness can be a hug or helping someone with their yard work. It can be gentle words to someone who needs to hear them or saving up your money to help someone.

Where patience asks us to wait to act, kindness requires action. Kindness is giving your time, talents, and resources to better the life of another person. Don't you love it when someone shows you kindness? Of course! So, if you like being shown kindness, do you think those around you like to be shown kindness? Absolutely. Love shows up in kindness. How can you show someone kindness today?

HOLY Qs!

- *Have I been jealous, grumpy, or really hard on anyone? What can I do about it?*
- *How can I keep from letting things like popularity or friends determine how I act?*

BLESSING

Go following the way of the Savior, walking in the truth of the King, and living the life of the Friend. May your thoughts, words, and actions reflect the love of Jesus.

Day 5
INJUSTICE FOR NONE

1 CORINTHIANS 13:4-7

Think of a time you saw someone treated unfairly. Verse 6 uses the word "injustice." Justice means "to make right." So, injustice is the opposite, it means things are *not* right or fair. Our world is full of lots of injustice. Sometimes there are individual people who aren't given justice. Sometimes whole groups of people are treated wrongly, or unfairly.

Look back at yesterday. Kindness is about actions. Because of God's loving kindness, when we see injustice in the world—people being treated unkindly or unfairly—it's our 1 Corinthians 13 duty to work for their justice. This is love. Pray today that God would show you injustices, so that you can show love.

Of course, sometimes you might be the one who isn't treated right. This isn't love. If someone isn't treating you right, it's okay to ask for help so you can feel safe again. God's love in the world means you have the right to be treated with kindness and justice. God loves you. You deserve justice too.

HOLY Qs!

- *What's a healthy or helpful way I can use my spare time?*
- *How can the way I spend my money reflect my relationship with Jesus?*

BLESSING

Go following the way of the Savior, walking in the truth of the King, and living the life of the Friend. May your thoughts, words, and actions reflect the love of Jesus.

Day 6
GOD IS ALL THIS

1 CORINTHIANS 13:4-7

Let's look at the big long list of the things love is not. You could probably make your own. Think of words to fill in the blanks (besides the ones in the passage). Love is not _____. Love is not _____. Love won't ever _____. You know why love isn't these things, or the things listed in the Scripture? Because God isn't these things. God is love. So this whole passage describes God. It's also a list of ways God's love forms us.

Paul is doing more than just telling people how to act. This is a hopeful list about the ways God's love shapes us. Love comes from God. Love is patient and kind because God is patient and kind. Love doesn't give up and is always hopeful, because God doesn't give up and is always hopeful. We can love these ways because God gives us the ability to love with God's kind of love. Read through the passage and replace the word "love" with "God." Let's thank God for His love today and for the way it shapes our lives with Jesus.

HOLY Qs!

- *When good things happen, how do I give God the credit?*
- *How does what I learned from Scripture inspire my thoughts and actions?*

BLESSING

Go following the way of the Savior, walking in the truth of the King, and living the life of the Friend. May your thoughts, words, and actions reflect the love of Jesus.

Day 7
LIVE GOD'S LOVE

1 CORINTHIANS 13:4-7

Think about the people you love most. What would you be willing to do for them because you love them? God's love for us is so strong that He gave His Son, Jesus, who went to the cross and conquered sin and death. God's love never quits on us. God's love is full of hope. Things can change. God's love is so powerful it can change lives. It made Zacchaeus turn his life around. It made Paul go from a person who killed Christians to a powerful follower of Jesus. It was out of love that God created the whole world, including you.

Pray this simple prayer, "Lord, fill me with Your love from the bottom of my toes to the top of my head until it pours out of me." This just means you're so full of love that you're sharing it with the world. Know that He loves you. Let God's love fill you up. Let your life with Jesus be lived in God's love.

HOLY Qs!

- *How can God's love give me confidence today?*
- *How does my relationship with Jesus impact my daily life in real ways?*

BLESSING

Go following the way of the Savior, walking in the truth of the King, and living the life of the Friend. May your thoughts, words, and actions reflect the love of Jesus.

JESUS ANOINTED AT BETHANY

It's a new week in your life with Jesus! Use the *5 What's or Lectio Divina* to guide your reading today. Enjoy God's love for you!

JOHN 12:1-11

¹ Six days before the Passover celebration began, Jesus arrived in Bethany, the home of Lazarus—the man he had raised from the dead. ² A dinner was prepared in Jesus' honor. Martha served, and Lazarus was among those who ate with him. ³ Then Mary took a twelve-ounce jar of expensive perfume made from essence of nard, and she anointed Jesus' feet with it, wiping his feet with her hair. The house was filled with the fragrance.
⁴ But Judas Iscariot, the disciple who would soon betray him, said, ⁵ "That perfume was worth a year's wages. It should have been sold and the money given to the poor." ⁶ Not that he cared for the poor—he was a thief, and since he was in charge of the disciples' money, he often stole some for himself.
⁷ Jesus replied, "Leave her alone. She did this in preparation for my burial. ⁸ You will always have the poor among you, but you will not always have me."
⁹ When all the people heard of Jesus' arrival, they flocked to see him and also to see Lazarus, the man Jesus had raised from the dead. ¹⁰ Then the leading priests decided to kill Lazarus, too, ¹¹ for it was because of him that many of the people had deserted them and believed in Jesus.

Day 2
PRICEY PERFUME

JOHN 12:1-11

What would you buy if someone gave you lots of money? Would it be big or small? There are tiny bottles of perfume that cost thousands of dollars. Do you smell bad enough to buy one of those?! In our Scripture this week, Mary had an expensive bottle of perfume. It was worth a whole year's pay! She poured the entire bottle on Jesus's feet (and on His head according to Matthew and Mark) and wiped his feet with her hair. Judas said she was wasteful and should have sold the perfume to give money to the poor. Jesus praised her actions, because she honored Him.

Does this mean you should go find something really expensive to celebrate Jesus? Not at all. It means that He is deserving of the greatest praise we can bring. What are some big ways you can worship Jesus without using any expensive perfume? He is worthy of your best!

HOLY Qs!

- *How can the way I spend my money reflect my relationship with Jesus?*
- *How does my relationship with Jesus impact my daily life in real ways?*

BLESSING

Go following the way of the Savior, walking in the truth of the King, and living the life of the Friend. May your thoughts, words, and actions reflect the love of Jesus.

NOT SO EMBARRASSING

JOHN 12:1-11

What's your most embarrassing moment? What was it about the moment that made you feel embarrassed? Many people were shocked by Mary's actions. Pouring a little perfumed oil on Jesus's head would have been considered kind, but she used the entire bottle. Wowza! She even put the perfume on His feet. Only lowly servants washed guest's feet. Did she stop there? Oh, no! She let her hair down and used it to wipe Jesus's feet. What?! A respectable woman would not let her hair down in public. People in the room must have gasped. Judas protested. But Mary didn't care. She was too focused on Jesus to be embarrassed or worried about what others thought.

A life with Jesus can sometimes lead to situations where people around us don't agree with our actions. Can you think of a situation where that could happen? What would it take for you to be so confident in your worship that you kept going, even if the people around you thought you were crazy for it?

HOLY Qs!

- *How can I keep from letting things like popularity or friends determine how I act?*

- *How does what I learned from Scripture inspire my thoughts and actions?*

BLESSING

Go following the way of the Savior, walking in the truth of the King, and living the life of the Friend. May your thoughts, words, and actions reflect the love of Jesus.

Day 4
DEVOTED, AND SMELLING LIKE IT

JOHN 12:1-11

What are some of your favorite smells? Cookies baking? Trees after it rains? Fresh cut oranges? Tacos? Check out verse 3. Lazarus's entire house was filled with the fragrance of Mary's perfume. Some of the sweet smell might have even drifted outside through open windows and doors. Mary used her hair to rub the perfume into Jesus's feet. The scent would have clung to her. Everywhere she walked, people would have smelled the rich fragrance. Through the aroma of the perfume, people would be reminded of her devotion to Jesus.

Can people watch your actions and tell that you worship Jesus? Can they listen to your words and hear what Jesus would say? People are watching your life. The Spirit may work through you in a way that others become very interested in following Jesus because of what they see in you. How will people watch your life and know that you are devoted to Jesus?

HOLY Qs!

- *Who in my life needs to hear about Jesus? How can they hear it from me?*
- *Have I been jealous, grumpy, or really hard on anyone? What can I do about it?*

BLESSING
Go following the way of the Savior, walking in the truth of the King, and living the life of the Friend. May your thoughts, words, and actions reflect the love of Jesus.

BE NOT DISTRACTED

JOHN 12:1-11

What distracts you? Judas told everyone that Mary was wasteful when she poured expensive perfume on Jesus. He said the perfume should have been sold and the money given to the poor. There were probably a few people in the room that nodded their heads in agreement. But not only did Judas miss that Mary was honoring Jesus, he was thinking that he could profit from the perfume sale. He already had been stealing from the disciples. It's no wonder that soon Judas would be the one to betray Jesus for 30 pieces of silver.

Judas lost his way. He let his weakness for money distract him. He ended up letting that distraction become most important to him, and he made some terrible choices because of it. What tries to call your attention away from Jesus? If you only think about yourself, it's easy to get confused. What does it mean, and what does it look like, to stay focused on Jesus?

HOLY Qs!

- *How can I be honest and trustworthy this week?*
- *What can I do to make wise choices this week?*

BLESSING

Go following the way of the Savior, walking in the truth of the King, and living the life of the Friend. May your thoughts, words, and actions reflect the love of Jesus.

Day 6
READY FOR BURIAL

JOHN 12:1-11

Jesus was going to die. He had said it before, but He was pretty clear about it in verse 7. Jesus surprised everyone by how He responded to Mary's act of worship. He said that pouring the perfume was a prophetic (prah-FEH-tick) act. In other words, this act of worship also gave everyone a look into the near future when Jesus would die and be buried. Why would perfume make them think of burial? Because when someone died, perfume was used in their burial ceremony.

Do you think Mary was thinking of Jesus's future burial when she anointed Him? What emotions do you think His friends went through, hearing that Jesus's death was coming? Jesus was a real person, with real friends, going to His very real death. Take a moment and think about that. Try to think like Mary. Like Lazarus. Like Jesus. Do you think He was afraid? Excited? You've considered the emotions of His friends. For a moment, consider the very real human emotions of the Savior.

HOLY Qs!

- *What have I been enjoying about prayer recently?*
- *What am I thankful for? How can I show how thankful I am this week?*

BLESSING

Go following the way of the Savior, walking in the truth of the King, and living the life of the Friend. May your thoughts, words, and actions reflect the love of Jesus.

LIKE LAZARUS

JOHN 12:1-11

Check out Week 37 for a quick refresher on Lazarus. We now get a glimpse of Lazarus after Jesus brought him back to life. How do you think his life was different after being brought back from the dead?

Jesus stayed in Lazarus's home. They ate dinner together. People came to see Jesus and Lazarus. The leading priests already hoped to kill Jesus, but they soon added Lazarus to their hit list. Lazarus was a walking miracle. The priests were mad that people started to believe in Jesus because of Lazarus.

If you hear the words, "Be like Lazarus," what do you think it means? Lazarus got a new life. When we begin a relationship with Jesus, He gives us new life too. (That's why you might hear someone call it being "born again.") Past mistakes are erased and we have a new life with Jesus. Sin doesn't control us. He's our Savior, King, and Friend. It's a new life. It's a good life! If you want to learn more about this, turn to page vii.

HOLY Qs!

- *Have my words matched my actions? Does who I say I am and how I act line up?*

- *How can I learn from others this week?*

BLESSING

Go following the way of the Savior, walking in the truth of the King, and living the life of the Friend. May your thoughts, words, and actions reflect the love of Jesus.

WEEK 43 Day 1
THE TRIUMPHANT ENTRY

It's a new week in your life with Jesus! Use the *5 What's or Lectio Divina* to guide your reading today. Enjoy God's love for you!

JOHN 12:12-16

¹² The next day, the news that Jesus was on the way to Jerusalem swept through the city. A large crowd of Passover visitors ¹³ took palm branches and went down the road to meet him. They shouted,
"Praise God! Blessings on the one who comes in the name of the LORD! Hail to the King of Israel!"
¹⁴ Jesus found a young donkey and rode on it, fulfilling the prophecy that said:
¹⁵ "Don't be afraid, people of Jerusalem.
Look, your King is coming,
 riding on a donkey's colt."
¹⁶ His disciples didn't understand at the time that this was a fulfillment of prophecy. But after Jesus entered into his glory, they remembered what had happened and realized that these things had been written about him.

HEADED TO PASSOVER

JOHN 12:12-16

What's your favorite holiday? What do you love about it? For thousands of years the Jewish people have celebrated a holiday called Passover to remember how God rescued their ancestors from slavery. The Pharaoh of Egypt would not let the slaves go free. So God had to send signs of His power to prove that Pharaoh needed to listen. (You can read the full story in Exodus 5—14.) The final sign was the worst. Death came across the land, and every firstborn Egyptian child died. But God warned the Jewish people. God told them to put the blood of a lamb outside their doors. This sign of obedience and sacrifice kept them safe, and death *passed over*. After this, Pharaoh saw the power of God and let the people go.

Passover celebrates God's protection from death, and rescue from slavery. Jesus celebrated this every year of His life. This is why He was coming into Jerusalem in this week's story. Is there anything in the story of Passover that reminds you of Jesus?

HOLY Qs!

- *What habits help me spend time getting to know God through Scripture?*

- *What can I do to make wise choices this week?*

BLESSING

Go following the way of the Savior, walking in the truth of the King, and living the life of the Friend. May your thoughts, words, and actions reflect the love of Jesus.

Day 3
DELIVER US

JOHN 12:12-16

Who leads your country? When Jesus lived, the Jewish people could not lead their own country. They were not slaves, but they weren't entirely free either. They were part of the Roman Empire, all the way in Italy. The Romans spoke a different language. They had a strong government, a very powerful army, and conquered countries all over the world. They sent soldiers and governors to make people follow the Roman rules. Judea, where Jesus lived, was one of the places Rome controlled.

The Romans were very harsh and cruel rulers. The Jewish people prayed all the time that God would deliver them from the Romans, like God delivered them from the Egyptians. They were waiting for God to send the Messiah—the *anointed one*—who would fight for them and give them back their country. Many people thought this is what Jesus would do.

How do you think the people of your city would welcome the person they thought was going to rescue them?

HOLY Qs!

- Is there anyone I'm struggling to get along with? What am I going to do about it?
- What's a healthy or helpful way I can use my spare time?

BLESSING

Go following the way of the Savior, walking in the truth of the King, and living the life of the Friend. May your thoughts, words, and actions reflect the love of Jesus.

Day 4
GOOD OLD DAYS

JOHN 12:12-16

What's the oldest city or building you've visited? Jerusalem is such an old city people call it *ancient*. It's so old, it was even old when Jesus was there!

Jerusalem was the capital city of Israel. It started to grow into a rich, important city because of King David. When he became king, he rode into the city with a victory parade and built a palace. (There are lots of interesting stories about him in the book of 2 Samuel.) The kings after him got into wars, and they forgot to follow God. So the Jewish people talked about the time of King David as "the good old days." And when the people saw Jesus riding into Jerusalem like King David did, they thought He was going to bring back "the good old days."

It's good to know old stories, and to like them. But God doesn't do old things; God does new things. The old stories won't happen again, but they can help us understand what God is doing now. What old stories help you understand things now?

HOLY Qs!

- *How have I been trustworthy recently?*

- *How can the way I spend my money reflect my relationship with Jesus?*

BLESSING

Go following the way of the Savior, walking in the truth of the King, and living the life of the Friend. May your thoughts, words, and actions reflect the love of Jesus.

Day 5
A DIFFERENT KIND OF KING

JOHN 12:12-16

Do you remember what the kingdom of God is? In Week 11 we learned that it's anywhere God is king, where things happen the way God wants. The prophets said all things will be made right when the kingdom of God comes to earth. And the people around Jesus thought this meant defeating the Romans. They wanted a mighty king to conquer their enemies, like the Romans had conquered them.

When Jesus rode into Jerusalem on a donkey, the people welcomed him like a king. They lined the streets like we do during a parade, waving leafy branches in the air. But Jesus is not the kind of fighting king they were hoping for. The prophet Zechariah wrote about God's peaceful king riding on a donkey. Fighting kings rode on mighty war horses, not donkeys. Jesus is the king bringing the kingdom of God. But He's a different king, and it's a different kingdom than the people expected.

Why do you think Jesus came as a peaceful king, instead of a fighting king?

HOLY Qs!

- *How does what I learned from Scripture inspire my thoughts and actions?*

- *Who in my life needs to hear about Jesus? How can they hear it from me?*

BLESSING

Go following the way of the Savior, walking in the truth of the King, and living the life of the Friend. May your thoughts, words, and actions reflect the love of Jesus.

WHAT JESUS KNEW

JOHN 12:12-16

Jesus knew something that others didn't. What's something you have known that other people didn't know until you told them? Jesus knew the people in Jerusalem wanted Him to be like King David. He knew they wanted Him to defeat the Romans and make their country strong again. But Jesus knew He wasn't that kind of king. He also knew some people would get angry at Him when they found out. Just a few days after people cheered for Him, they cheered *against* Him. (We'll hear the whole sad story over the next four weeks.) But Jesus knew what He was doing. He knew what kind of king He was. He knew God's love and purpose. And He knew listening to God's voice was most important.

Life with Jesus is learning to live in God's love and purpose, even if other people don't understand. Who does God want you to be? Who do other people—friends, teachers, neighbors—want you to be? Is there a difference?

HOLY Qs!

- *How can I keep from letting things like popularity or friends determine how I act?*
- *How can I be obedient to God this week?*

BLESSING

Go following the way of the Savior, walking in the truth of the King, and living the life of the Friend. May your thoughts, words, and actions reflect the love of Jesus.

Day 7
NOT WHAT WE WANTED

JOHN 12:12-16

Ever had something turn out a lot differently than you expected? Maybe you went somewhere new but it wasn't how you thought it would be. Maybe a book had a surprise ending. Or that new teacher was not anything like you thought he'd be. The people who cheered for Jesus and called Him king did not get what they expected. And as we'll learn next week, this made lots of them very angry. Humans still get angry with God for not doing what they want. But Jesus knows what we need, even more than we do. We need a king who brings us real peace with God, with each other, and with our enemies. We need a king who shows us how to love, not how to fight.

It can be disappointing when God does not give us what we want. But sometimes God knows that we need something *better* than what we want. We need to remember that God is God, and we are not. God's goal isn't always to give us what we want. What is God's goal for us?

HOLY Qs!

- *Is anything in my life really hard right now? Am I talking to God about it? Who else can I talk to?*

- *Have I been jealous, grumpy, or really hard on anyone? What can I do about it?*

BLESSING

Go following the way of the Savior, walking in the truth of the King, and living the life of the Friend. May your thoughts, words, and actions reflect the love of Jesus.

WEEK 44 Day 1
THE LAST SUPPER

It's a new week in your life with Jesus! Use the *5 What's or Lectio Divina* to guide your reading today. Enjoy God's love for you!

MATTHEW 26:20-28

20 When it was evening, Jesus sat down at the table with the Twelve. 21 While they were eating, he said, "I tell you the truth, one of you will betray me."
22 Greatly distressed, each one asked in turn, "Am I the one, Lord?"
23 He replied, "One of you who has just eaten from this bowl with me will betray me. 24 For the Son of Man must die, as the Scriptures declared long ago. But how terrible it will be for the one who betrays him. It would be far better for that man if he had never been born!"
25 Judas, the one who would betray him, also asked, "Rabbi, am I the one?" And Jesus told him, "You have said it."
26 As they were eating, Jesus took some bread and blessed it. Then he broke it in pieces and gave it to the disciples, saying, "Take this and eat it, for this is my body."
27 And he took a cup of wine and gave thanks to God for it. He gave it to them and said, "Each of you drink from it, 28 for this is my blood, which confirms the covenant between God and his people. It is poured out as a sacrifice to forgive the sins of many."

Day 2
HANGING OUT WITH JESUS

MATTHEW 26:20-28

What would you do if you could just hang out with Jesus for a day? He's always with us. But sometimes many of us wish that we could just sit at a table with Jesus like the disciples in this story. This was the Passover Feast. So, it was basically a holiday celebration that they were enjoying together. Can you imagine being there with Jesus? What do you think He'd sound like? What do you think He'd say?

This was something the disciples got to do a lot. As they traveled from town to town with Jesus, they'd camp, eat together, laugh, and tell stories. Jesus was a real person with real friends. Of course, now you can't sit at a table with Him, but Jesus still goes with us. He's present right now. Listen to Him and share your everyday life with Him. What are some ways today you could pause and remember that Jesus is right there with you?

HOLY Qs!

- How does what I learned from Scripture inspire my thoughts and actions?
- How can I be honest and trustworthy this week?

BLESSING

Go following the way of the Savior, walking in the truth of the King, and living the life of the Friend. May your thoughts, words, and actions reflect the love of Jesus.

SAY WHAT?

MATTHEW 26:20-28

How do you handle awkward moments? Do you get embarrassed, or laugh it off? It was certainly an awkward moment for the disciples when Jesus said, "One of you will betray me." Imagine their shock. Verse 22 says they were all "greatly distressed." This caused fear and confusion, and they didn't know what to say or do. They probably looked around at each other without knowing what to say.

We all make mistakes. The disciples knew this and each one immediately thought, "Maybe it's me." They each knew their own weaknesses. Each one wondered if they were strong enough *not* to betray Jesus. Do you ever feel like you might not be strong enough to handle something hard? That's okay. That's normal. A life with Jesus is full of times when we question ourselves. Like He did with the disciples, He stays with us even when we aren't feeling confident, when we make mistakes, and when we feel totally awkward.

HOLY Qs!

- *How can I be obedient to God this week?*
- *What habits help me spend time getting to know God through Scripture?*

BLESSING

Go following the way of the Savior, walking in the truth of the King, and living the life of the Friend. May your thoughts, words, and actions reflect the love of Jesus.

Day 4
JUDAS DID IT

MATTHEW 26:20-28

Can you think of a time when your friend didn't act like your friend? Maybe they chose to sit with someone else at lunch after they said they'd sit with you. Maybe they said something mean to you or embarrassed you in front of others. You might have felt betrayed. Betrayal is when someone you trust breaks that trust in a hurtful or harmful way. In this passage, that describes Judas.

Judas, after being with Jesus for so long, made some decisions to live his way and not Jesus's way. Remember, Judas was there when Jesus healed people, preached to the crowds, fed over 5,000 people in one day, was anointed, and changed Zacchaeus.

Judas made a selfish choice, and chose money over friendship. (He got paid to betray Jesus. Yikes.) Selfishness is still a temptation for us. Judas showed us what selfishness leads to. Let's pray today that our lives will be open to following Jesus, even when the selfish option is there tempting us.

HOLY Qs!

- *Have my words matched my actions? Does who I say I am and how I act line up?*
- *What can I do to make wise choices this week?*

BLESSING

Go following the way of the Savior, walking in the truth of the King, and living the life of the Friend. May your thoughts, words, and actions reflect the love of Jesus.

Day 5
RABBI OR LORD

MATTHEW 26:20-28

Who is your favorite teacher ever? Jesus was a great teacher too. But He was more than that. Look at verses 22 and 25. Judas called Jesus "Rabbi" (teacher), but the others called Him "Lord." This is an important detail. The disciples knew Jesus as Lord. He was the Son of God. Although they didn't understand everything, they were trying their best to follow Him. They surrendered to Him, their Lord.

Judas was different. He could only see Jesus as a teacher, a Rabbi. Nothing more. Jesus wasn't Lord of his life. It sounds like Judas had a life *near* Jesus. He didn't have a life *with* Jesus. Jesus isn't just a teacher of good things to think about. He's the Lord of the universe. He's the Lord of our lives. We don't just study the Bible to know more in-formation. We don't pray just to feel better. We do it because we are in a relationship with Jesus, our Savior, King, and Friend— the Lord of all!

HOLY Qs!

- *God cares about our whole life, not just the spiritual parts. What healthy habits do I need to work on?*

- *How can I learn from others this week?*

BLESSING

Go following the way of the Savior, walking in the truth of the King, and living the life of the Friend. May your thoughts, words, and actions reflect the love of Jesus.

Day 6
COMMUNION, PART 1

MATTHEW 26:20-28

What's the worst injury you've ever had? Broken bones? Lots of blood? Ew. Check out verses 26-28. Jesus told His disciples that His body was about to be broken, and His blood was going to be shed. But He told them this in a unique way. He took the bread, held it out, and broke it. He said, "This is my body, broken for you." Jesus is saying that pretty soon His body was going to be broken. And it was. He was beaten, whipped, kicked, stabbed, and His body was nailed to a cross.

He took the wine and called it His blood. He was about to bleed a lot, and it was going to be very painful. The wine wasn't really blood, and the bread wasn't really flesh. Instead, they represented those things. They were symbols of what was about to happen. Jesus knew the terrible things that were coming. It was going to hurt. It was going to be hard. Body broken. Blood spilled. But He did it anyway. Why?

HOLY Qs!

- *When good things happen, how do I give God the credit?*
- *What have I been enjoying about prayer recently?*

BLESSING

Go following the way of the Savior, walking in the truth of the King, and living the life of the Friend. May your thoughts, words, and actions reflect the love of Jesus.

COMMUNION, PART 2

MATTHEW 26:20-28

Have you ever taken communion? What's it like? Similar to this passage, communion involves eating a small piece of bread along with some juice or wine. Communion is one of the sacraments of the church. (Look at Day 3 of Week 9 for a refresher on what "sacrament" means.) When we drink the juice and eat the bread, we remember what Jesus did for us on the cross and remember His love for us. It's a way of receiving and embracing God's grace.

Communion is sometimes called Eucharist (YOO-kuh-rist). It's sometimes called the Lord's Supper. Some churches take communion every week. Others do it once a month. However often it is done at your church, we do it together. Communion is meant to be taken as a part of a community, like Jesus did with His disciples. When you take communion, remember that Jesus is Lord. He loves us, died for us, rose again for us, and lives for us. How does communion help you feel closer to Jesus?

HOLY Qs!

- *How can God's love give me confidence today?*
- *What am I thankful for? How can I show how thankful I am this week?*

BLESSING

Go following the way of the Savior, walking in the truth of the King, and living the life of the Friend. May your thoughts, words, and actions reflect the love of Jesus.

WEEK 45 Day 1
JESUS PRAYS IN THE GARDEN

MATTHEW 26:36-46

36 Then Jesus went with them to the olive grove called Gethsemane, and he said, "Sit here while I go over there to pray."
37 He took Peter and Zebedee's two sons, James and John, and he became anguished and distressed. 38 He told them, "My soul is crushed with grief to the point of death. Stay here and keep watch with me."
39 He went on a little farther and bowed with his face to the ground, praying, "My Father! If it is possible, let this cup of suffering be taken away from me. Yet I want your will to be done, not mine."
40 Then he returned to the disciples and found them asleep. He said to Peter, "Couldn't you watch with me even one hour?
41 Keep watch and pray, so that you will not give in to temptation. For the spirit is willing, but the body is weak!"
42 Then Jesus left them a second time and prayed, "My Father! If this cup cannot be taken away unless I drink it, your will be done." 43 When he returned to them again, he found them sleeping, for they couldn't keep their eyes open.
44 So he went to pray a third time, saying the same things again.
45 Then he came to the disciples and said, "Go ahead and sleep. Have your rest. But look—the time has come. The Son of Man is betrayed into the hands of sinners. 46 Up, let's be going. Look, my betrayer is here!"

Day 2
GRIEF AND PRAYER

MATTHEW 26:36-46

Think of something you were not looking forward to. You might be able to identify a tiny bit with Jesus in this passage. Of course, for Him, death was coming, and He knew it. Maybe you've dealt with something that heavy. Or, maybe your worst thing was just summer break coming to an end. Check out verse 38. "My soul is crushed with grief." You've got to be pretty sad to say words like those. Say them out loud, and slowly. They're heavy words.

While Jesus was fully God, He was also fully human. In His humanness, He was grieving the pain and suffering that was about to happen. So He went to pray. He drew His strength from His Father. His strength to obey. His strength to walk through the hardest thing He'd ever have to do. His suffering was very real. In the days leading up to it, His soul was crushed with grief. If you are grieving, look at Jesus's example. Pray. Ask for strength and comfort. God will give you what you need.

HOLY Qs!

- *How can God's love give me confidence today?*

- *Is anything in my life really hard right now? Am I talking to God about it? Who else can I talk to?*

BLESSING

Go following the way of the Savior, walking in the truth of the King, and living the life of the Friend. May your thoughts, words, and actions reflect the love of Jesus.

Day 3

WHOSE WILL?

MATTHEW 26:36-46

Ever had a hard time trusting someone? The trusted and loving adults in your life care about you, even if you don't always get where they're coming from. Check out verses 39, 42, and 44. What does, "Your will be done" mean?

"Will" is the power of choice. We all have a will. Our will is our desire to do what we want, or what we think is best. Jesus was giving over His will to God the Father. He was teaching us how to pray. Sometimes, our will can be a little too focused on ourselves—we're looking for whatever is best for us. God's will is always right, because everything God does comes from love.

So, when we're faced with a hard time or a tough decision, praying for God's will as Jesus did, is praying that we live in His plan and choose the most loving path. When you pray today, think about your own life and choices right now, and pray, "Your will be done."

HOLY Qs!

- *How can I be obedient to God this week?*
- *What have I been enjoying about prayer recently?*

BLESSING

Go following the way of the Savior, walking in the truth of the King, and living the life of the Friend. May your thoughts, words, and actions reflect the love of Jesus.

Day 4
WHO IS GOD?

MATTHEW 26:36-46

Do you understand everything you read in the Bible? God is Creator. God is love. God is . . . mysterious. One of the mysteries that people are still trying to figure out how to talk about is the Trinity. God is Father. God is Son. God is the Holy Spirit. We see evidence of the Trinity in verses 39 and 42, when Jesus—who is God—talks to God and calls Him Father. Wait . . . Jesus is God, but He's God's Son? God is the Father, but the Son is God? Check out Week 52. Then the Holy Spirit comes, who is also God.

Yes. It's confusing. Hear this: In your life with Jesus, you don't have to understand everything in the Bible to follow the God of the universe. Keep learning. Keep asking questions. But if you come across something in the Bible that's a mystery to you, like trying to understand the Trinity, it's okay. It just means there's more to learn. If you'd like to learn more about the Trinity, who could you talk to? Have you discovered anything else in the Bible you would like to learn more about?

HOLY Qs!

- *How can I learn from others this week?*
- *When good things happen, how do I give God the credit?*

BLESSING

Go following the way of the Savior, walking in the truth of the King, and living the life of the Friend. May your thoughts, words, and actions reflect the love of Jesus.

Day 5
CAN'T STOP, WON'T STOP

MATTHEW 26:36-46

What makes prayer easy? What makes prayer difficult? In 1 Thessalonians 5:17 Paul gives this simple advice, "Never stop praying." Never stop? But if you're on your knees at the altar, when will you play volleyball or eat pizza?! Obviously we can't kneel and pray 24/7, so what do you think it means?

Check out verse 41. Jesus wants the disciples to join Him in prayer, but they keep falling asleep. Whoops. Been there. Jesus's advice to them? "Keep watch and pray." Paul's advice? Keep praying. Seems like prayer is pretty essential to our faith journey. We are not going to know how to handle with wisdom what comes next in our lives if we're not praying. We stay connected with God through prayer. We listen to God's leading through prayer. "Never stop praying" means talking to Him throughout the day, and always being willing to listen. (You don't even have to close your eyes to pray!) What are some examples of "never stop praying" in your life?

HOLY Qs!

- God cares about our whole life, not just the spiritual parts. What healthy habits do I need to work on?

- How have I been trustworthy recently?

BLESSING

Go following the way of the Savior, walking in the truth of the King, and living the life of the Friend. May your thoughts, words, and actions reflect the love of Jesus.

Day 6
STAY READY

How do you get ready for something important, like a big game or a performance? How do you get ready to face temptation? Check out verse 41 again. We talked about it yesterday. Prayer helps us connect with God so we will be ready to act with wisdom. It also strengthens our life with Jesus, so when temptation comes, we can face it. Jesus knew Peter would be tempted. He wanted Peter to be ready. You're going to be tempted, too.

You will be tempted to choose selfishness. You will be tempted to choose to disobey. You will be tempted to be kind only to certain people. Being tempted is not sinful. Even Jesus faced temptation. But Jesus was in constant communication with His Father. He stood against temptation. You can too. You won't have a perfect score like Jesus, but Jesus will strengthen you to stand up to temptation. Keep letting Him in. Talk to Him. Listen to Him. Live in His love.

HOLY Qs!

- *What can I do to make wise choices this week?*
- *How can I keep from letting things like popularity or friends determine how I act?*

BLESSING

Go following the way of the Savior, walking in the truth of the King, and living the life of the Friend. May your thoughts, words, and actions reflect the love of Jesus.

Day 7
FACING THE BETRAYER

MATTHEW 26:36-46

What's an example of a dangerous situation a kid might be in? What's the best way to handle it? Check out verse 46. Jesus finds himself in a dangerous situation. His betrayer, the one who will hand Him over to His killers, is coming. Jesus could run. He's in a garden, so He could hide. He could fight. He could try to talk His way out of it. It's like all the choices you have if you're facing a bully. "Do I run, hide, talk, fight? What do I do?"

Jesus did none of them. Instead, He faced His betrayer. (See verses 47 and 48.) This isn't an example of how to handle danger. It's about Jesus. It's a story about Jesus accepting what He didn't deserve. He didn't try to escape. He was innocent, but He didn't fight back. You can bet He was afraid. He knew pain was coming. But this sacrifice was going to be done out of love. This story would be the ultimate proof of God's power and victory. How does this story make you feel about Jesus?

HOLY Qs!

- *How does my relationship with Jesus impact my daily life in real ways?*

BLESSING

Go following the way of the Savior, walking in the truth of the King, and living the life of the Friend. May your thoughts, words, and actions reflect the love of Jesus.

WEEK 46 Day 1
PETER DENIES JESUS

It's a new week in your life with Jesus! Use the *5 What's or Lectio Divina* to guide your reading today. Enjoy God's love for you!

MARK 14:66-72

66 Meanwhile, Peter was in the courtyard below. One of the servant girls who worked for the high priest came by 67 and noticed Peter warming himself at the fire. She looked at him closely and said, "You were one of those with Jesus of Nazareth."

68 But Peter denied it. "I don't know what you're talking about," he said, and he went out into the entryway. Just then, a rooster crowed.

69 When the servant girl saw him standing there, she began telling the others, "This man is definitely one of them!" 70 But Peter denied it again.

A little later some of the other bystanders confronted Peter and said, "You must be one of them, because you are a Galilean."

71 Peter swore, "A curse on me if I'm lying—I don't know this man you're talking about!" 72 And immediately the rooster crowed the second time.

Suddenly, Jesus' words flashed through Peter's mind: "Before the rooster crows twice, you will deny three times that you even know me." And he broke down and wept.

Day 2
DOG FIGHT

MARK 14:66-72

Ever seen a tiny dog that starts pulling its leash to bark at a larger dog? It's like the small dog is saying, "If my owner wasn't holding me back, I would get you. You big dog, you!" What do you think would really happen if the owners weren't there? Peter and the rest of the disciples also thought they were pretty strong. When they were with Jesus, they were confident. Before this passage, Jesus told the disciples that in the future they would desert Him, act like they didn't know Him. Jesus said Peter would deny Him three times before the rooster crowed twice. Peter argued back, saying he would die before that happened. As it turned out, without Jesus around, Peter wasn't as strong as he thought.

This week we discover Peter's overconfidence. Sometimes we get overconfident as well. We may think we can handle everything life offers on our own. You might have skills. You might have strength. But where does that strength come from?

HOLY Qs!

- *What habits help me spend time getting to know God through Scripture?*

- *How does my relationship with Jesus impact my daily life in real ways?*

BLESSING

Go following the way of the Savior, walking in the truth of the King, and living the life of the Friend. May your thoughts, words, and actions reflect the love of Jesus.

Day 3
NOT ALL ALONE

MARK 14:66-72

How does it feel to be surrounded by people but know that you are the only one who loves Jesus? That's how Peter felt. Peter was very bold when he was with Jesus and the disciples. He courageously told others about his beliefs. He even cut off a soldier's ear when the soldier tried to arrest Jesus. But Peter soon discovered that his bravery was gone. When alone and surrounded by people questioning him, Peter denied knowing Jesus three times.

Why is it important to be with other believers? We feed off each other's strengths and build each other up. The Christian life was never meant to be lived alone. You don't have to be with other Christians constantly, but their continual encouragement and support is vital to a life with Jesus. Going to church or meeting with Christian small groups lets you learn together. You gain wisdom together. You support each other. Where do you regularly spend time with other Christians? What do you need from those other Christians? What do they need from you?

HOLY Qs!

- *What's a healthy or helpful way I can use my spare time?*
- *How can I learn from others this week?*

BLESSING

Go following the way of the Savior, walking in the truth of the King, and living the life of the Friend. May your thoughts, words, and actions reflect the love of Jesus.

Day 4
SIN SNOWBALLS

MARK 14:66-72

What happens if you roll a snowball down a steep snowy hill? It rolls. It grows. It rolls. It grows. Peter's denial was like a snowball. Each time he denied Jesus, it made it easier to deny Him again. His denials grew. First, a servant girl accused him of being with Jesus. He pretended he didn't know what she was talking about. The second time, he denied it directly. The third time, he actually swore he didn't know Jesus.

Our sins can become like rolling snowballs if we let them. They grow and grow. So, how do we stop the snowballs? If you make a selfish decision, talk to Jesus about it. Pray about it. Don't just let it go, assuming you'll do better next time. He forgives us, and guides us through the next temptation. If we don't confess our sins and mistakes, they can get bigger and bigger until they're really hard to stop. As your Savior, King, and Friend, Jesus can help you stop the snowball. (Read more about this on page vii.)

HOLY Qs!

- *Have my words matched my actions? Does who I say I am and how I act line up?*
- *How can I be honest and trustworthy this week?*

BLESSING

Go following the way of the Savior, walking in the truth of the King, and living the life of the Friend. May your thoughts, words, and actions reflect the love of Jesus.

UNPOPULAR OPINION

MARK 14:66-72

Unpopular opinion alert! What's something you really like that people around you don't like? Or something you don't like that everyone else loves? The disciples were brave when they had Jesus to encourage them. Many people were open to what they had to say. But when Jesus was arrested, fear took hold of the disciples. Following Jesus not only became unpopular, it was dangerous! The disciples deserted Him. Peter denied Him.

There are times when following Jesus may be unpopular. In some places, it could even be dangerous. Have you ever been afraid or nervous to talk about Jesus or even live your life with Him? Do you sometimes find it easier to stay quiet and go along with everyone else? What situations might you face where choosing Jesus might be the unpopular choice? Ask for wisdom and courage in your prayer today.

HOLY Qs!

- *How can I keep from letting things like popularity or friends determine how I act?*

- *Who in my life needs to hear about Jesus? How can they hear it from me?*

BLESSING

Go following the way of the Savior, walking in the truth of the King, and living the life of the Friend. May your thoughts, words, and actions reflect the love of Jesus.

Day 6
JESUS IN MY HEAD

MARK 14:66-72

Are you good at quoting movies? Are you good at quoting Jesus? When Peter denied Jesus the third time, a rooster crowed again. Then check out the rest of verse 72. Jesus's words suddenly flashed through Peter's mind. His brain was quoting Jesus to him. It made Peter realize how he had failed Jesus—and himself—so he broke down and cried. He knew immediately that he had done wrong. Fortunately, this isn't all of Peter's story. He gets to hear Jesus's words again and gets another opportunity to follow Him (John 21:1-17).

Exploring and learning Scripture is super important to your life with Jesus. When you're really familiar with the words of Jesus, they can offer you hope and comfort in your challenges and mistakes. They can offer you wisdom when you are questioning something. They can give you words of praise in your worship. Memorizing Scripture can even be an act of worship. What Scripture could you work on memorizing this week? What words of Jesus do you want to remember?

HOLY Qs!

- *How does what I learned from Scripture inspire my thoughts and actions?*

- *Is anything in my life really hard right now? Am I talking to God about it? Who else can I talk to?*

BLESSING

Go following the way of the Savior, walking in the truth of the King, and living the life of the Friend. May your thoughts, words, and actions reflect the love of Jesus.

MAKING HOLY

MARK 14:66-72

Think of a time you felt guilty. Peter denied Jesus three times. Afterwards, he felt so guilty that he broke down and cried. Later, after Jesus rose from the dead, He appeared to Peter and the disciples. He gave Peter a second chance, the chance to declare his love three times (see John 21). Jesus never stopped loving Peter and He certainly didn't give up on him. His love is so perfect that He forgave Peter and chose him to keep sharing the good news of Jesus.

We all make mistakes. These don't make Jesus stop loving you. He knows your weaknesses, but He also sees your awesomeness. He will never give up on you. And here's the really good news: sin doesn't control you. Jesus changes you so completely that the desire to sin is taken over by the love for Jesus! We call that holiness, and it's a gift from God. God, through your relationship with Jesus, is making you holy! Pray a prayer of thanks today.

HOLY Qs!

• How can I be obedient to God this week?

• What am I thankful for? How can I show how thankful I am this week?

BLESSING

Go following the way of the Savior, walking in the truth of the King, and living the life of the Friend. May your thoughts, words, and actions reflect the love of Jesus.

WEEK 47 Day 1
DEATH OF JESUS

It's a new week in your life with Jesus! Use the *5 What's or Lectio Divina* to guide your reading today. Enjoy God's love for you!

LUKE 23:44-49

⁴⁴ By this time it was about noon, and darkness fell across the whole land until three o'clock. ⁴⁵ The light from the sun was gone. And suddenly, the curtain in the sanctuary of the Temple was torn down the middle. ⁴⁶ Then Jesus shouted, "Father, I entrust my spirit into your hands!" And with those words he breathed his last. ⁴⁷ When the Roman officer overseeing the execution saw what had happened, he worshiped God and said, "Surely this man was innocent." ⁴⁸ And when all the crowd that came to see the crucifixion saw what had happened, they went home in deep sorrow. ⁴⁹ But Jesus' friends, including the women who had followed him from Galilee, stood at a distance watching.

HOW DID WE GET HERE?

LUKE 23:44-49

Do you know why Jesus was killed? It's okay if it feels hard to answer. It's not easy to understand. In Week 39 we talked about the jealousy of the religious leaders, the Pharisees and Sadducees. In Week 43 we learned about the Romans who ruled over the Jewish people. These things are all important to understand why Jesus was killed.

The Romans had a cruel way of killing people who didn't obey them, called crucifixion. This is the way they killed people who broke laws or tried to fight the Romans. The Jewish religious leaders were so angry and jealous of Jesus that they wanted Him to die. But they couldn't legally kill Jesus themselves. So they made up a story about Jesus wanting to fight the Romans. The Roman governor, Pilate, didn't really believe it. But he didn't want to make the religious leaders mad at him, so he had Jesus crucified. Jesus was betrayed and lied about. How does it make you feel to know Jesus was treated so unfairly? What do you think Jesus was feeling?

HOLY Qs!

- How can I be honest and trustworthy this week?

- God cares about our whole life, not just the spiritual parts. What healthy habits do I need to work on?

BLESSING

Go following the way of the Savior, walking in the truth of the King, and living the life of the Friend. May your thoughts, words, and actions reflect the love of Jesus.

Day 3
STILL WITH US

LUKE 23:44-49

Can you remember a time when you felt lonely, afraid, or hurt? Every human knows these feelings. Jesus knew what these things felt like too. Do you remember when we talked about Jesus as *Immanuel*—the God with us? (Look back at John 1 in Week 3.) Even when He was dying, Jesus was *with us*. He joined in the loneliness, the pain, and the sadness that all humans feel.

Jesus knows what it feels like when powerful people use their power to hurt others. He knows what it feels like to be treated poorly by people who let jealousy and hatred fill them up. Jesus felt the pain of people abusing His body. Sadly, those kinds of things still happen to humans in our world. But even when terrible, painful things happen, *Jesus is with us*. And even when we feel all alone, *Jesus is with us*. He knows how we feel, and He has come to be with us. Say this out loud: *Jesus is with me.*

How can you talk with Jesus when you feel lonely, afraid, or hurt?

HOLY Qs!

- *What have I been enjoying about prayer recently?*
- *When good things happen, how do I give God the credit?*

BLESSING

Go following the way of the Savior, walking in the truth of the King, and living the life of the Friend. May your thoughts, words, and actions reflect the love of Jesus.

Day 4
TRUSTING

LUKE 23:44-49

What do you talk about with people you trust? Maybe you give them your ideas, your stories, or your questions. You can share with them honestly about how you feel, and what you think.

Jesus trusted God more than anyone else. He called God "Father," because He knew God loved Him, listened to Him, and cared for Him, like a good parent. For all of Jesus's life, He trusted God to give Him what He needed. Even when it was time for Jesus to die, even when He was in pain and very sad, Jesus trusted God. Look at what Jesus said right before He died (in verse 46). His life was in God's hands.

Because Jesus can trust God like this, we can learn to trust God like this too. When we are afraid to trust, we can ask Jesus to help us. We can even ask Jesus to teach us to trust. Is there anything that you have a hard time trusting God with?

HOLY Qs!

- *How have I been trustworthy recently?*
- *How can God's love give me confidence today?*

BLESSING

Go following the way of the Savior, walking in the truth of the King, and living the life of the Friend. May your thoughts, words, and actions reflect the love of Jesus.

Day 5
THE SACRIFICE

LUKE 23:44-49

What's the word "sacrifice" mean? A sacrifice is anything valuable that a person gives up for something even more important. What about the word "sin"? Even though it's a little word, sin is a big idea. Sin is anything that goes against God's perfect plan. God created things to be good, whole, and beautiful. Sin makes things broken, harmful, and ugly. God created life, but sin leads to death.

The Jewish people made sacrifices to God to remember what sin does. It might sound strange today, but animals like lambs were very valuable to people back then. When they brought a lamb to sacrifice in the temple, they asked God to forgive and heal their sin. There are many ways to understand what Jesus did when He died on the cross. One thing He did was offer *himself* as the sacrifice to forgive and heal our sin. Sin brings death, but Jesus never sinned. So Jesus picked up *our* sin and allowed death to come.

What questions or feelings do you have about this? Who could you talk to about it?

HOLY Qs!

- *Is anything in my life really hard right now? Am I talking to God about it? Who else can I talk to?*

- *How does my relationship with Jesus impact my daily life in real ways?*

BLESSING

Go following the way of the Savior, walking in the truth of the King, and living the life of the Friend. May your thoughts, words, and actions reflect the love of Jesus.

RIPPED CURTAIN

LUKE 23:44-49

Are there any places that are "off limits" for you? There was a place like that in the temple called the Holy of Holies that was closed off by a tall, thick curtain. No one could go in there, except one special priest on one special day of the year. The high priest went in there to make a sacrifice, and ask forgiveness for all the people of Israel. But when Jesus died, the curtain tore because no one needed to do that job anymore. Hebrews 10:12 explains it: *"Our High Priest [Jesus] offered himself to God as a single sacrifice for sins, good for all time."*

Jesus is the sacrifice *and* the high priest who goes between God and the people! This means we don't need anyone else to talk to God for us. This is the way Jesus loves us as Savior. He saves us from the power of sin and brings us back to God. God is never "off limits" for us. How does this impact your life with Jesus? Is there anything in your life that you have made "off limits" for God? You can talk to Him anytime, about anything.

HOLY Qs!

- *Who in my life needs to hear about Jesus? How can they hear it from me?*
- *What habits help me spend time getting to know God through Scripture?*

BLESSING

Go following the way of the Savior, walking in the truth of the King, and living the life of the Friend. May your thoughts, words, and actions reflect the love of Jesus.

Day 7
WHAT THE SOLDIER SAW

LUKE 23:44-49

What's something you have learned from someone different than you?

Check out verse 47. The people standing near the cross were probably surprised to hear what the Roman soldier said about Jesus. They probably figured the soldiers wouldn't even try to understand Jesus. But what did that soldier say? He got it right! In our translation the soldier says, "Surely this man [Jesus] was innocent." In Greek, the word "innocent" really means "righteous." Righteous means doing what's totally right and totally full of love. The Roman soldier had watched many people die like Jesus did. But as Jesus was dying, He still loved the people who betrayed Him and killed Him. The soldier noticed.

Some people think Jesus was weak because He didn't fight back when these things happened. He's not weak. His strength is where it should be. His strength is love. Humans have never seen someone so strong in love as Jesus. Even the strongest Roman soldier saw and believed this. How does the cross reveal His loving strength?

HOLY Qs!

- *How can I learn from others this week?*

- *How will I be a good friend and listener?*

BLESSING

Go following the way of the Savior, walking in the truth of the King, and living the life of the Friend. May your thoughts, words, and actions reflect the love of Jesus.

WEEK 48 Day 1
RESURRECTION (EASTER)

MATTHEW 28:1-9

¹ Early on Sunday morning, as the new day was dawning, Mary Magdalene and the other Mary went out to visit the tomb. ² Suddenly there was a great earthquake! For an angel of the Lord came down from heaven, rolled aside the stone, and sat on it. ³ His face shone like lightning, and his clothing was as white as snow. ⁴ The guards shook with fear when they saw him, and they fell into a dead faint.

⁵ Then the angel spoke to the women. "Don't be afraid!" he said. "I know you are looking for Jesus, who was crucified. ⁶ He isn't here! He is risen from the dead, just as he said would happen. Come, see where his body was lying. ⁷ And now, go quickly and tell his disciples that he has risen from the dead, and he is going ahead of you to Galilee. You will see him there. Remember what I have told you."

⁸ The women ran quickly from the tomb. They were very frightened but also filled with great joy, and they rushed to give the disciples the angel's message. ⁹ And as they went, Jesus met them and greeted them. And they ran to him, grasped his feet, and worshiped him.

Day 2
A NEW DAY!

MATTHEW 28:1-9

What's the best part of waking up to a new day? Check out verse 1. A new day represents new opportunities. New hope. Whatever tough things happened the day before, it doesn't have to be that way on this new day. Friday, Jesus was hung on a cross and died. It was the worst of days. Everyone was devastated. They thought it was over. They were confused. It felt hopeless. They wondered if they missed something. They were afraid.

Three days later, Jesus's tomb was empty. He was alive! He rose from the dead. Death couldn't keep Him down. In Jesus we can have hope. There's always a new day. There's always a reason to not give up because there's always Jesus, our risen Savior! Is there anything in your life that seems hopeless? Anything you are down about? Anything you are afraid of? Place your hope in a new day with Jesus.

HOLY Qs!

- *How does what I learned from Scripture inspire my thoughts and actions?*

- *How does my relationship with Jesus impact my daily life in real ways?*

BLESSING

Go following the way of the Savior, walking in the truth of the King, and living the life of the Friend. May your thoughts, words, and actions reflect the love of Jesus.

Day 3
NOT AFRAID

MATTHEW 28:1-9

What makes you feel afraid? Check out verses 4-7. It starts with these big, brave Roman soldiers. They've been in battles and war. They are considered the toughest guys around. And they literally passed out in fear from seeing the angel. Then, when the angel appeared to the women, how did they handle it?

They're all good. Mary and Mary stood and listened to the good news the angel had for them. They had seen amazing things while being with Jesus. Miracles. They knew Jesus. Their time spent with Jesus had them better-prepared to handle a situation that put two Roman guards out like lights. Like these women, time spent with Jesus can prepare us to handle scary situations. It doesn't mean we'll never be afraid, but when we are afraid we know where our hope and help comes from.

HOLY Qs!

- *Is anything in my life really hard right now? Am I talking to God about it? Who else can I talk to?*
- *What habits help me spend time getting to know God through Scripture?*

BLESSING

Go following the way of the Savior, walking in the truth of the King, and living the life of the Friend. May your thoughts, words, and actions reflect the love of Jesus.

Day 4
VICTORY

MATTHEW 28:1-9

Jesus actually died. He wasn't faking it. He wasn't taking a nap or passed out. Even though He was the Son of God who raised others from the dead, He did not use that power for himself that day. Out of love, He really died. But Friday's death brought Sunday's life!

Imagine this: Jesus. Laying in the tomb. Dead a couple of days. Sits up, fully alive! Fully healed and victorious over sin and even death. Then He walks out. The stone that took several Roman guards to move into place just rolled away! In church, pastors and songwriters love to talk about death not being able to hold Jesus. This is what it means. He took on real death, but real death was no match for His life. We will see victory, because of His victory!

HOLY Qs!

- *When good things happen, how do I give God the credit?*
- *What can I do to make wise choices this week?*

BLESSING

Go following the way of the Savior, walking in the truth of the King, and living the life of the Friend. May your thoughts, words, and actions reflect the love of Jesus.

Day 5
GO!

MATTHEW 28:1-9

Have you ever had good news that you just couldn't keep in? Like maybe you couldn't wait to tell your friends what you got for your birthday or for Christmas. Or maybe you hit a home run in last night's game and can't wait to tell your friend at school. Check out verses 7-8. The angel wasted no time. He told Mary and Mary to go. "Go and tell others. Don't wait. Go tell everyone He's alive! For those who thought He lost, He won. For those who think it's over, it's just begun. For those who are sad, be joyful! For those who feel stuck, He has the power to save. Don't wait!"

And the same is true for you and me. Go! God has good news for all. Our King and Savior is alive. Let's share the good news. Let's be like Mary and Mary. They did exactly what they were told to do. They left to tell the story. Who do you want to tell?

HOLY Qs!

- *God cares about our whole life, not just the spiritual parts. What healthy habits do I need to work on?*

- *What's a healthy or helpful way I can use my spare time?*

BLESSING

Go following the way of the Savior, walking in the truth of the King, and living the life of the Friend. May your thoughts, words, and actions reflect the love of Jesus.

Day 6

HE GOES TOO

MATTHEW 28:1-9

Do you ever get afraid when you feel like God is asking you to do something? Do you think "what will happen?" or "what if they think I'm weird?" or "what if I fail?" These are all okay questions to ask. God doesn't get mad because you have them. Talk with Him about these things. Now, check out verse 7: "He is going ahead of you to Galilee."

He has gone ahead of you. In other words, He's already reaching out to people in your life. The places you will go. The people you will talk to. God's reaching out to them too. It's kind of like walking through the woods with a trail guide. You might be a little scared in the woods. But you've got a guide who knows the trail because He's walked it before. He created it. Every time God calls us to do something, we do it with God. How does this give you confidence?

HOLY Qs!

- How can I keep from letting things like popularity or friends determine how I act?

- Who in my life needs to hear about Jesus? How can they hear it from me?

BLESSING

Go following the way of the Savior, walking in the truth of the King, and living the life of the Friend. May your thoughts, words, and actions reflect the love of Jesus.

Day 7
RUN RUN RUN

MATTHEW 28:1-9

What would get you so excited that you would actually run to get to it? Check out verse 9. Jesus has been dead. The disciples have felt defeated. They were confused about all the good news He had been talking about for the last three years. They were left without a leader, without direction, and without their friend. Then He showed back up. And they ran.

What if you were so excited about your relationship with Jesus, so in love with your Savior, that you would run to Him? Maybe that already describes you. Since Jesus isn't actually walking around on two feet, you can't literally run to Him. But the emotions can still be there. This is part of what it means to give our all to Jesus. Everything we have, including our emotions. We recognize how powerful His love is and we "run" with excitement to be a part of it. What gets you excited about Jesus?

HOLY Qs!

- *How can God's love give me confidence today?*
- *How does what I learned from Scripture inspire my thoughts and actions?*

BLESSING

Go following the way of the Savior, walking in the truth of the King, and living the life of the Friend. May your thoughts, words, and actions reflect the love of Jesus.

WEEK 49 Day 1
JESUS APPEARS TO THE DISCIPLES

It's a new week in your life with Jesus! Use the *5 What's or Lectio Divina* to guide your reading today. Enjoy God's love for you!

JOHN 20:19-23

19 That Sunday evening the disciples were meeting behind locked doors because they were afraid of the Jewish leaders. Suddenly, Jesus was standing there among them! "Peace be with you," he said. 20 As he spoke, he showed them the wounds in his hands and his side. They were filled with joy when they saw the Lord! 21 Again he said, "Peace be with you. As the Father has sent me, so I am sending you." 22 Then he breathed on them and said, "Receive the Holy Spirit. 23 If you forgive anyone's sins, they are forgiven. If you do not forgive them, they are not forgiven."

Day 2
NOT HOME ALONE

JOHN 20:19-23

The disciples were afraid. Jesus was gone. After three years of amazing miracles and great preaching, He was dead and they were scared. Jesus wasn't just killed by murderers in the street. He was killed by the government, and the government had the law on their side. That meant the disciples, friends of Jesus, had to hide. Check out verse 19. There they were, locked in a room, afraid.

What goes through your head when you feel alone? What about when you feel afraid? The disciples were probably feeling those same emotions. They didn't realize yet that everything Jesus said was true, and He was already alive. We sometimes forget, too. Sure, we know it. But we can get so down on ourselves that we feel like we're totally alone. We forget there's a risen Savior who is always with us. When you start to feel like the disciples did that evening, remember you aren't alone. How does Jesus help you feel less alone?

HOLY Qs!

- *What habits help me spend time getting to know God through Scripture?*
- *How does my relationship with Jesus impact my daily life in real ways?*

BLESSING

Go following the way of the Savior, walking in the truth of the King, and living the life of the Friend. May your thoughts, words, and actions reflect the love of Jesus.

Day 3
STAY READY

JOHN 20:19-23

What does it mean to have peace? Check out verses 19 and 21. Jesus decided peace was so important He wanted to say it twice. Peace can be used to describe a nice, clean, quiet house. It can be used to describe a walk in the woods. It can be used to talk about a time when there is no war. All of these might include what Jesus was talking about here, but they don't quite define Jesus's version of peace in these Scriptures.

Peace is knowing Jesus is real. He's alive. Peace is knowing Jesus loves you. Peace is knowing Jesus will guide you. Peace is knowing Jesus will comfort you. When Jesus showed up to the disciples after His resurrection, all of these truths became real to them. Everything He had ever said was true. Peace, real peace, comes from knowing and being with Jesus. Then, when we have that peace, we offer it to others. Christian, in your life with Jesus, how can you be a bringer of peace?

HOLY Qs!

- How will I be a good friend and listener?
- How can I keep from letting things like popularity or friends determine how I act?

BLESSING

Go following the way of the Savior, walking in the truth of the King, and living the life of the Friend. May your thoughts, words, and actions reflect the love of Jesus.

Day 4
LIVING PROOF

JOHN 20:19-23

Do you have any scars? Scars usually come with stories. What's your scar story? The scar is the proof that the story really happened. Sometimes those stories end with, "and I've got the scar to prove it." You've got scars. Chances are, you'll end up with a few more. Jesus had them, too. Look at verse 20. Actually, this Scripture says wounds, not scars, but wounds like those become scars.

Showing the wounds was proof to the disciples that Jesus wasn't appearing as a ghost. He wasn't just sent from heaven to talk to them one last time. The death was real and the resurrection was real. And Jesus has the scars to prove it. In the following Scriptures, Thomas, one the disciples, wouldn't believe until he had touched the scars himself. He wanted proof! And Jesus gave it. Sometimes it's a little harder to offer proof that Jesus's story is completely real because He's not here next to us with His scars. In what other ways can we know Jesus is real?

HOLY Qs!

- *When good things happen, how do I give God the credit?*
- *How can I learn from others this week?*

BLESSING

Go following the way of the Savior, walking in the truth of the King, and living the life of the Friend. May your thoughts, words, and actions reflect the love of Jesus.

Day 5

JOY SPREADER

JOHN 20:19-23

What's the difference between happiness and joy? Check out verse 20. The disciples were filled with joy. Joy runs deeper than happiness. It's like joy comes from deep down and lasts longer. The joy the disciples felt probably filled their whole bodies. They felt relief. Things were the way they should be. Their future was bright again. Their leader was back. Happiness just wouldn't be a big enough word!

Jesus is the great bringer of joy still today. Take a look at Week 20. Joy is a fruit of the Spirit. The Holy Spirit brings real joy to our life with Jesus. That's how Jesus is present with us today. He's with us in the Holy Spirit. The disciples experienced joy when Jesus was present. Since Jesus is always present with us, joy is present with us each day, too. Wouldn't it be great to live a life of joy every day? Jesus is the bringer and spreader of joy!

HOLY Qs!

- Have my words matched my actions? Does who I say I am and how I act line up?

- Have I been jealous, grumpy, or really hard on anyone? What can I do about it?

BLESSING

Go following the way of the Savior, walking in the truth of the King, and living the life of the Friend. May your thoughts, words, and actions reflect the love of Jesus.

Day 6
SO EXCITED

What's something that got you so excited that you wanted to tell everyone about it? One kid got her ears pierced and told friends, family, and complete strangers about it for days. She was so excited! In verse 21, after being filled with joy, the disciples are told they were being sent. It makes sense that these two verses come one right after another. They experienced great joy, and now they're being sent to tell the world about it!

A disciple is a follower of Jesus. That means you are a disciple. That means you have been sent. We can't just learn about Jesus and grow closer to Him in private. The more filled with His love and joy we are, the more we're going to want to tell others about Him. And we are being sent into the world to do that very thing. Don't do it because you have to. Do it because you want others to know the love, joy, and peace that you have with Jesus. How does your life with Jesus bring you joy?

HOLY Qs!

- *Who in my life needs to hear about Jesus? How can they hear it from me?*

BLESSING

Go following the way of the Savior, walking in the truth of the King, and living the life of the Friend. May your thoughts, words, and actions reflect the love of Jesus.

Day 7
CATCH HIS BREATH

JOHN 20:19-23

When's the last time you were out of breath? What were you doing? Look at verse 22. This might sound a little weird, but Jesus . . . breathed on the disciples so that they would receive the Holy Spirit. Considering we read a story in Week 29 where Jesus did some spit healing, maybe breathing isn't that weird. But, why would He need to breathe on the disciples?

The Greek word "pneuma" (NOO-ma) and the Hebrew word "ruach" (ROO-ahk) are both used in Scripture when talking about the Spirit. Both words mean "wind." In Acts 2, when the Holy Spirit comes, there's a sound like a wind. Here, Jesus uses His breath to create wind. Wind is invisible, but you can see its effects on the world. The Spirit is invisible. People could see and touch Jesus. But now, Jesus was going to be everywhere all the time like the *pneuma* or *ruach*. We won't see Him, but we feel Him. How do you feel Jesus impacting yourself and others?

HOLY Qs!

- God cares about our whole life, not just the spiritual parts. What healthy habits do I need to work on?
- What's a healthy or helpful way I can use my spare time?

BLESSING

Go following the way of the Savior, walking in the truth of the King, and living the life of the Friend. May your thoughts, words, and actions reflect the love of Jesus.

WEEK 50 Day 1
THE GREAT COMMISSION

It's a new week in your life with Jesus! Use the *5 What's or Lectio Divina* to guide your reading today. Enjoy God's love for you!

MATTHEW 28:16-20

16 Then the eleven disciples left for Galilee, going to the mountain where Jesus had told them to go. 17 When they saw him, they worshiped him—but some of them doubted!

18 Jesus came and told his disciples, "I have been given all authority in heaven and on earth. 19 Therefore, go and make disciples of all the nations, baptizing them in the name of the Father and the Son and the Holy Spirit. 20 Teach these new disciples to obey all the commands I have given you. And be sure of this: I am with you always, even to the end of the age."

Day 2
NERVOUCITED

MATTHEW 28:16-20

Describe the end of your favorite movie. Here we are at the end of an important chapter in our story. This is Jesus's last big meeting with His disciples. They are being sent on an important mission, but He will no longer be with them physically like He had for the last three years. They had seen Him die. They were seeing Him now, alive. He won. He beat death. Some worshiped Him. Some doubted Him. He met them on a mountain and gave them instructions on what was next. It's a pretty solid ending.

Even though it felt like the end of that story, it was really just getting started. In the coming books, Jesus was about to take His church to the next level. This thing was gonna blow up. Huge. To do that, He had to inspire the disciples and put them in action. The disciples were probably nervous and excited. What about following Jesus makes you nervous? What makes you excited?

HOLY Qs!

- What habits help me spend time getting to know God through Scripture?
- What am I thankful for? How can I show how thankful I am this week?

BLESSING

Go following the way of the Savior, walking in the truth of the King, and living the life of the Friend. May your thoughts, words, and actions reflect the love of Jesus.

Day 3
DISCIPLE DOUBT

MATTHEW 28:16-20

The 11 disciples saw Jesus after He rose from the dead. He stood right before them like He had promised. But check out verse 17. Some of them still doubted. Following Jesus had always been a little mysterious, and required trust. When Jesus first asked the disciples to follow Him, they were asked to trust and obey without knowing the details. Then, as they followed Him, they witnessed and did amazing things. Now, a small number of them were uncertain, but they still followed.

The disciples actually got to see Jesus and everything He did, and they still struggled with doubt. It's no wonder people still doubt today. In your life with Jesus, it's not a bad thing if you find yourself doubting from time to time. Doubt makes us ask questions. In your questioning, read Scripture. Talk to a Christian friend, and find the answers together. What else can you do if you struggle with doubt? (Jesus isn't scared off by your doubt. He loves you and wants you to ask questions.)

HOLY Qs!

- *How can I be obedient to God this week?*
- *How does my relationship with Jesus impact my daily life in real ways?*

BLESSING

Go following the way of the Savior, walking in the truth of the King, and living the life of the Friend. May your thoughts, words, and actions reflect the love of Jesus.

Day 4
WHO HAS THE AUTHORITY?

MATTHEW 28:16-20

Who has authority in your life? Let's back up. What is authority? It's the power to give orders to others and make decisions. What sort of authority do you have? Check out verse 18. Jesus was God on earth and had all the authority to send the disciples on their mission. He wanted them to help Him change the world. They came under His authority. They gladly did what Jesus told them. This doesn't mean they weren't ever scared, but they knew they were a part of something big.

We serve a powerful Savior. What an honor to be able to share life with Him, follow Him, and do all that He wants us to do. He sends us to the world to share His love and tell His story with our words and actions. When we know Him really well, following His authority actually becomes what we want to do, not what we have to do. How do you follow His authority?

HOLY Qs!

- *How does what I learned from Scripture inspire my thoughts and actions?*
- *When good things happen, how do I give God the credit?*

BLESSING

Go following the way of the Savior, walking in the truth of the King, and living the life of the Friend. May your thoughts, words, and actions reflect the love of Jesus.

ALL THE NATIONS

MATTHEW 28:16-20

How many countries and languages can you name? In verse 19, Jesus told His disciples to go and make disciples of all the nations. This was actually kind of a big deal. Up to this point, most Jewish people thought the Messiah was just for them. When Jesus said "all the nations" that would have made some people gasp. "Jesus, surely you don't mean . . . *all* the nations. Even our enemies? Even people in far away lands? Aren't you just *only our* God?"

Nope. He's not. He's God for everyone. Not only that, but He's given us the responsibility of loving all people too. We get to tell everyone, *all* the nations, the good news of Jesus. We get to show them how to live a life with Jesus. This means your family and friends, sure. But also people you haven't even met yet. And that cousin you don't get along with very well. All people. Who do you need to pray about reaching for Jesus today?

HOLY Qs!

- *Have I been jealous, grumpy, or really hard on anyone? What can I do about it?*
- *How will I be a good friend and listener?*

BLESSING

Go following the way of the Savior, walking in the truth of the King, and living the life of the Friend. May your thoughts, words, and actions reflect the love of Jesus.

Day 6
THE GREAT COMMISSION

MATTHEW 28:16-20

What would you do if you were given a stack of treasure maps and were told that everyone you knew could have their own treasure chest of riches? Before Jesus returned to heaven, He told the disciples to share the gift of salvation with others. He told them to make disciples of all nations, to baptize them in the name of the Father, Son, and Holy Spirit, and to teach them to obey His commands. We often refer to this as the "Great Commission." Commission means a direction given with authority. So, Jesus was using His authority to send the disciples out to do an important job—share that great treasure!

The Great Commission wasn't just for the disciples. It's for all Christians. We know Jesus as our Savior, King, and Friend, so let's do this. Check out page vii for a reminder about how to talk about a relationship with Jesus. Practice talking about Jesus as your Savior, King, and Friend with someone today. The more you do it, the easier it gets!

HOLY Qs!

- *How can God's love give me confidence today?*
- *Who in my life needs to hear about Jesus? How can they hear it from me?*

BLESSING

Go following the way of the Savior, walking in the truth of the King, and living the life of the Friend. May your thoughts, words, and actions reflect the love of Jesus.

Day 7

ALWAYS AND ALWAYS

MATTHEW 28:16-20

What's one thing you are learning from someone else that someday you'll have to do on your own? The disciples had an easy answer to this question. Jesus was with His disciples for three years. They were able to watch, listen, and learn from Him. Now they were being told to spread the good news on their own. They were probably nervous. That's why verse 20 is important. Jesus told them that He would be with them always. He was about to return to heaven, but His Spirit was coming to be with them everywhere, all the time.

Jesus is always with you, too! He is with you when you are happy, sad, excited, nervous, and afraid. He is with you as you tell others about your relationship with Him. He will give you the strength, wisdom, and peace you need to keep growing. You can live life knowing that He is with you every step of the way. He'll give you what you need.

HOLY Qs!

- *God cares about our whole life, not just the spiritual parts. What healthy habits do I need to work on?*

- *Is anything in my life really hard right now? Am I talking to God about it? Who else can I talk to?*

BLESSING

Go following the way of the Savior, walking in the truth of the King, and living the life of the Friend. May your thoughts, words, and actions reflect the love of Jesus.

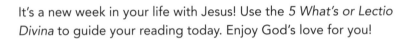

WEEK 51 Day 1
JESUS'S ASCENSION

It's a new week in your life with Jesus! Use the *5 What's or Lectio Divina* to guide your reading today. Enjoy God's love for you!

ACTS 1:6-11

[6] So when the apostles were with Jesus, they kept asking him, "Lord, has the time come for you to free Israel and restore our kingdom?"
[7] He replied, "The Father alone has the authority to set those dates and times, and they are not for you to know. [8] But you will receive power when the Holy Spirit comes upon you. And you will be my witnesses, telling people about me everywhere—in Jerusalem, throughout Judea, in Samaria, and to the ends of the earth."
[9] After saying this, he was taken up into a cloud while they were watching, and they could no longer see him. [10] As they strained to see him rising into heaven, two white-robed men suddenly stood among them. [11] "Men of Galilee," they said, "why are you standing here staring into heaven? Jesus has been taken from you into heaven, but someday he will return from heaven in the same way you saw him go!"

THE WRONG QUESTION

ACTS 1:6-11

How does a triangle smell? What color is 24? If you don't know the answer, it's because those questions don't make sense! Kind of like the question the disciples asked Jesus about the kingdom.

Remember, the people of Jerusalem thought Jesus was going to be a fighting king that made the nation of Israel strong again. (Look back at John 12 in Week 43.) Jesus was not going to be that kind of king. But after Jesus was raised from the dead, the disciples *still* thought Jesus was going to make Israel strong again. They didn't understand that the kingdom of God was much bigger than Israel. They didn't understand how Jesus was making things right—even if the Romans were still in control of their country. God's kingdom would be built through God's love.

Jesus was patient with them, even though they didn't get it. He didn't give them the answer they wanted, but He did tell them what they needed to know. What questions have you asked Jesus? What questions do you still have for Him? How does Jesus answer us?

HOLY Qs!

- *Have my words matched my actions? Does who I say I am and how I act line up?*
- *What can I do to make wise choices this week?*

BLESSING

Go following the way of the Savior, walking in the truth of the King, and living the life of the Friend. May your thoughts, words, and actions reflect the love of Jesus.

Day 3
WITNESS THIS

ACTS 1:6-11

What does it mean to be a witness? A witness is a person who sees something, and then tells others what he or she saw. Jesus told the disciples that they would be witnesses about what they saw with Jesus.

Everything that we know about Jesus has come from those disciples. They told people about Jesus in Jerusalem. They told people about Jesus in the nation of Judea (or Israel). They told people about Jesus in the next-door country of Samaria. And in a few years they told people about Jesus in places like Italy, Greece, and Ethiopia. The disciples of Jesus invited new people to become disciples. And those people invited other people, and they invited others! That has been happening now for almost 2,000 years. Who told you about Jesus? Who told that person about Jesus?

Even though you haven't seen Jesus with your own eyes, you can be a witness too. What can you tell others about what you have learned, read, or felt in your life with Jesus?

HOLY Qs!

- Is there anyone I'm struggling to get along with? What am I going to do about it?
- Who in my life needs to hear about Jesus? How can they hear it from me?

BLESSING

Go following the way of the Savior, walking in the truth of the King, and living the life of the Friend. May your thoughts, words, and actions reflect the love of Jesus.

Day 4

MORE THAN US

ACTS 1:6-11

What's a job you can't do alone? Jesus told the disciples they had an important job to do. They were going to be witnesses for Jesus. But they couldn't do that job right away. They had to wait. Jesus promised that the disciples would be given power when the Holy Spirit came. We'll learn more about that next week. The Holy Spirit is how we see and know God's love and power on earth. The Holy Spirit helps us live a life with Jesus. God gives all disciples (Christians) what we need to be His witnesses.

Jesus invites us into His work, and asks us to be witnesses. But He never asks us to do these things alone. In fact, we *can't* do them alone. We can only join in Jesus's work if we stay close to Jesus. Jesus shares His power, His love, and His words with us. So our first work is to listen to Jesus. How does listening well help us with His work?

HOLY Qs!

- *How can God's love give me confidence today?*
- *What habits help me spend time getting to know God through Scripture?*

BLESSING

Go following the way of the Savior, walking in the truth of the King, and living the life of the Friend. May your thoughts, words, and actions reflect the love of Jesus.

Day 5
ALL AROUND US

ACTS 1:6-11

Where is heaven? For a long time people thought that there was a land of heaven above the sky. But then astronauts went into outer space. They found a moon, and they saw stars, the sun, and other planets. But no one has ever found heaven. Does that mean it isn't real? Nope. It just means heaven is more than we can even imagine.

When Jesus lived, people didn't think of heaven like a place on a map. They understood heaven was not a place you could just walk over to. Heaven was everywhere God was, right alongside the places we can see and travel to. So when Jesus went up into heaven, He didn't go far away. He went to a place no one can see, but a place that is close to us. Sound confusing? You're not alone. This is another mystery that we can't fully explain. The most important thing to know is that Jesus is not far away from us. He's actually much closer than we think.

HOLY Qs!

- God cares about our whole life, not just the spiritual parts. What healthy habits do I need to work on?

- Have I been jealous, grumpy, or really hard on anyone? What can I do about it?

BLESSING

Go following the way of the Savior, walking in the truth of the King, and living the life of the Friend. May your thoughts, words, and actions reflect the love of Jesus.

Day 6

INVISIBLE POWER

ACTS 1:6-11

Can you think of something that has power, even if you can't see it? We can't see the wind, but we can see the wind blowing things, so we know it's there. We can't see WiFi, but we know it connects our stuff to the internet.

When Jesus lived on earth, He could only be in one place at a time, just like every other human. But since Jesus went to heaven, He doesn't have the same limits. Like wind or WiFi, Jesus, through the power of the Holy Spirit, can move into places a body can't. And He can be in all different places. He can be with you here, and at the very same time Jesus can be with another kid on the other side of the world. And He can be in all the places in between!

The disciples were probably sad and confused to see Jesus going away. But Jesus's power and love wasn't going away. When have you felt the love and power of Jesus, even if you couldn't see it?

HOLY Qs!

- Is anything in my life really hard right now? Am I talking to God about it? Who else can I talk to?

- What am I thankful for? How can I show how thankful I am this week?

BLESSING

Go following the way of the Savior, walking in the truth of the King, and living the life of the Friend. May your thoughts, words, and actions reflect the love of Jesus.

Day 7
IN BETWEEN

ACTS 1:6-11

Can you remember a time when you were in between two important events in your life? While you were on break from school, you were in between two different grades. When you're traveling to see family, you're in between home and your grandparents' house. And even right now, you're in between two important events. All of us are. We are in between the time Jesus came to earth, and the time when He will come back.

This week's story is what we call the ascension (uh-SEN-shun) of Jesus. Ascension just means "the going up." And like we learned this week, heaven isn't just above us—it's all around us. But that's not where Jesus will stay. The angels told the disciples that one day Jesus would return to earth again with a body. You might hear this called "the second coming." That's when God will make earth and heaven new again. That's when all will be healed and made right—forever.

What do you think Jesus wants us to do until He comes back?

HOLY Qs!

- *What's a healthy or helpful way I can use my spare time?*
- *How does what I learned from Scripture inspire my thoughts and actions?*

BLESSING

Go following the way of the Savior, walking in the truth of the King, and living the life of the Friend. May your thoughts, words, and actions reflect the love of Jesus.

WEEK 52 Day 1
PENTECOST

It's a new week in your life with Jesus! Use the *5 What's or Lectio Divina* to guide your reading today. Enjoy God's love for you!

ACTS 2:1-13, 38-41

¹ On the day of Pentecost all the believers were meeting together in one place. ² Suddenly, there was a sound from heaven like the roaring of a mighty windstorm, and it filled the house where they were sitting. ³ Then, what looked like flames or tongues of fire appeared and settled on each of them. ⁴ And everyone present was filled with the Holy Spirit and began speaking in other languages, as the Holy Spirit gave them this ability.
⁵ At that time there were devout Jews from every nation living in Jerusalem. ⁶ When they heard the loud noise, everyone came running, and they were bewildered to hear their own languages being spoken by the believers.

7 They were completely amazed. "How can this be?" they exclaimed. "These people are all from Galilee, 8 and yet we hear them speaking in our own native languages! 9 Here we are—Parthians, Medes, Elamites, people from Mesopotamia, Judea, Cappadocia, Pontus, the province of Asia, 10 Phrygia, Pamphylia, Egypt, and the areas of Libya around Cyrene, visitors from Rome 11 (both Jews and converts to Judaism), Cretans, and Arabs. And we all hear these people speaking in our own languages about the wonderful things God has done!" 12 They stood there amazed and perplexed. "What can this mean?" they asked each other. 13 But others in the crowd ridiculed them, saying, "They're just drunk, that's all!"

38 Peter replied, "Each of you must repent of your sins and turn to God, and be baptized in the name of Jesus Christ for the forgiveness of your sins. Then you will receive the gift of the Holy Spirit. 39 This promise is to you, to your children, and to those far away—all who have been called by the Lord our God." 40 Then Peter continued preaching for a long time, strongly urging all his listeners, "Save yourselves from this crooked generation!" 41 Those who believed what Peter said were baptized and added to the church that day—about 3,000 in all.

WHAT COMES NEXT?

ACTS 2:1-13, 38-41

Jesus was . . . gone . . . again. The disciples were all gathered together, probably trying to figure out what to do next. They had spent three years with Jesus before His death and 40 days with Him after His resurrection. Then Jesus ascended into heaven. He told them He'd give them a Comforter. But none of them knew what that meant.

There's probably no way the disciples could have expected what would come next. They may have been feeling pretty down. Maybe not quite as bad as the three days Jesus was dead, but still pretty lonely with Him gone. Lonely and without much direction. What were those three years for? What were all the miracles for? What were all the lessons for? What were they supposed to do NOW? Oftentimes it's the same way in our lives. We know God has been at work, but the next part of the plan isn't clear. We just have to be ready for God to lead us to act. Pray today that God would reveal to you what He wants you to do next.

HOLY Qs!

- *How can I be obedient to God this week?*

- *How does my relationship with Jesus impact my daily life in real ways?*

BLESSING

Go following the way of the Savior, walking in the truth of the King, and living the life of the Friend. May your thoughts, words, and actions reflect the love of Jesus.

Day 3

MORE THAN VEGGIES

ACTS 2:1-13, 38-41

Does your town have any big parties, parades, or festivals? What are they like? Check out verse 1. Pentecost was a celebration of the harvest. People threw a big party to celebrate that the crops they planted were ready to be picked and eaten. It was time to eat some veggies! More importantly, it was a celebration of God providing. Everyone traveled to Jerusalem to celebrate together. School was out. No one worked. They enjoyed the party and the plentiful harvest.

It's very fitting that the Pentecost that we now celebrate started as a party to celebrate what God provided. At this particular Pentecost in Acts, God would provide in a brand new way. Besides crops, do you know what God provided at that Pentecost in Acts? Yep, the Holy Spirit. Pentecost is still a celebration of God giving us what we need. Particularly, we celebrate God giving us the Holy Spirit, just like Jesus promised. What can you discover about the Holy Spirit from this passage? What else do you know about the Holy Spirit?

HOLY Qs!

- *Is anything in my life really hard right now? Am I talking to God about it? Who else can I talk to?*
- *When good things happen, how do I give God the credit?*

BLESSING

Go following the way of the Savior, walking in the truth of the King, and living the life of the Friend. May your thoughts, words, and actions reflect the love of Jesus.

Day 4
GOODBYE CURTAIN

ACTS 2:1-13, 38-41

When Jesus died, something interesting happened. Go back to Day 6 of Week 47 for a quick refresher. The curtain in the temple ripped in two. This curtain's job was to separate regular people from the holiest place where God's presence was on earth. Only priests could go to God in the holiest place in the temple. Not everyone had access. But when Jesus died, the curtain ripped open. Why? Any guesses before you keep reading?

Fast-forward to Pentecost. The Holy Spirit came to everyone who was gathered. From there, the Holy Spirit would go with all the people; God's presence was now a constant part of their lives.

That's veeerrry different from the time when the curtain separated people from God. Instead of just a few people, now everyone had access to God. They could go to God anytime and any place. The Holy Spirit is God's presence. He is still with you now. God is always there for you, caring for you, and shaping you with His love.

HOLY Qs!

- *How does what I learned from Scripture inspire my thoughts and actions?*

- *What am I thankful for? How can I show how thankful I am this week?*

BLESSING

Go following the way of the Savior, walking in the truth of the King, and living the life of the Friend. May your thoughts, words, and actions reflect the love of Jesus.

Day 5
NO LIMITS

ACTS 2:1-13, 38-41

How many different languages do you think are spoken in the world? Take a guess. (We'll get to the answer later.) If you can pronounce all those different lands in verses 5-11, bonus points for you. Why do you think all these different languages were suddenly spoken?

Language was important in Jesus's story because each language represented a different group of people. Remember, up until Jesus came, there was a very specific group of people—the Israelites—that were chosen by God. But on this day of Pentecost, God's Spirit was present among all these people, and suddenly they were hearing the good news of Jesus in their own language. In other words, that good news wasn't just for certain people. It was for everyone! The Holy Spirit's friendship, Jesus's saving grace, and God's loving Kingship is for everyone. Countries, languages, and cultures don't matter when it comes to the good news. (By the way, the world has about 6,500 different languages!) How do you think people around the world hear the good news of Jesus?

HOLY Qs!

- *What's a healthy or helpful way I can use my spare time?*
- *Who in my life needs to hear about Jesus? How can they hear it from me?*

BLESSING

Go following the way of the Savior, walking in the truth of the King, and living the life of the Friend. May your thoughts, words, and actions reflect the love of Jesus.

WE ARE THE CHURCH

ACTS 2:1-13, 38-41

What do you like most about going to church? Every Sunday God's people get together for worship. We all show up at a building we call the "church." We learn more about who God is. We share our lives together. But here's the thing: that place you go on Sundays isn't actually the church. Don't flip out. Read on.

The church isn't a building. The church God started on this day of Pentecost had nothing to do with a parking lot, sanctuary, or classrooms. We—the believers and followers—are the church. Listen again: *We* are the church. The church is people. After this story, Peter preached and 3,000 more became believers. The church got bigger by 3,000 people. The church grew and grew . . . and there wasn't even a building. A building can be a blessing, but as part of the community of believers, *you* are the church. God's presence isn't just waiting for you in the sanctuary. Pentecost teaches us that the Spirit's presence goes with the church anywhere! So, what does it mean to be the church?

HOLY Qs!

- *What have I been enjoying about prayer recently?*
- *Have I been jealous, grumpy, or really hard on anyone? What can I do about it?*

BLESSING

Go following the way of the Savior, walking in the truth of the King, and living the life of the Friend. May your thoughts, words, and actions reflect the love of Jesus.

Day 7
I DON'T BELIEVE YOU

ACTS 2:1-13, 38-41

Think of something you just didn't believe until you had proof. Maybe you have an uncle who is always telling you jokes and you're never sure what's true and what's not. Check out verse 13. There were many who heard the disciples and believed, but there were also people who made fun of them. They didn't believe it. Maybe they thought it was a joke.

As you live your life with Jesus, you will run into plenty of people who have no interest in Jesus. They just don't believe in God. Maybe they think the whole thing is a joke. Sometimes people don't believe in the miracles of Jesus. They don't believe the good news is true. Some people have had a lot of struggles in their life, and believing that God is good is really hard for them. It's not going to be easy. Pray that God will give you the loving attitude to continue your life with Jesus and present the good news to people, even when they don't believe it.

HOLY Qs!

- How can God's love give me confidence today?
- How can I keep from letting things like popularity or friends determine how I act?

BLESSING

Go following the way of the Savior, walking in the truth of the King, and living the life of the Friend. May your thoughts, words, and actions reflect the love of Jesus.

YOU'RE DONE!

You made it through the whole book! Wow. Call your grandma. Email a college president. Tell someone. You've spent a year or more diving into 52 different passages of Scripture and getting to know Jesus in brand new ways. Hopefully your life with Him is deeper, richer, and full of things to celebrate because of your devotional time spent this year. Let's reflect a little bit.

Take a look at the list of Holy Qs on page iii. Which ones were easy to answer? Which ones were hard? Why is it important to ask yourself these kinds of questions?

Take a look at the list of Scriptures on page ix, or just flip back through the book. What stands out about what you learned or how you grew? What do you remember?

Now, you get to do it again. You're a year older, and you're going to connect with the devotions in this book in brand new, older-you ways. Get ready to dive back into the life of Jesus. Your Savior, King, and Friend still has so much to tell you.

HOLY Qs!

- *How does my relationship with Jesus impact my daily life in real ways?*

BLESSING

Go following the way of the Savior, walking in the truth of the King, and living the life of the Friend. May your thoughts, words, and actions reflect the love of Jesus.

Author Bios

James Abbott

James Abbott is a follower of Jesus, husband, and dad to two amazing boys. He is a Pastor to Children and Families in Olathe, KS. He's an avid outdoorsman along with his sons. He enjoys Taco Tuesdays and baseball, though they don't have to be at the same time.

Tami Brumbaugh

Tami Brumbaugh is a teacher and an author of over 30 books and numerous articles. She loves spicy food, playing ukulele, and painting with watercolors. She lives in Kansas with her husband, two daughters, and an assortment of pets.

Michaele LaVigne

Michaele LaVigne is a mom, pastor, author, and ordained elder in the Church of the Nazarene. She serves as pastor of spiritual formation at 8th Street Church in Oklahoma City where she lives with her husband, son, and daughter.

Kyle Tyler

Kyle Tyler is a dad, husband, pastor, author, musician, sports fan, and lover of burritos. He likes to read books, ride his bike, and drink coffee. He lives in the Kansas City area with his wife, two daughters, and obese cat.